"*Every so often a management bo*...... *...ong that rocks your world, in every sense. Viral Change is a management book that radically shifts your thinking around a familiar concept. It progressively and compellingly convinces you that many of your most dearly held beliefs about change have always been wrong.*"

**Kieron Shaw,
for Strategic Communication
Management (Melcrum)**

"*Nonconformist in its writing as in its ideas, Viral Change stands out from other literature on change.*"

Business Digest

"*A welcome challenge to the view that big change requires big programmes. It was pleasing to come across an approach to change that doesn't advocate the top-down, project-based, all-singing-all-dancing methodologies that tend to dominate current management thinking and practice.*"

Chris Rodgers, Informal Coalitions

"*Through Viral Change, the employees discovered the depth of their potential and new methods of working together. The team became more resilient and knew how to continue with the positive dynamic it had acquired.*"

**Pierre A. Morgon, experienced
pharma industry executive,
having successfully tried the Viral
Change approach twice**

VIRAL CHANGE™

VIRAL CHANGE™

The alternative to slow, painful and unsuccessful management of change in organisations

Second Edition

Leandro Herrero

meetingminds
ideas worth printing

Disclaimer

Published by:
meetingminds
PO Box 1192, HP9 1YQ, United Kingdom
www.meetingminds.com

First edition 2006 – ISBN 978-1-905776-01-6
Second edition 2008

ISBN Paperback edition:
10 - Digit: 1-905776-05-5
13 - Digit: 978-1-905776-05-5

A CIP catalogue record for this title is available from the British Library

Never doubt that a small group of thoughtful, committed citizens can change the world. Indeed, it is the only thing that ever has.

Margaret Mead, anthropologist

The philosophers have only interpreted the world, in various ways; the point is to change it.

Karl Marx, philosopher

"Do you want to spend the rest of your life selling sugared water or do you want a chance to change the world? (…) Let's make a dent in the universe"

Steven Jobs of Apple offering the job of CEO to
John Sculley, at that time President of Pepsico

Q: Five frogs are sitting on a log. Four decide to jump off.
   How many frogs are on the log?
A: Five, because deciding and doing are not the same thing.

A riddle

Waiting for the barbarians

By Constantine P. Cavafy (1904)

What are we waiting for, assembled in the forum?

      The barbarians are due here today.

Why isn't anything happening in the senate?
Why do the senators sit there without legislating?

      Because the barbarians are coming today.
      What laws can the senators make now?
      Once the barbarians are here, they'll do the legislating.

Why did our emperor get up so early,
and why is he sitting at the city's main gate,
on his throne, in state, wearing the crown?

      Because the barbarians are coming today
      and the emperor is waiting to receive their leader.
      He has even prepared a scroll to give him,
      replete with titles, with imposing names.

Why have our two consuls and praetors come out today
wearing their embroidered, their scarlet togas?
Why have they put on bracelets with so many amethysts,
and rings sparkling with magnificent emeralds?
Why are they carrying elegant canes
beautifully worked in silver and gold?

      Because the barbarians are coming today
      and things like that dazzle the barbarians.

Why don't our distinguished orators come forward as usual
to make their speeches, say what they have to say?

      Because the barbarians are coming today
      and they're bored by rhetoric and public speaking.

Why this sudden restlessness, this confusion?
(How serious people's faces have become.)
Why are the streets and squares emptying so rapidly,
everyone going home so lost in thought?

> Because night has fallen and the barbarians have not come.
> And some who have just returned from the border say
> there are no barbarians any longer.

And now, what's going to happen to us without barbarians?
They were, those people, a kind of solution.

DEDICATION

I want to dedicate this book to all clients that over the years have trusted me and my team to help them with the design and implementation of change. And in particular to those who started out sceptical, but went on to become VIRAL CHANGE™ advocates and activists. To all Change Champions in organisations: those who bear that title and those who behave as such, but without the label. To those who share my passion for environments that enhance the individual, that bring out the best in us and that host our talents and our dreams. To all activists, deviants, sceptics and non-conformists who often have a hard time navigating an artificially predictable organisation. To those who build organisations in perpetual quest mode, those who are not stuck in the past, or worse, in suspended animation, waiting for the barbarians (next reorganisation, next M&A, next budget, next CEO) to solve their problems, create change, bring ideas, innovate or simply move forward. In short, it is dedicated to those brave souls who have decided not to wait...

PROLOGUE TO THE SECOND EDITION

The terms 'viral change' or 'behavioural change management' have increasingly been linked to our work as any Google search for these terms will show you. And I am delighted that there is a growing interest - from many sectors of the business and organisational life - in understanding the viral model of change management that we pioneered and its applications.

Since the first edition, we have continued building on our VIRAL CHANGE™ experience, both in large scale interventions and in its applications in medium-sized organisations. Additional work on viral leadership has also taken place and some extra notes on this topic have been added in this second edition. Viral leadership goes beyond communication ('viral communication') to engage others to champion the new idea, the new process or the new behaviours. We are so used to equating change to good communication that sometimes people think these two things are not just connected, but interchangeable. However, they are not the same.

I have also added some notes on influence mechanisms. In recent months, it became fashionable to question the true role of 'influencers', for example, in marketing.

In this second edition, I have stressed how any virally induced cultural change recognises a combination of mechanisms: influencers ('the opinion leader model'), the first followers ('the early adopters model') and the fact that a critical mass of 'new culture practitioners' ('the critical mass model') is powerful enough in itself to induce another critical mass, no matter what the initial trigger was. Social copying leads the way. This is incredibly important for me as a practitioner of VIRAL CHANGE™ (as opposed to a simply theoretical advocate), because I am more interested in the infection of new ideas and behaviours being spread and leading to new routines within the organisation ('new cultures') than in the socio-arithmetical ability to measure whether 20% of those were due to mass social imitation or direct Change Champion, peer-to-peer work. The best (cultural, organisational) VIRAL CHANGE™ in action is the one that has used multiple mechanisms of influence.

Every day I encounter more and more people in organisational life who are tired of yet another corporate initiative with a change management angle. The mechanistic top-down model (push from the top of the organisation, get results at the bottom) is still what people think of: a burden you have to endure at some point, one way or another. This model is past its sell-by date. Making no apologies for stealing the slogan of a European mobile communications company, I'd like to proclaim that 'the future is bright, the future is viral'. I really believe that the viral model of change is the only hope for a tired, overwhelmed, over-managed, predictable, commanded-and-controlled, straight-jacketed and initiative-inundated corporate life.

Leandro Herrero
May 2008

Contents

INTRODUCTION: CHANGE BEHAVIOURS, GET CULTURE

This is a real story. Andrew X was the CEO of a flagship company. Still in his forties, he was young for a CEO. He had been headhunted from a different industry sector and had arrived at the pharmaceutical company with a reputation for past achievements. Though he was friendly - to a point - he wasn't the type of guy to hang around the executive floor having informal conversations with corporate officers and staff. He meant business. He was busy. He was always busy.

He was replacing Dr Peter Y who, at 55, had taken an early retirement. Peter had been at the helm for more than fifteen years and used to be a 'young CEO' as well. But industry turmoil, failed acquisitions and a weak research and product development machinery had taken the company into very unsettled times. The Board decided that a fresh approach was needed. They found Andrew with a track record of 'results' in a meteoric career and they sent Peter to play golf with a generous pension scheme.

I met Andrew several times after he arrived. He seemed to have clear ideas about the need for a lean business and for cutting unnecessary fat and waste. And that 'fat and waste' could include anything from travelling in business class to 'big supporting functions' and 'that bad habit of breakfast meetings in the cafeteria'.

For his VPs on the exec floor and their immediate staff in headquarters, what was most noticeable about Andrew wasn't his speeches about strategy or his apparent appetite for asking people who used to have one job now to do three and earn the same as before. The most noticeable thing about Andrew was how different from Peter he was. As simple as that. From his very first weeks on the tenth floor, whenever I approached any of his senior VPs direct reports and asked, "*How is it going?*" the answer would be, "*different, very different*". As if all those PhDs, MBAs, MDs, senior heads of R&D, Finance, Operations, International Marketing, etc., were suddenly short of vocabulary and could not articulate it any better than that. 'Very different'. Here are some of those differences:

- The old CEO, Dr Peter Y, loved inclusive meetings and presentations with lots of PowerPoint slides and 'progress reviews' and an average audience of 30. Andrew performed on a one-on-one basis ("*If I need something, I'll come to you*") and rarely called meetings (*"Having an executive committee once a month is more than enough, don't you think?"*)

- Dr Peter Y was an 'email distributor'. He loved email communications in its neatly structured way with lots of people in the 'cc' box (*"Let's make sure that everybody in my circle gets as much information as I do"*). Andrew's email was short-and-sharp without many greetings and polite endings. No 'Dear John' or 'Dear Mary', or sincerely or kind regards. Just: *"Need to have that plan for Wednesday now Tuesday evening would be great please send to Barbara, tx A"*. And that would be a long one.

- Dr Peter Y was a visiting, apostolic CEO. In the early days, when the company had a corporate jet, he would travel extensively that way. Most recently, a more modest first class in a commercial airline would take him to the affiliates worldwide for 'review meetings'. Andrew wasn't averse to travelling but, apparently, this was not his favourite way of managing internationally. He was very fond of teleconferences. Video conferences were another 'waste' for him.

To be fair, it wasn't that extraordinarily hard for the VPs to adapt. Andrew wasn't particularly difficult, or nasty, or unfriendly, nor did he make their life miserable. Andrew was, hey, 'different'.

Five months after Andrew's arrival, a series of anecdotal observations were made by middle managers in the IT department, the International Marketing group and the in-house travel agency (the latter having miraculously survived an outsourcing attempt). When all these observations were put together, the facts were solid and unquestionable:

- Overall email traffic 'at the centre' (the official jargon for headquarters) had decreased by 25%
- Total number of meetings had decreased by 30%
- Travel budget was within budget for the first time since, well, since there was a travel budget.

At that time, I didn't spend much time at their premises but, intrigued by these figures - 'compiled' by a data hungry, clever summer intern doing an MBA project - I tried to find opportunities to discuss them with senior, and not so senior people, sometimes in passing, sometimes as a topic of conversation on the back of my totally unrelated consulting project. What I got back sounded as follows:

> Andrew has made it very clear that we should be more agile and fast and that there was a bit of a waste in the way we were doing things. Nothing wrong, but, hey, new times!

> He wants straight, simple communications. We were a cosy-cosy family, I suppose. Now we are learning fast to involve only those who need to be involved, you know, the 'on-a-need-to-know-basis' that Andrew preaches. And frankly, it's great.

> We were travelling a lot, too much. This new environment is great. I welcome it. We can do lots of things on the phone. Sometimes one tends to forget.

We are certainly in big culture change mode, far more entrepreneurial, more 'fit for purpose' as Andrew likes to say. He wants less meetings and more work done! And he is right! And we've got rid of the practice of monthly reports. To the relief of my troops, I must say! He says he doesn't need them.

One evening, Andrew and I were invited to the same social event. He was unusually chatty and towards the end we found ourselves in an animated private conversation:

- What a big cultural change you are driving, Andrew, I said.
- What do you mean?
- Well, all these...how should we call it, streamlined processes…?
- Yes, we needed to simplify the budget process.
- I was talking more about the emails, and the number of meetings and…
- What emails?
- Well, IT has put together some figures and claim that email traffic has gone down by 25 %.
- Why? Do we have a problem? I thought we had just upgraded our servers?

At that point, I was beginning to look uncomfortable and I was wondering if he was trying to take me for a ride. So I tried:

- Andrew, seriously, are you kidding me? (Actually, I used different words). This young guy from the business school, summer intern, is writing a dissertation and has compiled what he calls

5

'efficiency statistics' for the period since you arrived. And they included email traffic 'at the centre' down by 25%, total number of meetings decreased by 30% and, incidentally, within budget in travel expenditure. And surely you must take credit for these efficiency targets. I have seen a draft of the dissertation and you figure there as a case study under the title *A case of fast cultural change by the introduction of key efficiency measures: the role of transformational leadership.*

Andrew looked at me in a strange way: eye contact but semi-catatonic face, surprised, uneasy, solemn. Then, a few seconds of silence that felt like minutes. Suddenly, he changed and smiled a lot as if everything had been revealed in the way those hidden cameras show in TV programmes where people have been tricked big time, only to finally realise that they'd been set up by their best friend.

> – Right! Nice! But I don't really know what you are talking about.

I had to take over the conversation flow of that evening - I thought - or we would both go home with a strange embarrassment and a feeling that it was too much chardonnay after all.

> – Are you telling me, I said, that you have not orchestrated these changes? That you haven't issued guidelines on the need to have less meetings, sharper conversations, less dependence on email pollution and cutting down on travelling?

This is what your people are telling me, and, by the way, they are delighted.

- Well, I am glad they are, but I haven't done anything!
- What about email traffic?
- What about it?
- The reduction across the board.
- I don't like emails; I think they are an excuse for recording everything 'just in case'. But I haven't said to anybody that we should use less email because I appreciate that this is a bit personal and many people are used to this way of communicating. I just don't want my inbox full at seven o'clock in the morning! But I am not in the business of dictating how many emails should land in somebody else's inbox. Do you think I am such a control freak?
- But your people say that you don't even reply to many emails…
- I don't reply to any email in which I am 'cc', that's for sure, let alone bcc, but I haven't asked others to 'follow me'. Quite frankly, I hope they will find better things to follow me upon!
- They said that when you presented the 'only-on-a-need-to-know' philosophy…
- I have never presented such a thing. I hate the term. How can I know what others need to know? Isn't it a bit of an arrogant view of the world?
- Travel budget is under-spent…
- Good! My fault as well?
- They said you have strong views about how abusive travel had become in the organisation and that it wasn't acceptable.

7

–   I seem to remember that at an early Exec Committee I mentioned that, in my previous job, I had felt 'abused' by having to travel too much, particularly on week-ends, and that many discussions don't need the five or more hours on a plane. But I had not discussed travel policy with anybody. I don't think it is appropriate to travel business class for a couple of hours' flight. I personally would travel economy in those cases! But I am not aware that we have formally reviewed travel policy. Now that you mention it, perhaps we should…

–   Well, you seem to have a new one! What people seem to be most grateful for is for what they see as your personal efforts to cut meeting time. I know that in the previous regime they spent their day in meetings: corporate, international, project management, finance, reviews, you name it.

–   I am not a meeting person…

–   They figured that out now.

–   But we have never discussed in the monthly executive committee anything about 'less meetings'. In my first senior manager job, many years ago, management imposed upon us an initiative of 'no meetings on Friday' and a target of reduction of meetings across the board by one third. I thought it was a stupid idea. There are things that need meetings and things that don't. In my position I want to believe, perhaps with some arrogance, that I don't have to be involved in endless reviews on the security of our warehouses or the pre-pre-pre Marketing plans, or the agenda arrangements for the launch of a product! I hate that waste! But I hope that those involved in those topics meet as much or as little as they need to have secure warehouses, good marketing plans and a b….y good product launch!

- There are no monthly reports anymore…
- Why?
- Because you don't want them.
- I don't need them! Other managers may…
- You have launched an efficient mini-reengineering initiative by amalgamating jobs…
- Give me a break! We had four HR VPs in the country, one for each of the sites. I asked to have one, and challenged them to convince me on the need for four. Nobody has. If this is *reengineering*, so be it. I call it common sense! I also happen to believe that we have an IT department capable, in numbers, of controlling a space shuttle launch but with too many chiefs and no Indians who can fix my laptop! But this is another conversation.
- Ok, but, wait a minute, this is not only your people. I still remember our early conversations. You despised 'breakfast meetings' …
- I can't do business and eat breakfast. Is that a problem?
- You told me it was a bad habit.
- Being half European, I see breakfast meetings as a bad American export. So, if I share this with you, are you going to stop having business discussions over breakfast?
- I am not on your payroll, otherwise I might, I continued. So none of this has been Machiavellically orchestrated and skilfully crafted

from your tenth floor office? People think that you have a sort of supreme gift for pulling strings and expressing yourself with clarity about what is expected and that there is a significant cultural change programme of some sort going on. A senior person reporting to you used the term 'crusade'. That MBA guy thinks you are a transformational leader injecting strong efficiency measures. And you are telling me that you were not aware of this?

- Look, I very much welcome all the good things happening. We are lucky if all this is true, I mean, the rational improvements etc. But I am not Machiavelli. My name is Andrew and what I am really, really good at is…
- Don't tell me, teamwork and organisational re-engineering, I said, pushing my luck.
- Investor relationships. Yes, I did enjoy the City of London when I was in Europe and now Wall Street. I have many venture capital friends. I talk to them. I am close to them. And, let me tell you, this is a big change for this company. In the previous regime, as you called it, they used to ask junior people to prepare some PowerPoint slides and send those to them. They felt treated badly. And we paid for it! This is my forte. Once I get this done as a priority, I will start thinking about changes that perhaps I need to make in the organisation. Do you fancy another drink?

>> ACCIDENTAL TRANSFORMATION

Andrew the CEO may not have been a transformational leader, but the organisation had been transformed in only a couple of months. One year, later most of the changes - plus others that followed as a natural consequence of these - were still in place. Many other 'efficiency measures' were still working. The copy-writers of that year's Annual Report drafted things such as:

- 'We have focused on efficiencies across the board'
- 'Become a fast and agile organisation'
- 'Rational approach to communication between sites'
- 'Concerted focus on controlling operating expenses'
- 'New entrepreneurial spirit'
- 'Significant cultural change and a new north'

and, of course:

- 'Far better relationships with investors!'

Let's not take this lightly. If you work or have worked in an organisation with high levels of information pollution, email-itis and 'reply-all pandemic', non-stop 9-to-5 meetings, Outlook calendars with no blank spaces until 2023, weekly, monthly and quarterly reports and pervasive bureaucracy, and if for just one second you could imagine an organisation exactly the opposite, you would feel an immense relief just by the simple use of your imagination and visualisation of this utopia! You, citizen of Average Company - or manager, CEO, business leader, HR professional, organisational consultant, etc. - know what I am talking about.

Cultural changes and broad organisational changes are very often discussed (and taught in business education) with a long list of caveats including: 'make sure that the change is not transitory, that it is not superficial'. Agreed. And - from people who always *know*- 'it's going to be long, painful, and massive'. Also, for many of those people, only Big Planned Changes are real change. For some reason, changes in Andrew's organisation became pretty 'stable'. He didn't plan much in the first months, although later on in his tenure he formalised some specific changes. And as for having to be long and painful... Does it have to be? It didn't happen in Andrew's company.

> The problem is that our stereotypes of 'management of change' or 'cultural change' usually include experiences or images of extremely complicated systems mapped on big flipcharts and encapsulated in a myriad of PowerPoints and Post-its, the content and philosophy of which seems to desperately be trying to emulate quantum physics.

>> VIRAL CHANGE™: INFECTIONS IN THE ORGANISATION'S PLAYGROUND

This book presents an approach to management of change - including 'cultural change'- that includes the concerted use of some of the mechanisms present in Andrew's accidental change management programme: the one that never was, but that de facto created a new culture. Some of these mechanisms have labels such as imitation, diffusion of new practices, reinforcement of new behaviours, creation of 'tipping points, 'language frames' and others.

In Andrew's case, a cascade of assumptions, imitations, triggers, etc., created a snowball effect. Perhaps the changes were 'desired' by many. Perhaps they were ready. I don't know. Andrew's vignette is a showcase of some of those powerful mechanisms. The key is to move from 'accidental' to 'orchestrated'....

In other words, I am not suggesting for a second that we leave the spread and development of change to the kind of uncontrolled cascading down of the behaviour of a single person at the top. Or that we rely on that kind of role model to be mirrored across the organisation. This would be naïve to say the least. But we can't ignore the power of influence (which is different from the power of authority) and, in particular, mutual influence between individuals within the organisation. Engineered and distributed influence is a key engine of change, one that this book will have at its core.

Beyond those labels described before, which I will explain later in the book, the messages that I'd like to leave are clear and simple:

- You can do it!
- It's not about a massive deployment of a legion of external consultants.

- It's not about an incredibly long and massive 'exercise'.
- It doesn't have to be painful, although people tend to make it so.

I am going to take you through it.

I call this approach VIRAL CHANGE™. It is based upon the combination of mechanisms that have been 'discovered' over many years and that blend traditional Behavioural Sciences with more modern Social Sciences and recent Network Sciences.

> VIRAL CHANGE™ is unconventional. It sees and creates the diffusion of new ideas, new processes, new behaviours and changes within the organisation like 'infections in the corporate playground'. And VIRAL CHANGE™ achieves more than massive communication programmes with dozens of Town Hall meetings.

In VIRAL CHANGE™ mode, 'change management' effectively means the orchestrated creation of an internal epidemic of success. I am not in the business of telling you what your success has to look like. You define that.

To achieve this, you don't need the step-by-step, sequential, orderly processes mapped and sold by many consultants and academic gurus with a multi-million dollar price tag.

I am going to redefine your business! You - (change) manager, CEO, HR partner, consultant, project leader or organisational-development-transformation-rethinking-renewal-leader - need to get into the infectious disease business, even if you didn't know it, and epidemiology wasn't in your business education curriculum.

>> MAKING SUCCESS FASHIONABLE

VIRAL CHANGE™ is about contagious behaviours that spread. Perhaps a bit slowly at the beginning (or at least it may look like that) but then they suddenly seem to reach a tipping point and become 'the norm'. And this can be achieved with a relatively small number of behaviours. It's also about specific networks of an also relatively small number of individuals, carrying the infection and creating the fashion. Fashions and infections have many things in common. After all, fashion is the infection of ideas or habits.

I believe that real, successful management of change is not about preaching change, the need for change, the importance of change and the consequences of not changing. It is not about massive communication and training programmes. It is not about 'cascaded-down' management retreats to engage absolutely everybody on earth. Behind VIRAL CHANGE™ is a fundamentally different way of understanding, not only how organisations work but also how change is induced and made sustainable. Schematically, the differences are articulated in the graph on page 16.

VIRAL CHANGE™

TRADITIONAL (ME TOO) CHANGE MANAGEMENT PROGRAMME

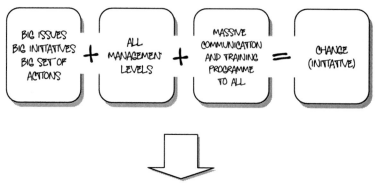

VIRAL CHANGE™

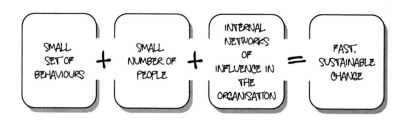

>> NEW IDEAS ABOUT THE ORGANISATION

As it often happens with the historical development of many disciplines, they sometimes tend to go their own way without talking to each other. The current business world is a good example. It sometimes looks like isolated, tribal silos talking to themselves. HR people go to HR conferences. IT people to IT conferences. R&D people to whatever techie conferences they need to go, etc. You won't find these tribes mixed up other than at internal-company-jamborees.

Also, social sciences in general don't get serious air time in corporate life. If anything, it sounds like 'HR stuff', which provides an immediate alibi for management and leadership to 'devolve the initiative to the function'.

In recent years, we have seen a great deal of convergence of disciplines and approaches in areas that just a few decades ago were thought to be unrelated. Today, we know quite a lot about how the organisation works. And we know that a key part of its functioning has to do with the internal fluid connections between people that could loosely be called internal networks. Many good things happen on those hidden highways, although
what we see is mostly what happens in visible structures such as teams and committees. But today we also know quite a lot about how networks work; any network, whether physical, electronic or human/social. This knowledge gives us a tremendous advantage in understanding not only how organisations work, but how to manage change.

A group of unlikely fellow travellers are coming together on an intriguing journey. Mathematics, biology, complexity theory, conventional social sciences, computer sciences, and socio-economics, for example, are becoming closer and closer as if in a new *philo-sophos* era. In today's world, the excuse 'I haven't been trained in those things' is no longer a valid one!

What we can learn and apply to the management and leadership of organisations and 'management of change' is simply fascinating. VIRAL CHANGE™ firmly borrows from those convergent disciplines and applies a framework that creates fast, sustainable change.

>> THE PILLARS OF VIRAL CHANGE™

(1) THE ONLY REAL CHANGE IS BEHAVIOURAL

There is no 'change' in the organisation until there is behavioural change in the individuals; no matter how many new processes and systems or new enabling technologies have been mapped and 'implemented'. Your wall may be full of post-its of new processes, the new IT system may be launched or the new re-organisation declared live, but if people continue with their 'old ways of doing', you will be kidding yourself by calling that change. And what's more: intellectually, your people may get it! Emotionally, they may or may not get it. But even if they do, there is still no guarantee that behaviours will change, that change will occur.

(2) BEHAVIOURS CHANGE CULTURE, NOT THE OTHER WAY AROUND

Example 1: There is no such a thing as 'an entrepreneurial culture'. There are cultures where people behave in a manner of A, B, C, obtaining an organisational benefit of X, Y, Z and a personal gain of 1, 2, 3. When all these things happen, we have habits, routines, norms, ways of doing things, etc., that we can call entrepreneurial (or we can have a debate about a better term!).

Example 2: Do you want 'a culture of accountability'? You can preach the importance of accountability, describe to people the advantages of accountability (personal and organisational), communicate the risk of lack of accountability, train them with packages describing the five components of accountability, produce posters, stickers and mugs with the slogan 'we need to be accountable', go to the country-house hotel and repeat that message times twenty, and then pray. Or you can define specific, visible behaviours of individuals that when (a) seen, (b) practiced and (c) properly reinforced, will create habits and ways of doing which you would be happy to describe as 'showing accountability'. Then you'll have a culture with that label.

> If you want cultural change with a label, define the behaviours needed, install them, make them live and sustainable and you'll get 'that culture'. Then, well, you can keep the original label or you may even find a better one!

Margaret Thatcher once declared: "*There's no such thing as society. There are only individual men and women and there are families*". You wouldn't expect less from the Iron Lady sitting on the right-hand side of the political arena where individualism is king and collectivism is bad for your health.

My temptation to steal the line is strong. Here it is: in the organisation, forget the culture, there are only behaviours. These are accepted or unaccepted, expected or unexpected, sanctioned or not. There are established ways of doing things, ways of talking, ways of thinking and ways of gluing people. There are also visible windows to the world such as logos, colours, objects, symbols and other paraphernalia usually called 'artefacts' by scholars. But, above all, there are people - single, in pairs, in trios, in groups, in teams, in networks and any other multiples - who *do* and *don't do* things. This is as visible as it can get: how people behave in a particular environment. And this *is* culture.

(3) ORGANISATIONAL CHANGE, INCLUDING CULTURAL CHANGE, IS NOT A LONG-TERM AFFAIR

You can change culture 'now' and see results in a few months. Andrew's organisation was progressively transforming itself in significant terms and with visible and measurable outcomes as early as four months after some *mechanisms* were in place in that otherwise accidental 'programme'. These changes were not short-term, ephemeral, so called 'win-wins'. They lasted beyond his first and second year and created a platform for many others.

For many business people, changing culture is a far away utopia. All very well in terms of 'cultural change', they say, but we have needs now: the strategic plan, the business plan, and then Christmas, and then the New Year, and, incidentally, a January full of conferences! We'll focus on these short-term things for now. Cultural change is a long-term initiative; we'll tackle this as soon as we can. Unless the sky has fallen down, there will always be a winner between this year's business plan actions to implement and 'the culture thing'. And you know what? The winner always looks like a spreadsheet.

(4) A FEW 'HOT POINTS' ARE THE KEY TO FOCUS THE ENERGY UPON

Long-term, fast and sustainable change in organisations can be achieved by putting energy and effort into some 'hot points', not by pouring them into a massive, across the board declaration of intentions, involving all processes and systems; colossal communication programmes or, above all, exquisite planning to predict what exactly will be happening at well-defined points in time.

Andrew's changes were achieved via a (invisible and initially un-planned) 'programme' which contained no Town Hall meeting, no road shows, no corporate communication projects and no country-house retreats to 'explain', 'motivate', 'engage' and 'empower' employees. A few 'measures' plus a great deal of imitation, assumptions about what the boss would like to see and presumably reward, had the power to snowball changes. What happened in Andrew's company during his initial months as CEO wasn't trivial. Yet, it didn't come from a six-month assessment period and a two-year change management programme. If only we could learn from these dynamics!

>> FIRST KEYWORD: IT'S BEHAVIOURS, STUPID!

Let me go back to behaviours. This is at the core of VIRAL CHANGE™ because the infection must be mainly behavioural! It could not be otherwise: we have just said that unless behaviours change, there is no proper change!

2

Actually, I don't agree with Thatcher. I do believe that there is such a thing as society and that this collective entity matters. But I would agree that 'society' as a concept, important as it may be, has limited operational value. To put it bluntly, I don't know what to do with 'society', while I do know a lot about 'the individual men and women' and those little groups called 'families'. People, institutions, the government, etc. give money or take money away from individuals, and create laws to protect or punish them. In doing so, they are framing and shaping 'the society thing'. But all this is done because of the individual or their groupings. The shape of 'society', whatever that may be, is depending on all those things that we do or don't do with individuals and their natural (family) and artificial (company, institution) groupings.

Thatcher's point was that society can only be described in terms of its components. My copycat point is that while culture in an organisation can be described in many terms, many of them serve as artefacts (logos, buildings) while others are labels that have great difficulty in achieving any degree of reliability. In plain words, labels such as 'entrepreneurial culture', or 'mature culture', or 'culture of fear', or 'high trust culture', mean next to nothing until you start describing what you mean, which usually happens in the corridor and the cafeteria!

These things mean different things to you and me. And as soon as you start to seriously describe and articulate them, you are bound to describe what people do or don't do, what they are or aren't allowed to do, which behaviours are established, which ones are non-negotiable, which behaviours would take you places and which ones would take you nowhere. You will progressively be talking about behaviours.

The only cultural parameters that really count as far as being able to do something about/with them are the behaviours of the individuals or groupings that exist within such a thing as 'the culture of the organisation'.

I can hear people saying: *"Wait a minute; this sounds a bit like a reductionism approach. What about norms, beliefs, attitudes, values, hopes, expectations, emotions?"* Yes, of course the culture also has norms, many of them tacit. But norms are the mirrors for behaviours. Yes, people in that culture also have attitudes, beliefs, values, hopes, expectations, emotions and all that. I agree. The problem is that, if you push me, I would declare all of those to be pretty intangible, compared to what I can (or cannot) see people doing or not doing, i.e. their behaviours.

I am stretching the argument here on purpose and taking a pretty fundamentalist psychological position called behaviourism. For many folks in and out of the psychological and social sciences world, behaviourism is a sort of Thatcherism of psychology and, as in politics, not everybody's cup of tea. We could spend hours on this very interesting discussion within the social sciences arena and that would be great. But, if you are like me, a business practitioner, the reality is that we would need concrete things to work with. Many of the reasons why people take a rather cynical approach to mission statements and declarations of values is because they are full of non-operational concepts, apparently all of them designed to make it impossible to disagree with. If your value statement contains a list of words such as integrity, honesty, creativity, trust, pro-activity and customer focus, you are at the top of the bell curve. The question is: *"What does all that mean?"* Yes, sometimes there are explanations, but, incidentally, rarely at the behavioural level. What is it that people have to do or not do around here to be called honest? What behaviours are acceptable or unacceptable under 'integrity'? What does trust mean? And so on.

Behaviours are actionable, values are not. Behaviours-only with no reference to values is like bits of information in the computer that only make sense when you put them together. Values-only with no reference to behaviours just implies naked labels open to an attitude of pick-your-own interpretation. Culture of an organisation defined in values-only mode is nice, but not actionable. Culture defined in terms of behaviours may not have the glamour of many grandiose value statements but provides clear frameworks and boundaries for people, with the advantage that (a) you can always refer to a value system in the background and (b) we know a lot about the 'social life of behaviours – how they are formed, why they fade, how we can make them stick, how they can create environments.

In VIRAL CHANGE™ we don't dismiss the importance of values and beliefs and the lexicon around attitudes, qualities, mindset and other 'intangibles'. But VIRAL CHANGE™ works with behaviours. It is up to you, to us, to translate any intangible into its behavioural reality. That's why VIRAL CHANGE™ is behavioural change.

>> SECOND KEYWORD: CHANGE. 15 ASSUMPTIONS TO CHALLENGE

This book would like to help any manager and leader working in any organisation - large or small, in the private or public sector - to explore, understand, digest and embrace some counter-intuitive ways of dealing with 'change'.

I am using the word 'change' in a broad sense because - unless you have been in a corporate coma for a while - you would agree right from the start that change is constant in any organisation.

To a great extent, one of the two words in the expression 'change management' is actually redundant. Change Management is management or it is not management at all.

But you and I are also aware that people often give the label 'change management' or 'management of change' to a formal process or series of processes that try to get the organisation from A to B. There is a myriad of books on the topic, there is formal training at business schools, scholarly literature, management gurus specialised in this, countless consulting services, etc. Last time I Googled 'change management', it showed me more than 27 million entries; 9 million if you narrow it down to 'organisation'.

If you are – or have been - involved in any of these 'change-labelled processes' - either as top leader, manager, HR practitioner or part of Organisational Development - you will have been exposed to a lot of the above. This build-up of interest and specialisation has inevitably created lots of assumptions about 'how change works'. Many of them have become dogma, and many of them are simply myths.

Throughout this book and through the glasses of VIRAL CHANGE™, we will address these frequent assumptions:

1 Big change requires big actions

2 Only change at the top can ensure change within the organisation

3 People are resistant to change

4 Cultural change is a slow and painful long-term affair

5 Everybody needs to be involved in the change

6 Communication and training are the vital components of change

7 New processes and systems will create the new necessary behaviours

8 People are rational and will react to logical and rational requests for change

9 There is no point in creating change in one division without the rest of the company participating

10 Sceptical people and enemies of change need to be sidelined

11 Vision for change needs to come from the top and cascade down

12 After change, you need a period of stability and consolidation

13 Short-term wins are tactical but they do not usually represent real change

14 There will always be casualties – people not accepting change – and you need to identify and deal with them

15 People used to not complying with norms will be even worse at accepting change

I'd like to make a suggestion before you read the rest of the book. Take a few minutes and try to establish your position on these 15 assumptions. At the end of this introduction you can write down what you think of them and whether you agree or disagree. And above all, if you can, write down an example from your own organisational life or experience that supports or challenges the assumption. When you have finished the book, I would like to ask you to go back to these, your initial notes and see if your position has changed in one way or another. That would be the greatest measure on how this book will have helped you!

>> READING THIS BOOK

The first five chapters of this book lay the foundations for the practicalities of VIRAL CHANGE™.

Chapter 1 explores the often confusing world of 'change management' or 'management of change'. In this world, the language of change is used in ways that suit practitioners, and it represents different, not always well-defined angles and approaches. A bit of terminology clean-up is necessary in order to understand how to create change.

In Chapter 2, I share why, in my view, many 'change management' initiatives fail. The track record of programmes created under such a label is unimpressive. We think we know why. You'll also see why VIRAL CHANGE™ is such an attractive alternative.

Chapters 3 and 4 open the curtains of the organisation to understand what's going on inside! Any approach to change has a 'model of the organisation' behind it. We all have conventional and traditional views on 'how the organisation works'. Our view of change is a logical consequence of these views. However, we have recently accumulated a great deal of knowledge about 'organisational life' that challenges conventional wisdom. Discovering this fascinating world is the pre-requisite to creating and managing change.

Chapter 5 puts all the insights together and articulates the significant differences between the traditional view -, still the backbone of most academic and consulting frameworks - and VIRAL CHANGE™.

I have grouped all the above chapters under the heading 'In theory for the pragmatists' because many so-called 'practitioners' rush into the application of off-the-shelf processes, systems and templates (including downloadable ones form the internet) without a proper understanding of the fabric of the organisation. Those 'pragmatists' could do with a bit of re-thinking of what we really know about organisational life. The following chapters are grouped under the heading 'In practice for the theorists', because they take VIRAL CHANGE™ to the real life implementations. Inversely here, people with affinity to conceptual frameworks, could well do with 'some action'!

This second section deals with the four components of VIRAL CHANGE™: language (chapter 6), new behaviours (chapters 7, 8 and 9), creation of tipping points (chapters 10, 11 and 12) and rules and routines (chapter 13).

VIRAL CHANGE™ has tremendous flexibility in its application. Different managers, leaders or change practitioners may apply it in somehow different ways. In chapter 14, the 'process' I offer and discuss is far from dogmatic but represents a good overview of my own experience in applying VIRAL CHANGE™.

Chapter 15 revisits the 15 change management assumptions that I introduced here in the introduction, to see if, after reading and digesting this book, we are in need of qualifying or challenging them.

I finish with an epilogue on the role of labels such as 'change' or 'culture' in our day-to-day organisational life.

Come on, let's go!

TAKE A FEW MINUTES. TRY TO ARTICULATE YOUR POSITION ON EACH OF THE ASSUMPTIONS. WRITE DOWN WHETHER YOU AGREE OR DISAGREE. IF YOU CAN, THINK OF AN EXAMPLE FROM YOUR OWN EXPERIENCE TO SUPPORT, QUALIFY OR CHALLENGE THE ASSUMPTIONS. WHEN YOU HAVE FINISHED THE BOOK, GO BACK TO YOUR INITIAL NOTES AND SEE HOW OR IF YOUR POSITION HAS CHANGED IN ONE WAY OR ANOTHER

15 POPULAR AND ESTABLISHED ASSUMPTIONS ABOUT MANAGEMENT OF CHANGE		
	YOUR POSITION	EXAMPLE FROM YOUR EXPERIENCE
(1) BIG CHANGE REQUIRES BIG ACTIONS		
(2) ONLY CHANGE AT THE TOP CAN ENSURE CHANGE WITHIN THE ORGANISATION		

	YOUR POSITION	EXAMPLE FROM YOUR EXPERIENCE
(3) PEOPLE ARE RESISTANT TO CHANGE		
(4) CULTURAL CHANGE IS A SLOW AND PAINFUL LONG-TERM AFFAIR		

	YOUR POSITION	EXAMPLE FROM YOUR EXPERIENCE
(5) EVERYBODY NEEDS TO BE INVOLVED IN THE CHANGE		
(6) COMMUNICATION AND TRAINING ARE THE VITAL COMPONENTS OF CHANGE		

	YOUR POSITION	EXAMPLE FROM YOUR EXPERIENCE
(7) NEW PROCESSES AND SYSTEMS WILL CREATE THE NEW NECESSARY BEHAVIOURS		
(8) PEOPLE ARE RATIONAL AND WILL REACT TO LOGICAL AND RATIONAL REQUESTS FOR CHANGE		

	YOUR POSITION	EXAMPLE FROM YOUR EXPERIENCE
(9) THERE IS NO POINT IN CREATING CHANGE IN ONE DIVISION WITHOUT THE REST OF THE COMPANY PARTICIPATING		
(10) SCEPTICAL PEOPLE AND ENEMIES OF CHANGE NEED TO BE SIDELINED		

	YOUR POSITION	EXAMPLE FROM YOUR EXPERIENCE
(11) VISION FOR CHANGE NEEDS TO COME FROM THE TOP AND CASCADE DOWN		
(12) AFTER CHANGE, YOU NEED A PERIOD OF STABILITY AND CONSOLIDATION		

	YOUR POSITION	EXAMPLE FROM YOUR EXPERIENCE
(13) SHORT-TERM WINS ARE TACTICAL, BUT THEY DO NOT USUALLY REPRESENT REAL CHANGE		
(14) THERE WILL ALWAYS BE CASUALTIES – PEOPLE NOT ACCEPTING CHANGE – AND YOU NEED TO IDENTIFY AND DEAL WITH THEM		

	YOUR POSITION	EXAMPLE FROM YOUR EXPERIENCE
(15) PEOPLE USED TO NOT COMPLYING WITH NORMS WILL BE EVEN WORSE AT ACCEPTING CHANGE		

IN THEORY, FOR THE PRAGMATISTS

(1)

THE CHANGE MANAGEMENT 'SPEAK'

"We trained hard… but it seemed that every time we were beginning to form up in teams we would be reorganised. I was to learn later on in life that we tend to meet any new situation by reorganising, and a wonderful method it can be for creating the illusion of progress while producing confusion, inefficiency and demoralisation".

This is not a quote from the latest biography of a retired CEO, or from a recently published book found in an airport bookshop. It was written in AD 65 by Caius Petronius, who apparently had an insight or two into organisational development.

In 513 BC, Heraclites observed: *"There is nothing permanent except change."* And in the 16th century, in *The Prince*, Machiavelli stated, *"There is nothing more difficult to take in hand, more perilous to conduct, or more uncertain in its success, than to take the lead in the introduction of a new order of things."* So there you are! Change and reorganisation were sort of invented by the Roman army, had already been accepted as inevitable by the Greeks, and have continued ever since. But don't despair if you are part of a painful change, even Machiavelli conceded that it is difficult. But how difficult?

>> PEOPLE ARE RESISTANT TO CHANGE

I can't think of any other statement more used in management conversations than 'people are resistant to change'. By repeating these like parrots, we end up taking it at face value. If you hear somebody in the company saying that people are *not* resistant to change, your first reaction would be to call in the men in white coats!

Look around you: there are legions of consultants and academics saying this. A whole industry of books, tapes, conferences and motivational speakers delivering 'how to' (change) solutions. All under the premise that people need to be pushed, otherwise they would prefer to be static. The Machiavelli school of change management is the official one:

it's going to be difficult, pain is inevitable, people don't like it, push or else.

There is a particular sector of the organisation that has repeatedly won the Oscar for Best Resistance to Change. It's called middle management. Apparently, there is this layer in the organisational sandwich, somewhere in the middle, that blocks everything, resists everything and that, quite frankly, we would be better off without. And this is what happened in the last decades under the lean-and-mean-corporate-clean-up.

> Hierarchical corporate structures have become flat pancakes. Those battalions of unhelpful managers in the middle - blockers of change, gatekeepers of information flow, obstructive individuals, corporate parasites and ugly people in middle management ranks - have left big corporations to resurface as top managers in smaller firms, enablers of change, providers of information and knowledge, facilitators of change, and beautiful consultants selling services to their ex-employers at a premium.

'People are resistant to change?' You don't have to be a biologist to understand how intrinsically contradictory this statement is with the very nature of what we are: sophisticated beings in constant adaptation to changes in the environment, from cradle to grave.

Again, think about it. You, yourself may be married and have children. You have perhaps changed jobs three or four times, if not more; moved house a couple of times, perhaps even moved countries a while ago. Look at your neighbours, they may be in a similar situation and, if not, surely you know others like you. And perhaps now you feel a bit older, you have stopped doing things that you did when you were younger, but you may also have started doing new things that you didn't do until just a little while ago. Perhaps you stopped smoking. Perhaps you have remarried and started a second family. If not, you know somebody who has.

You may have seen your children go through primary and secondary school, abandon you for university (and providing you with that spare room that you always wanted) and have boyfriends and girlfriends, who always looked different from what you expected. You may have seen the death of your parents and the birth of your grandchildren; or you are now spending more time than ever with your surviving parents.

If you look around, what you see is a symphony of change. People, emotions, attachments and geographies sometimes change with the rhythm of the four seasons, other times with the violence of earthquakes. There is a name for all this. It's called life.

From a biological viewpoint we are not resistant to change because we *are* change. You can't say that a baby resists becoming a child and a child resists becoming an adolescent. Life and change are synonymous. There are different degrees of pain associated

with the transitions but we are always
in transition; we are transition.
And, incidentally, any transformation
from pain to misery is largely in our
own hands.

>> CHANGE MAY BE INEVITABLE BUT MISERY IS A CHOICE

Sloppy, insensitive, mismanaged, unnecessarily prolonged change initiatives and programmes in companies - whether on the back of a merger or an internal reorganisation - create misery out of possible pain. Creating unnecessary uncertainty by lack of clarity or openness produces anxiety that could evolve to misery.

We are not talking here about the need for suppression of all forms of pain but the unnecessary hi-fi of pain. We all know that a deviant form of obtaining pleasure is to produce pain. We have a name for this: sadism.

There are managers who believe
that part of their role in times of
change is to turn on the pain hi-fi for
those under them. That would apparently
make them powerful.

I know a few of them. They have a tremendous ability to create a sense of fear and misery around them. They belong to a spectrum of deviant management that on one end has the benign macho and at the other the malignant macho, often disguised as 'it's not me, it's the system'.

>> ME AND YOU IN THE 'CHANGE PLOT'

So, if we, people, are 'changing' all the time - biological age, psychological maturity, social circumstances - and we are somehow still convinced that we have some sort of genetically predisposition not to change, what is it that happened - particularly in the business world - that convinced us of this? The answer may be found in experimental psychology. In classical experiments, two monkeys are equally subjected to a minor, inoffensive electrical shock, delivered to both with the same pattern and intensity. Both of them are equally restrained but only one of them has been given the choice of pushing a little lever that can temporarily stop the shock. Only one of them produces peptic ulcers. Yes, that's it, the one who is not able to 'control' the environment.

> It is not change per se that is a problem, but the ability to have some sense of control over events. For control, read also information, knowing what's going on, the objectives of 'the change programme' or simply personal involvement in the process.

I suggest that many statements like 'we are resistant to change' are short of an end and just need adding: 'when we are not real protagonists'.

In my experience, three broad factors trigger so-called 'resistance' in the management of change in the organisation:

(1) THE TENDENCY TO AVOID LOSS Any process of change has double dimensions. On one hand, we gain something (a better system, a more agile organisation, new leaner processes, etc.). On the other hand, we always lose something: sometimes part of our identity, a portion of history and memory, some emotional attachments. In many cases, the perception of the loss takes over, even when it may be unjustified.

(2) UNPREDICTABLE OUTCOMES Change may take us to terra incognita and we don't quite know what's going to happen. Unpredictability and uncertainty may lead us to defend ('to exhibit a resistant behaviour'), not because we *are* resistant by nature but because we can't visualise the future.

(3) CORPORATE INDUCED PARANOIDISM A variant of the above, people suspect that behind the language of change ('we have to change', 'we have to adapt to the market', 'we need to change to be customer-focused') there is reorganisation (and job losses) even if nobody has the guts to articulate it. Many organisations generate 'paranoid behaviours' because there is no clarity and transparency in the culture and because nobody trusts 'the change speak'.

We are certainly not resistant to change but there is no question that one observes lots of 'resistant behaviours' in organisations. They seem to block, postpone, dismiss or protect against doing things differently.

47

What we see as 'resistance' is what people do to protect themselves, not something that they intrinsically are. This is far from a semantics discussion. Believing that 'we are', inevitably focuses 'the problem' on 'us-as-a-human-nature' and not on the nature of the organisational change. This creates a total distraction from the reality and a potential alibi for disingenuous management.

Most of the resistant-things we see are symptoms of something else. One has to look at those 'signs of resistance' with some detachment and think, "*Why is this? What does it mean? What are the fears behind all this? If it looks like defensive behaviour, what's the aggression?*"

There are classical compilations of 'expressions' that will be very familiar to many. The following list has been taken lightly many times, but it is full of true mechanisms in organisations. I am sure you can add from your own vintage.

- We must not rush things
- We are too small for that
- We do not have the power
- It needs sleeping on, let's think about it
- Not my job or not my priority
- Impossible, not the way we do things here
- It will not work here
- We are too large
- Not in the (public) interest
- No-one has ever done it before

- Someone else (we) tried it before
- From a theoretical viewpoint, yes, but it will not work in practice
- We are not ready yet
- We do not have the resources
- We will get into trouble

>> INSIDE THE 'CHANGE MANAGEMENT' CHURCH: TERMINOLOGY CLEAN-UP

'Change management' has become a specialty in itself amongst the consulting and academic offerings. However, it has also become one of those terms that needs a lot of qualifications in order to understand the real meaning. VIRAL CHANGE™ applies to many scenarios but it is important that we first understand the confusion around these terms. People often refer to 'change management' as a formal programme of activities. Other people and practitioners speak of it in generic terms. Sometimes too generic and as a pure 'speak' hiding many other things. Frequently, 'change management' is equated to some tools or IT-driven process. Here is a useful map (see graph on page 50):

(1) 'MANAGEMENT OF CHANGE' In the sense of generic day-to-day management of the organisation, management equals change management. All ingredients of the conceptual framework behind VIRAL CHANGE™ - as described in this book - and the use of the learnings from the behavioural, social and network sciences are valid and even present.

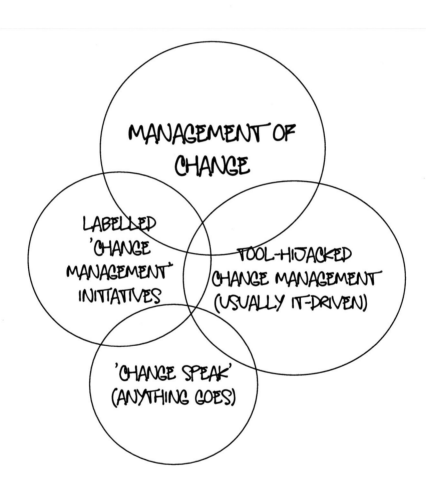

MANAGEMENT OF CHANGE

LABELLED 'CHANGE MANAGEMENT' INITIATIVES

TOOL-HIJACKED CHANGE MANAGEMENT (USUALLY IT-DRIVEN)

'CHANGE SPEAK' (ANYTHING GOES)

(2) FORMALISED 'CHANGE MANAGEMENT' INITIATIVES AND PROGRAMMES

These are designed processes 'to go from A to B', usually in one or more of these situations:

- Merger and acquisition, or re-organisation for other reasons.
- Implementation of new processes and systems - sometimes enterprise-wide - such as Customer Relationship Management (CRM) or Enterprise Resource Planning.
- Other implementations of fundamentally different ways of working, usually (but not always) associated with an IT tool (centralised HR processes, a territory management system for the sales force, a new 'protocol' in a hospital, etc.)
- 'Problem-solving' change management or initiative. Although the word 'problem' could be associated with almost any of the above and other areas, I tend to refer in this case to programmes and initiatives that at least at the start are clearly focused on specific 'needs for fixing'. The most typical are:

  - Improve productivity, with specific desired outcomes more or less defined.
  - Gain efficiency and/or effectiveness; these may or may not have been quantified.
  - So-called 'execution problems'. In these scenarios the organisation very often feels that there is no problem with strategy or almost anything else, it is just a question of implementation and delivery.

- Cultural (or transcultural). These are often described as the developing of a 'culture of' (entrepreneurship, accountability, innovation, speed, etc.).
- Unifying people across the world. That is synchronising processes, systems, ways of working and 'people' in an often fragmented or geographically diverse company.

Inevitably most of these 'formal activities' are heavily focused and biased towards 'processes and systems change' with assumptions of collateral damage. Collateral damage is what people tend to remember:

- 'People will have to change' (or else).
- There will be different roles and responsibilities (will I have a job?).
- Efficiencies will have to be gained (= redundancies, cost cutting)

(3) TOOL-HIJACKED 'CHANGE MANAGEMENT' In my experience, as soon as there is a big IT piece in the middle of the changes (CRM, for example) this driver will take over, with a strong tendency to ignore the people and organisational angles of the change. Also, IT practitioners are largely responsible for the popularisation of the concept of 'change management'. There are offers that read more or less like this: *"This software delivers proactive, automated, user-friendly change management. It is a complete solution that will increase ROI by automating and managing your change process better via a web-based process. It will create change by significantly contributing to your organisation's strategic planning process"*. To which I cry: *"Give me a break!"*

(4) LOOSE SPEAK This is an extremely loose use of the term 'change management' that can mean almost anything and that generates the 'paranoidism' described before.

Next time you talk about management of change or a 'change management programme', please define it!

>> A VERY, VERY SIMPLIFIED CLASSIFICATION FOR THOSE WHO NEED ONE

In terms of 'types of change', you'll find endless classifications, all of them created for a reason! Leaving aside those of mainly academic interest and other more or less pretentious ones, let me share with you the two dimensions that really matter to me (see graph on page 54):

(1) DIRECTION OF THE CHANGE:

In terms of direction, change programmes, initiatives or other less formalised attempts can be conceived in three ways:

 # TOP-DOWN The top leadership team dictates the way to go and everything cascades down via the managerial grid. This usually involves a series of communication programmes with the aim of reaching most people in the organisation.

 # BOTTOM-UP Changes sometimes start in some teams or divisions that perhaps had originally been charged with looking into a particular

53

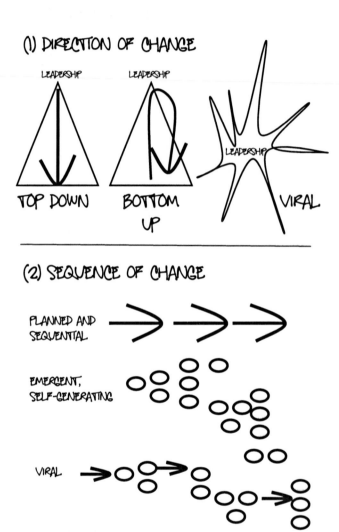

(1) DIRECTION OF CHANGE

LEADERSHIP   LEADERSHIP

LEADERSHIP

TOP DOWN   BOTTOM UP   VIRAL

(2) SEQUENCE OF CHANGE

PLANNED AND SEQUENTIAL

EMERGENT, SELF-GENERATING

VIRAL

problem. Or an employee satisfaction survey (surely initiated at the top) has resulted in team activity that interprets the need for changes. They 'report back' and 'report back' and eventually the leadership at the top absorbs this, integrates it and translates it into a top down 'reaction'. You could say that in terms of the 'physics of change', what goes up inevitably comes down again!

 # DISTRIBUTED (VIRAL CHANGE™) Leadership at the top may initiate the process and give directions but very soon change becomes multi-directional and the leadership of change is effectively 'distributed' across the organisation. The real 'leaders' become people in formal or informal groups, at different levels, often labelled as 'Change Champions'. VIRAL CHANGE™ aims at the synergy between the role of management and the power of those internal networks of committed people.

(2) SEQUENCE OF THE CHANGE

In terms of sequence of change, we also have three main categories:

 # PLANNED AND SEQUENTIAL Changes take place in a particular order. Kotter's steps for change, for example, read[1]: establishing a sense of urgency, creating a guiding coalition, developing a vision and strategy, communicating the change vision, empowering a broad base of people to take action, generating short-term wins, consolidating gains

---

[1] Kotter, John P., 1996, *Leading Change*, Harvard Business School Press, Boston

55

and institutionalising new approaches in the culture. There you have it: follow the steps, add salt and pepper, put it in the oven and change will be produced. Command and control managers love it.

 # EMERGENT AND SELF-GENERATING

The proponents of this kind of change come from many places which were considered esoteric until now (i.e. 'complexity theory' or 'systems thinking'). Fundamentally, they believe that change can not be planned and that it needs to occur in a 'biological' self-generating way that evolves progressively and the outcomes of which are not totally predictable. Not popular amongst command-and-control managers.

 # VIRAL CHANGE™

This is a different category because it acknowledges the role of 'planning', but does not support the sequential-fundamentalism of the traditional A→B→C (the ones that generate hundreds of Gant charts and pretend to define what exactly will be in place on the afternoon of Wednesday the 17th July in 2008). For those of us in the VIRAL CHANGE™ business, this oracle-like capacity of prediction is safely left in the hands of the Big Consulting Groups and some Big HR Departments who have special genes for this.

>> SUMMARY: WHERE VIRAL CHANGE™ STANDS

From the myriad of classifications on 'change', I have picked up three well-established names and 'models' that you may or may not have come across, because they provide a particularly good mirror to see what VIRAL CHANGE™ may look like.

(I)   Kotter's - and Kotter-like - frameworks would work for me if we could establish a sense of urgency at the same time as creating a guiding coalition, and at the same time as developing a vision and strategy, communicating, empowering, generating wins, and consolidating gains, all in one and in parallel, all boiling and backwards and forwards. I know this is counterintuitive, but not impossible. VIRAL CHANGE™ proves it, and I have been practicing it for years with success. Thank you. In plain English, and paraphrasing Woody Allen on London ("*all seasons in one afternoon*"), we need Kotter's eight steps in one afternoon.

VIRAL CHANGE™ has a hard time understanding a sequential, orderly business organisation world when what we see every day is a chaotic, multidimensional, network-centric, but otherwise very rich one. The boiling life within the organisation, the pressure of challenges, the shortening of product and market cycles, the speed of technology reinventing itself, the 24/7/365 life of information and knowledge, the ephemeral nature of many products and the compressed time and space that, whether you like it or not, characterises business life today, forces us to look at things as 'whole systems' as opposed to 'a sequence of events'. To tackle a chaotic, unpredictable, fast-moving, multi-directional and multi-dependent world with a Ten-Sequential-Steps-Orderly-Change-Programme is the squaring of the circle in management terms. But:

'When the only tool you have is a
hammer, everything looks like a nail'.
When the method you have is a 10-steps-
5-modules-change-management-programme,
everything will look like activities and
initiatives that fit into the
consultant's PowerPoint templates.

(2) Some of the sequences historically described are more modest. Kurt Lewin, for example, described a three-stage process called 'unfreezing' (recognise the need for change, develop alternatives and create messages) 'implementation' and 'refreezing' (creating new approaches). Kurt Lewin, a great pioneer of many things in the social sciences, just about missed the opportunity of labelling things in a different way. The commercial microwave was introduced in 1947. I wonder whether Lewin could have called it 'defrosting' instead of 'unfreezing'. At least defrosting implies unfreezing and cooking at the same time! It would be at least closer to the 'all seasons in one afternoon'! The fifties were very different from today, not only in our cooking possibilities but in the concept of space and time.

If you were trained in sequential
change management (unfreezing-
implementing-refreezing-style) in your
MBA or your executive development as
taught in the 50's, you'll be shocked
when faced with the real life
organisation of today, where sequences
(of any kind!) only work in the
ephemeral life of the flip chart.

(3) Harvard guru Rosabeth Moss Kanter differentiates between 'Bold Strokes' and 'Long Marches'. Bold strokes are drastic changes imposed by 'people above' such as a big reorganisation, merger or acquisition, selling of a division, etc. They may or may not produce changes in the long term, but they are usually injected as a short-term measure. Long Marches are composed of small changes developed over time in what is a long process needing the involvement of 'the organisation'. VIRAL CHANGE™ is neither bold stroke nor long march. VIRAL CHANGE™ is Bold March. It does not have the patience of the long-term incremental process (if VIRAL CHANGE™ had a headquarters, the motto above the door would be: 'life is short') but proves that 'small changes' can create 'big change' relatively fast, provided that a viral network is ready; i.e. an organisational network through which the changes are imitated, diffused and 'fashioned'.

There are hundreds of other classifications on the nature of change[2], the type and the pace of change and the conceptual frameworks behind them. I mean literally hundreds. They all try to encapsulate 'the process of change' in one way or another. They were all conceptually born for a reason. There are very good sources to dip into if this is what you want. Otherwise, let's keep moving.

---

[2] A very good and readable academic graduate book is Bernard Burnes' *Managing Change* (Financial Times Prentice Hall, 2004, London)

>> WHAT ABOUT 'BEHAVIOURAL CHANGE'?

If management of change or 'change management' is almost totally absorbed by 'the organisation territory' (organisational development, management, HR practices, consulting services, organisational academics), then 'behavioural change' is very different. As a discipline, it has its roots in experimental psychology and what subsequently became behaviourism. For a long time, the new science of behaviours never lost either the experimental flavour or the presence of rats, pigeons or other animals as main characters. Progressively, we gained the knowledge of fundamental laws that seem to work across complex living organisms. That includes you and the organisation you work for. Its core and often crude historical basis also became embellished by the connection with social sciences. Today, a world of 'applications' are better known than the core experimental science.

If you Google 'behavioural change' or 'behavioural change management'[3], you will find a combination of very different topics. Amongst them:

- Applications for socio-medical issues such as addictions.
- Social and community programmes 'to change behaviours' (adolescent anti-social behaviour, for example).
- Epidemics, change of (social) behaviours (needed) in AIDS management, for example.

---

[3] Please be aware that results will be different depending on whether you use the US or UK spelling of the word 'behaviour'.

- Psychological-Clinical issues, mainly in the area of so called 'anxiety disorders': anxiety management, phobias, etc.
- Child behavioural problems.
- Education topics.
- Safety, health and safety (in the workplace, for example).
- Coaching and/or leadership (to change behaviours).
- Some aspects of 'performance management' in business organisations.

It really does look like a broad church!

> The application of behavioural and social sciences to the day-to-day management in organisations in general, and, in particular to formal programmes or initiatives of change, still has very limited visibility.

Later in the book, we will see that the use of 'the language of behaviours' does not necessarily guarantee that a true behavioural approach is taken. In any case, if something needs big changes, it's 'change management'. In the next chapter, we'll see how VIRAL CHANGE™ constitutes the only modern alternative to the traditional, conventional and mainly sequential-linear approaches, which, as we'll see next, have an incredible record of failure!

(2)

HOW TO FAIL EXPENSIVELY

Perhaps, you have been involved in corporate programmes that have started with great fanfare. Some of them may have disappeared from everybody's radar screen in months if not weeks. Why? The intentions were good. The communication was good. The retreat at the country-house hotel was good. The speeches were good. The external consultants were good. So, what happened? The life cycle of many 'initiatives' - including the ones labelled 'change management' - resemble the variety of patterns in the graph on page 64: peaks, disappearance, resurrections, parallel lives and more peaks…

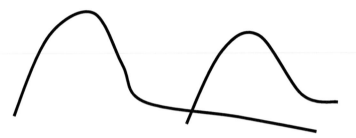

Initial peak of excitement and 'adoption' followed by progressive fading and disappearance, at which time probably another 'corporate initiative' is born

Peaks, disappearance and resurrections of multiple initiatives running in parallel, none of them fully established or implemented

Very erratic process with occasional premature declarations of death. However, it's stable over time

>> THE BIG IT HIJACK

In recent years, 'enabling technologies' (often a fancy term for big IT) have become both sophisticated and pervasive. Many corporations of some size that have experimented with growth, some times via M&A, have been compelled to install enterprise-wide new processes and systems, very often - if not almost always - hand in hand with a new IT system or IT architecture. SAP, ERP and CRM have become familiar soup letters on the company's menu.

CRM (customer relationship management) in particular has become a big area across many industries. Both in IT terms and 'process terms' it is a sub-industry and sub-specialty in its own rights! But many people across industries would agree that many of those efforts have failed to meet expectations. As in any other IT-driven or IT-heavy implementation of new processes and systems, reality can be split into three:

(A) THE NEWS FROM THE SOFTWARE VENDOR'S SIDE
- Company X chooses product Y to roll out in all EU countries. Successful implementation of Z across all affiliates of N.
- Another pharma company chooses A and its product for its global sales strategy realignment.

(B) THE NEWS FROM THE MANAGEMENT'S SIDE
- 70% of executives surveyed disappointed in the performance of X.
- The 'change' has not fulfilled its promises.
- ROI being questioned by senior management.

(C) THE ACTUAL (REAL) NEWS

- 50-70% of the system under-used
- IT and product blamed: 'It doesn't live up to its promises'.
- Successful implementation in country A. Same product, same process for country B, here it fails miserably (Tip: and it has nothing to do with the country's culture).

What's going on? A criticism often heard is that implementers fail to involve stakeholders and therefore 'they' (employees, for example) didn't feel the ownership. My experience in this area is completely different, actually exactly the opposite. Stakeholders are usually over-included. You find Project Teams, Users Teams, Specification Teams, Steering Committees and other management paraphernalia that cushion the implementation. And, still, the implementation is over-budget, over-time, under-used and in many cases over-hated. The same applies to 'change management programmes' with a smaller (or even no) IT component. The only difference is that when you have an expensive IT system at the centre of it all, the whole thing just has greater visibility.

>> THREE WAYS TO FAIL

I see three reasons for this widespread organisational fiasco. And they have nothing to do with the technical process of describing 'specifications' and 'rolling out the product', or even with the efforts to map new processes and systems.

(1) FOCUS ON WHAT'S VISIBLE OR MANAGEABLE, EVEN IF THE SOURCES OF PROBLEMS LAY ELSEWHERE

Probably 85% of issues in the implementation of formal 'change management programmes have to do either with vision or with people. 15% or so are strictly speaking issues related to technology or new processes. Yet, we spend 85% of the budget on the 15% that is more visible and manageable: the IT packages and the mapping and developing of the associated (new) processes and systems. Management has traditionally always had a term for that 85% of the trouble. They call it the soft stuff. The 'soft' is sometimes unpopular, sometimes simply scary for people who do not know how to navigate through the muddy social and psychological waters. Many managers behave as if the sole parameter to apply to 'the people issue' is hope. Which leads me to the second source of fiasco:

(2) WE TREAT BEHAVIOURS AS A BY-PRODUCT OF THE CHANGE PROGRAMME, SOMETHING THAT 'WILL HAPPEN' AS A NATURAL CONSEQUENCE

This is a universally held assumption about the role of people's behaviours. Consciously or unconsciously, many people use a thought process that is fundamentally flawed. We expect people's rationality. We design processes, systems and implementation on the assumption of that rationality. Something that reads more or less like this: "*We move from old, bad system A to new, good system B, which delivers more advantages, i.e. X, Y and Z. People will adapt their behaviours accordingly. They will do new things, will use the system*".

ASSUMPTION

STRATEGY

↓

PLANNING
(+ SPECIFICATIONS
IF IT PROGRAMME)

↓

MAPPING OF
PROCESSES AND
SYSTEMS

↓

COMMUNICATION
TRAINING
IMPLEMENTATION

↓

NEW BEHAVIOURS
WILL FOLLOW
ACCORDINGLY

STRATEGY

↓

PLANNING
(+ SPECIFICATIONS
IF IT PROGRAMME)

↓

MAPPING OF
PROCESSES AND
SYSTEMS

↓

COMMUNIC...

REALITY

↓

PEOPLE CONTINUE
TO BEHAVE AS
BEFORE. LOW
ADOPTION, HIGH
REJECTION, POOR
ROI, BIG EXPENSE

In other words, for many people behaviours are, consciously or unconsciously, a by-product, a consequence of the new process and system. However, after many new processes and systems have been put into place, very often people seem to continue to 'do as before'! In behavioural terms, the above assumption is nonsense.

> The 'position' of behaviours is misplaced. New processes and systems and 'the changes' per se do not *produce* new behaviours. On the contrary, you need to have new behaviours in the system so that they can sustain the new processes and systems. Not the other way around! This simple paradigm has tremendous implications for the management of change (see graph p. 68).

Although I am including an IT-driven or IT-heavy new process change in my argument, the same principle also applies 100% when IT is not a key ingredient.

You'll understand the fiasco better now with the following case! 'Collaboration' is a behavioural example that I am using later on in the book as well. Imagine that a new, sophisticated, CRM system requires that people - for example in your sales force - input data gathered from the market into the electronic system (i.e. activity in the field, competitor intelligence, customer assessment, changes in personal details of the customer, etc.). Imagine that this data is crucial to feed the system and make it work.

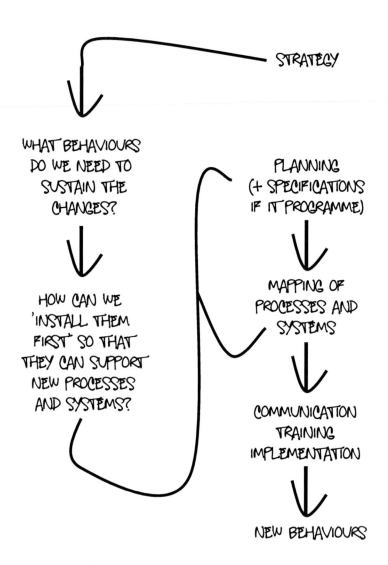

Behaviours as a pre-requisite to support changes,
not as a consequence

That's the only way for other salesmen, for example, to benefit from that crucial information. Or for marketing to change gears, or for management to allocate resources flexibly.

The design of the system is perfect. The analysis it can provide is very sophisticated. But you will be making an important assumption: that the salesmen will enter the data!

In the previous, pre-CRM era, for example, all salesmen carried their own notes. They 'owned the data'. Now we are asking them to collaborate with each other and share the data! This is a significantly different behaviour. Rationally, it's difficult to disagree! However, in reality, the system is underused. Why? The sophisticated, highly analytical, sexy new CRM system *does not produce* collaboration! It needs collaboration instead! It is the other way around. The graph on page 70 illustrates the correct 'position' of behaviours.

(3) IN MANY LARGE ORGANISATIONS THERE IS A SATURATION OF (CHANGE) INITIATIVES AND A CLUTTERED MANAGEMENT SPACE

In medium and big-sized companies, corporate life is very often punctuated by a series of continuous 'initiatives' that are launched to provide the workforce with frameworks, guidance, rules, strict dictation on what is possible/acceptable and what's not, new directions, new focus, new emphasis or new requirements. They all come on top of more permanent frames of reference.

For example, there is usually a pre-existing 'value system' of some sort, with perhaps a set of half a dozen of those declared values and their definitions. There is also most likely a performance management system in place, used to measure the achievement of individual annual goals and objectives. You may recognise your company in this picture.

The linkage of permanent frameworks is assumed. It may be assumed, for example, that somewhere in that annual appraisal, under the performance management system, there is a reference to the value system. But this is sometimes one hell of an assumption. In many cases, these two frameworks, are not connected, or at least not in an obvious way. The corporate value system sits somewhere in the background, while the performance management system speaks the day-to-day language of operational goals and objectives. To put it modestly, the two 'systems' may not talk to each other at all.

If you are in the sales force, you will probably have a 'sales system' as well, that perhaps will have been branded as unique to the company. Let's call it 'Company X Sales Process and Performance – XSPP'. It will map some steps in the selling process, from planning to closing the sale. It will have a full training programme associated with the framework. Any new recruit will have to graduate from that training programme and embrace the method. A performance management system in that sales force is likely to incorporate measurements on how the individual is doing on the XSPP system, together with measurements on the individual targets on sales quota and other operational objectives.

For that sales force professional, that's a different set of measures and a particular reference framework on top of corporate values and their descriptions. So, to follow the logic, we now have three frameworks that should 'talk to each other'. It would be logical to expect that the sales force division follows the corporate value system, therefore the XSPP should be 'compatible with it' and the performance management should incorporate both. Are you with me? So far, we have at least the following components of the metrics: how that individual meets its sales targets, how he does this following XSPP, and how he lives up to the corporate values.

It may be that the company has embarked upon an enterprise-wide cost-cutting initiative, under an umbrella label of 'change management'. The company may have other parallel frameworks or 'initiatives' such as a Quality System, perhaps a resurrected Six-Sigma programme, which is another 'change management' initiative in itself. This has another superimposed matrix of declarations of purposes, language, metrics, processes and expected ways of working. If you are still able to follow the above sales force example, you should expect that somewhere in the company's Sales Management, the Quality System comes in and superimposes itself on the previously described processes.

I haven't finished. Let's imagine that, as an example, we are talking about a big corporation with a big HR function and that there is a Leadership Development system in place, perhaps an internal Leadership Institute. Chances are, there is a 'leadership framework' that details the quality of desired leadership, its taxonomy and perhaps a set of, let's call it, 'leadership qualities'.

This is another framework, another language and another set of measures, not forgetting another set of booklets, guidelines, CDs and 'workbooks' on offer which managers are supposed to use with the troops at some point. Would this Sales

Management in my example above ignore the crucial dimension of leadership qualities? Surely not! They will have to be incorporated somewhere.

So, if I can still count correctly, I now have five different frameworks/programmes/initiatives superimposed on one another, besides the perhaps overriding 'Working Smart' or any other down/right-sizing programme.

Bear with me! Let's continue and imagine that you are visiting the Marketing division. They have their own 5 year 'renewal plan' that contains 5 strategic goals across the division, leading to 12 critical success factors (CSFs). Each section within the division (International Marketing, New Products Marketing, Strategic Marketing and Product Life Cycle Marketing) is supposed to absorb the 12 CSFs and create their own action plan to make sure that they are driving in the appropriate direction.

The Marketing division's leadership team has also crafted a change management programme. It is defined by a small set of far-reaching 'drivers' expressed like this: 'Customer-centric focus', 'Smart Connectivity' (with other parts of the company) and 'Living the Brands'. These are the three dimensions that this leadership team has decided are to be placed above everything else. Each of them has been described in some detail and each of them contains CSFs that are linked to the other more operational CSFs. The Sales division, which we just left above with at least five different managerial frameworks, has a similar strategic construction on the strategic/operational side but with different language.

The R&D division has another change management programme under a triad: 'Time to market', 'Smart Projects' and 'Knowledge Networks', each of these with a similar pattern of definitions, universal goals, CSFs and the associated 'translation' for each of the sections such as product development, external affairs, etc. There is always a training package and workshops associated with these frameworks.

If you can't identify yourself with all the above and you think this is just an exaggeration, you should consider yourself lucky about the way daily life is conducted in your company.

> It is not unusual that a professional in the managed-by-framework-type of company finds himself 'framed' (what better word to use if you have so many frameworks?) into at least four or five different systems of reference, all of them with their own language and metrics.

A great percentage of those 'initiatives' and their associated frameworks would be labelled - formally or informally - as 'change management' and/or leaders would see themselves in the business of 'managing change'.

Half of these initiatives may seem vaguely connected. For the rest, if the intention was to connect them, that connectivity may not be obvious in reality. But even if the connections are there, the individual language for each of the initiatives is sometimes so different for the average employee that these initiatives and frameworks seem to have a life of their own.

> Each of the 'change initiatives',
> new or old, came about for good reasons.
> All of them have so-called 'sponsors' at
> high levels to ensure that people get
> the message that the company is serious
> about them. Many of them will be talking
> about 'management of change'.

Because of their multi-centric origin, these initiatives have their own epicentre of energy. The HR division is pushing leadership programmes, workshops and associated materials for managers. These managers are also getting the standard presentation toolkits and workshops of the Quality System sponsors. Their own division has its own programme of training all managers on, say, 'customer-centric practices' and 'smart connectivity'. This brings another set of activities (workshops, meetings) and another set of visible frameworks (templates, posters, booklets, workbooks).

>> NEW CHANGE INITIATIVE? SURE, WHATEVER...

Confronted with all these packages, schemes, frameworks, programmes, appraisal systems, declared sets of values, dozens of CSFs, dozens of actions and ever emergent agendas, and with having to follow corporate projects, to attend workshops, to read PowerPoints, plus daily cost-cutting hunting, the average employee feels bombarded by a constant campaign of friendly fire! Management sometimes explains it all (the complexity) by saying that they want the workforce to understand the corporate objectives so that people can be aligned with them. The employee sometimes only needs a single word to comment on it all: "*Whatever!*"

"Alignment? Alignment with what?" people seem to be saying. The daily life of the employee takes place in a forest with so many trees that they perhaps decide it's easier to deal with one tree at a time. Much of company life is spent inwards, managing internal processes and systems and refining and re-oiling the internal machinery. Companies often suffer from framework exhaustion, initiative saturation and multi-metrics fatigue.

>> METRICS SATURATION AND DEATH BY TEMPLATE

This is often more visible in the Sales Force, where more often than not a complex Incentive System is in place, that - on top of everything else (yes, I didn't finish my list before) - gives top bonuses to the top and lesser bonuses to the next layers in a scaled system often called 'forced ranking'. Incidentally, one of the reasons why incentive programmes are one of the most useless management tools on offer is that they are often based upon pristine benchmarking market data: data provided by compensation and benefit consultants with an incredible lack of knowledge of behavioural sciences, leading to immensely flawed behavioural assumptions.

For example, a 'forced ranking' system that gives a bonus of 10,000 dollars to the top 20% over-achievers, 8,000 to the next 15% and 5,000 to the next group down, is based upon the assumption that individuals are rationally seeking more money all the time.

Meet Joe Bloggs, senior rep, seven years with the company, proud of his job. Bombarded with a quality programme, 12 CSFs, a performance management system, four leadership drivers, ten principles to 'live the brand', sales targets, an advanced sales training course, and one hour a day of sending 'activity data' to the Customer Relationship Management System (CRM) from his laptop at home, Joe has thrown in the towel a long time ago and professes (so far only in private) that awful, terminally ill 'whatever'.

He is doing his job and he knows that he will do a good job, but he is happily settling for the 10% overachievement and he has no intention whatsoever of killing himself for the 20% and the associated bonus excess. *"Do you want to rate me?"*, Joe says, *"OK, do it, but don't force me to understand the metrics. Last time I tried, I got terminally exhausted."* *"But, Joe, please, look at this, we need to follow the new ten quality principles"*. *"Sure, whatever."*

> The initiative fatigue and multi-framework approach that we are seeing – particularly in medium and big sized corporations – operates like a machine gun of friendly fire that kills any hope of so-called 'alignment' because it is impossible to know what to align with. Many so-called 'change management programmes' are associated with these mutually competing initiatives in the already immensely cluttered environment.

It is the death-by-template approach that expands like the plague, very often with senior people on the 10th floor totally ignorant of its associated toxicity. Each of the 'sponsor groups' would report back on the marvellous achievements of their initiatives but perhaps nobody would point out that the troops are exhausted and wounded and that the lethal 'whatever' is now spreading rapidly.

>> ANTIBODIES TO 'THE NEXT CHANGE'

An unintended consequence of all this is that this fatigue operates like a reinforcement. That is, the next time a new initiative comes in - even if this one is the one that will make the difference - employees can't distinguish it from anything else and will treat it with extreme cynicism. The level of initiative-antibodies soars and any new intruder is welcomed with the 'whatever' salute.

Given the temptation of small sized companies to imitate the medium sized ones, it is not unusual to see some caricatures of this problem in those small enterprises. Which is scary. It is leadership at the top of any company that has the duty to look at all those 'initiatives' and see if they provide any real meaning and direction. But they may be busy with a boardroom initiative of their own.

> The best new corporate initiative that money can buy is Simplicity. The best leadership output is Meaning. And the next senior management vacancy to fill in is Vice President of Cleaning-up Frameworks.

Believe me, 'whatever' is deadly and spreading fast.

>> IN SUMMARY

The following three:

- wrong focus of attention with premium on technology instead of people's behaviours
- wrong assumptions about the role of behaviours, expecting that they will 'appear' as a result of new processes
- a cluttered corporate environment where multiple initiatives and 'processes' are running in parallel

are the main reasons why many 'change management' processes fail. The failure is usually expensive, painful and prolonged, despite which 'managers-of-failed-change' seem to have an incredible ability to keep their jobs.

But, let's be fair to many of them. A great part of the problem is caused by a concept of the organisation and its management of change that is conventional, traditional, old and totally unsuitable to today's environment. We must go back to the drawing board and challenge some of our sacred assumptions about 'how organisations work' and 'how people do things'. There is no way we will produce a quantum leap in our progress from failure to success, unless we are prepared to shake one or two pillars.

In the next chapters, we'll try to see 'what's going on' inside the organisations. And there are enormous possibilities for modern management and leadership when we see things with completely different glasses. It's time to adjust our focus.

(3)

BEHIND THE CURTAINS OF THE ORGANISATION CHART

The greatest risk we could take, and that is embedded in many traditional 'change management approaches, is to assume that (1) we all have a common, shared understanding of 'how the organisation works' and (2) this organisation is the one we 'see', the one somehow represented in the organisation charts.

Before we expand on how fast and sustainable VIRAL CHANGE™ will work, we need to stand back and review fundamental *misconceptions* of daily life within organisations. And this is probably an understatement. Perhaps we should call it 'fundamental misconceptions about what the organisation *is*'.

And a good starting point is to throw away the organisation chart. Let me explain.

Meet John. First day at the office was a typical one: introductions, lunch with his new staff, credit card, formal inheritance of a secretary and a car park slot, and chat with the boss to go through the organisation charts. It didn't take John long to realise that the real communication lines in daily life, the information flow between groups and people with influence, or even the obvious working relationship of the established multidisciplinary matrix teams, had little to do with that organisation chart. Beyond the otherwise useful information on who reported to whom, and how many bosses away from the Big One he was, the organisation chart or, as he used to call it in his previous company, the *organigramme*, was largely irrelevant.

> The entire daily dynamics in the company could be better represented in the form of a monster 'influence diagram', which would look more like a London underground map or a web. Certainly it would not look like the PowerPointed little boxes on a Christmas tree.

Incidentally, John soon also learnt another thing. What applied to the organisation chart could also be said of his job description and his initial set of objectives. Since he joined, things had evolved fast, and 'the goals of the job' had become a moving target. New assignments were coming in weekly. His original set of annual objectives, although the same on paper, had been substantially modified. Some of them were now brand new. Others became obsolete pretty fast. Progressively, the 'organisation on paper' and the 'real organisation' had gone their different ways. They soon became divergent companions.

Welcome to the 21st century business organisation. 'The organisation chart is dead'. 'The job description is dead'. But don't panic! The death of 'the structure' may have been grossly exaggerated.

>> FIRST STOP: BIOLOGY

Like biological organisms, organisations are in continuous adaptation to stimuli (external and internal environments), and must change and evolve accordingly. But we apply to them rather static, linear or artificial borders, processes and checks. Think about it. Biological organisms do not understand *one year* budget cycles, *quarterly* reporting on activity, *one-off* post-retreat reorganisations, *static* organisation charts, two-page-*forever* job descriptions, or *annual* objectives set up in January and assessed in December.

They grow, move, reproduce, generate antibodies, get smaller or bigger, and die at different paces and rhythms. Their 'ultimate structure' is created by their functionality ("*The function creates the organ*," anatomy professors say). Also, they can not be fully explained without reference to another ('bigger') system to which they belong or are connected to.

In fact, they are complex systems that are better understood through the glasses of complexity theory. Business organisations may be just the same. What happens inside them can't be followed with the static organisation chart and the job description manual.

> The different components (people, groups, teams, networks of influence and power, etc.) are linked by an information flow which is far from static. In fact, the organisation *is* an information network.

Cells form organs, organs form human beings, human beings form groups and organisations. Wouldn't this be a natural progression to consider in order to understand how all these entities work, including 'an organisation'?

If that is the case, biology, not scientific management (or so-called management science) should be a more appropriate discipline to understand how organisations work; a pre-requisite to understanding how *change* in organisations may work! But, biology is not a conventional part of an MBA curriculum.

> Our understanding of organisations is largely mechanistic. Machines are a good model for the command and control of physical things, but they may not be such a good model for associations of human beings.

Fritjof Capra is a physicist, whose books are mainly found on New Age shelves. He is an advocate of 'systems thinking' and ecology (or both), and has written multiple books and other writings on the connections between physics and the environment. He is a speaker in a broad circuit that expands from ecology, greens, 'management', self-help to the celebrity and political arena. His book *The Hidden Connections: a Science for sustainable living*, (Harper Collins, 2002) deals - among other things - with a 'biological model' of organisations.

The idea that the organisation is better understood as a living system is not new[4], but Capra embraces it to stress the differences between a *machine approach* and *a living system* approach.

> A machine, Capra says, can be *controlled*; a living system can only be *disturbed*. Organisations, he says, can be influenced by giving impulses rather than instructions.

Living systems 'choose' what to notice and what to react to. The model - the basis and logic of which can hardly be challenged - has tremendous implications. For example, he says:

> "Working with the process inherent in living systems means that we don't need to spend a lot of energy to move an organisation. There is no need to push, pull or bully it to make a change; force and energy are not the issue, the issue is meaning. Meaningful disturbances will get the organisation's attention and will trigger structural changes".

---

[4] See also De Geus, Arie, 1997, *The Living Company*, Harvard Business School Press, Boston.

But, hey, don't read over this too fast. In terms of management of change, something important has just been said above, almost unpretentiously, almost in passing: *"There is no need to push, pull or bully it to make a change; force and energy are not the issue, the issue is meaning"*. Bookmark this please!

Regarding people and management, Capra also says:

> "Giving meaningful impulses rather than precise instructions may sound far too vague to managers used to striving for efficiency and predictable results, but it is well-known that intelligent people rarely carry out instructions exactly to the letter. They always modify and reinterpret them, ignore some parts and add others of their own making. Sometimes it may merely be a change of emphasis, but people always respond with new versions of the original instructions".

Wow! I am not sure what to say, Mr Capra, but we have just done a multi-country roll-out of 13 Town Hall meetings with an average of 300 people each, the CEO has come along to all of them (all of them! Isn't that commitment?) and he has stressed that *"the train has left the station and the question is whether you are on it"*. That was a nice threat that our HR department called 'burning platform'. We have a communication programme with ready-made PowerPoints, DVDs, web casts, standard workshops and Outlook calendars blocked for the next twelve months.

We have slogans, pocket cards, posters, mugs and pencils by the hundreds, reminding people of the key messages for change. We have engaged the best Big Change Management

Consulting Group that we could find. This is big! This is powerful! VPs will cascade this down to directors in each country via weekend retreats. Directors to Managers. Managers to staff. Every single person, I repeat, *every* single person has been engaged.

We want to make sure that every corner of the firm understands the reason for change, that we have engaged all hearts and minds, that everybody is involved (or we won't be completely successful) and that everybody is also aware of the consequences of not 'jumping onboard', you know, the wagon thing. And you are telling me that *"there is no need to push, pull or bully it to make a change; force and energy are not the issue, the issue is meaning"*? Give me a break!

The main point about a living organism theory of the firm is that beyond the superficial, anecdotal or, as many people may see it, just 'a clever way to talk', there is an inevitable truth: we are talking about people after all. People are living organisms, and their groupings must be living organisms as well! If that's the case, life in organisations may have more to do with a life cycle (birth, adolescence, maturity and in some cases senility and certainly death) than with an engineering model of bits and pieces that fit together with standard operating procedures and unchangeable quality systems written down in a manual.

Perhaps the main consequence of the 'living company' metaphor when applied to leadership in organisations is that over-detailed plans to act may be intrinsically alien to the living organism that is the organisation.

Following the model, leadership must be more about setting a framework and directions and literally leaving it up to people to figure out how to act, acknowledging that there will be a fair amount of re-interpretation and re-framing. It also must be about creating an environment for these important 'conversations' to take place and to protect them.

Perhaps the CEO is in fact the Chief neurobiologist of the firm and the flow of information and knowledge throughout the firm is better understood in terms of a 'central nervous system'.

Many managers, perhaps you as well, may choose to dismiss these metaphors as something fancy or as New-Age thinking. But the beauty of metaphors is that they get us close to understanding reality through analogy.

Ok, so it's all biology! If we are into the 'living organisms' model - and it seems reasonable to accept this model as plausible (!) - then something needs to be recognised from the start:

> The mechanistic concept of the organisation plus its associated 'way of management' is going to be hard to square with a dynamic, ever evolving and adapting living entity. But this 'mechanistic model' is at the core of the very traditional understanding of organisations, the one that is in our minds: one of a relatively hierarchical top-bottom plumbing system of data, information, dictations, point checks, actions and outcomes.

We have this model in mind, consciously or unconsciously, in:

- the way many strategic planning and budget processes work.
- the way many 'reporting systems' work (bottom-up, up the pipes of the 'plumbing system' in the more or less hierarchical organisation.
- the way corporate information and communication is cascaded down (note the terms used).
- the way the web of annual goals and objectives starts at the top and, again, cascades down, taking one objective from one VP and translating it into 3 objectives each for his directors' direct reports, at which level any objective will consequently be translated into two or three more at manager level and so on. If you associate a few Critical Success Factors (CSFs) with each of the components of the planning system, you end up with a bottom line in the spreadsheet that contains an enormous amount of 'tasks' or 'actions'. Last time I counted them at one of my clients, I found six corporate objectives becoming eighteen strategic objectives leading to forty or so 'goals and objectives' for the divisions, which in their turn added thirty-five critical success factors, resulting in eighty or so 'critical actions'. I was told that this year was 'an easy one' with a more simplified process and system.

This fabulous cascade that flows through the 'management plumbing system' creates an illusion of pristine architecture with all the pieces being 'consistent with the strategy'; leading to a very rewarding 'sense of completion' once you have gone through the PowerPoints several times. There is also an implicit hidden belief that 'success must surely be the sum of all actions'. Hmm? Eighty critical actions? What happens if you only hit seventy-five? Less success? No success?

Exactly the same mechanisms are seen in conventional 'change management programmes' where all is mapped: from strategy to plans to actions to outcomes to timing to metrics. The same illusion of control is created.

> We have to admit that there is something mechano-hydraulic in the way we tend to understand the organisation, something that makes people feel comfortable. Push strategy at the top, go down the pipes, adjust the valves (CSFs) and you'll get the outcomes. It seems aesthetically acceptable and managerially correct to people.

>> SECOND STOP: BEYOND THE VISIBLE WORLD

In a 'living organism', surely the self-adaptation or self-emergence of functions or structures is very relevant. Indeed, although organisations are rich in elements 'by design' (we create structures, management teams, reporting lines, etc.) what may matter 'more' is how its 'living components' (if I may refer to you and me like this) interact beyond what has been designed for them. This is relevant to understand not only 'how the organisation works', but also imperative to understand 'how *change* in the organisation works!'

> Individuals in organisations establish clusters or networks of interactions and communications. Some of them are 'official' and 'designed': teams, task forces, committees, etc. But more interesting are the ones that may be formed in an 'emergent way': clusters of individuals, not designed by the boss, but 'self generated' by the interactions between them.

Some of this 'organisation-outside-the-organisation-chart' has been recognised in recent years.

- *Self-managed teams* are often interpreted in terms of semi-spontaneous associations that don't need a formal boss to achieve their objectives.

- The 'knowledge management' movement has created the term *'communities of practices'*[5] to describe networks of individuals linked by a common objective or interest (including the finding of solutions to an organisational problem).

- People following the systems approach represented by Peter Senge[6] and the concept of 'the learning organisation' tend to refer to *'networks of commitment'*, here with more emphasis on the

---

[5] Wenger, Etienne, 1999, *Communities of Practices: Learning, Meaning and Identity*, Cambridge University Press, Cambridge.
[6] Senge, Peter, 1993, *The Fifth Discipline: Art and Practice of the Living Organisation*, Random House Business Books

mobilisation of motivation and energy in the organisation.

- *'Emergent teams'* is another generic term frequently used to describe loose, 'self-created' teams.

- More on the spontaneity side, *'hot groups'*[7] have been described as a mobilisation of individuals with common interests and drivers of real organisational creativity.

- *'TeamNets'* have been introduced in many places as a 'way of encouraging voluntary relationships in team formation, information exchange and problem solving.'[8]

Three questions come to mind:

- First, is all this another piece of organisational jargon ready for the consulting industry to capture, commoditise and commercialise? Yes and no. No, because these networks - whatever one may want to call them - *do* exist (at least, they have been described). Yes to the second part of the question: this is indeed a risk!

- Second question: what do all those 'emergent groups' have in common? Despite the different labels, probably a lot. For a start, *they live outside the*

---

[7] Lipman-Blumen, Jean, Leavitt, Harold J., 1999, *Hot Groups: Seeding them, feeding them and using them to ignite your organisations*, Oxford University Press Inc., USA
[8] Battram, Arthur, 1998, *Navigating Complexity*, Spiro Press, London

organisation chart with different degrees of both independence and spontaneous formation. It may be that they are somehow invisible at the beginning of their life and it is not until some level of interaction has been reached that they manifest themselves as a proper system.

- Third: if these 'organisations within the organisation' do exist (in the way that the literature suggests), do they matter anyway? I suggest they do.

>> SOCIAL CAPITAL IN THE BANK

The condition of 'associability' is perhaps one of the main sources of the so-called 'social capital' of the firm. It is worth distinguishing between 'associability' and 'sociability'. No, it's not semantic gymnastics. Whilst 'sociability' has to do with the universal propensity to socialise, 'associability' is defined by the 'willingness and ability of individuals to subordinate personal goals and associated actions to collective goals and actions.'[9]

In other words, a sociable environment where people meet, discuss, interact and interchange communication, is a prerequisite for 'associability' but it does not necessarily lead to the enormous added value of the 'association'. Associability can be designed, but also happens spontaneously. (See graph on page 94).

---

[9] Leana, Carrie R., van Buren, Harry J. III, 1999, Organisational Social Capital and Employment Practices, *Academy of Management Review*, Vol. 24, No. 3: pp. 538-555

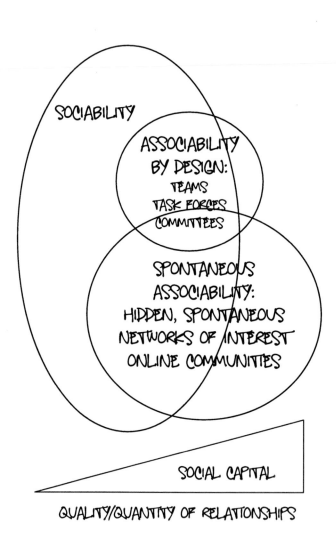

SOCIABILITY

ASSOCIABILITY
BY DESIGN:
TEAMS
TASK FORCES
COMMITTEES

SPONTANEOUS
ASSOCIABILITY:
HIDDEN, SPONTANEOUS
NETWORKS OF INTEREST
ONLINE COMMUNITIES

SOCIAL CAPITAL

QUALITY/QUANTITY OF RELATIONSHIPS

The social capital of the firm is based upon internal and external *relationships*. It produces mutual benefits, for the individual and for the organisation. It is an asset different from other forms of capital such as bricks and mortar (physical capital) or knowledge and technical ability of the individuals (human capital). As an asset, should it not be managed like other types of capital? In some 'low social capital' organisations, any form of leadership appeal to collective goals becomes a contradiction in terms! Individuals may get on with their jobs (as per 'their job descriptions'), and even do them well, but they may not be interested in anything else, certainly not in any form of *collective collaboration* that, in most cases, entails 'going the extra mile', beyond formal responsibilities. And it is in those circumstances that the real added value is generated and real difference is made!

But, is this 'semi-invisible' world of connections anything new? People in organisations have always talked to each other and communicated on a variety of topics, not necessarily directly related to the operational parts of the job! For a long time, we have known about grapevines and gossip. Yes, we know that there are communication flows all over the place but, what is management supposed to do? First of all, some of this is fairly 'invisible' and second – the traditional manager may say - most of the information traffic may be noise and waste, and if it's not, well, people are just doing their jobs.

This is naïve, to say the least. Ignoring the greatest percentage of information flow and the richness of influence mechanisms going in every direction, including perhaps the greatest part of knowledge sharing within the organisation, is 21st century organisational blindness. The trouble is that, as we said before, traditional management is 'mechanistic management'.

It feels very comfortable and concerns itself with the designed part of the organisation: structures, systems, reporting lines, organigramme and boxes. It does not pay much attention to the non-designed, 'emergent', self-managed part of the organisation, the organisation you can't see.

If mechanistic management is blind to that very rich part (the hidden connections between people, the networks of common interest, or simply informal networks) it is not surprising that traditional 'change management' (grown up on the back of this view of the firm) is also mechanistic. It simply mirrors the above conceptual framework of the organisation.

>> THE ORGANISATION AS COLLABORATIVE SPACE(S): TEAMOCRACY AND NETWORKRACY

What follows is in part a summary and recap of the above conversation in an attempt to formalise what we know today about these visible and invisible worlds in the organisation. This is a way to explore and understand the variety of forms of association and collaboration that are hosted by 'the organisation'. And it is precisely in this variety that clues for fast and sustainable management of change live.

Consider the organisation from a structural viewpoint as the sum of all possible forms of 'collaborative spaces'.[10] (Figure on page 98)

---

[10] Herrero, Leandro, *Teamocracy and its discontents* (To be published by meetingminds)

COLLABORATIVE SPACE 1: DESIGNED AND FORMAL COLLABORATION

It represents the *designed organisation* composed of teams, formal structures, reporting lines, etc. It is the one represented in the organisation chart. I call this space 'teamocracy' to refer to *the star* of the organisational collaboration: the team. 'The team' has literally hijacked our thinking about people collaboration! It is rather structured and visible. Most of the traditional management thinking, day-to-day management and the huge literature about 'the organisation' assumes that it is all happening in this visible, shiny, approachable, manageable, managed and quantified Space 1.

COLLABORATIVE SPACE 2: SPONTANEOUS BUT FORMALISED COLLABORATION

This space wasn't created by design. It represents spontaneous associations of people inside the firm, whether this is ephemeral and transient, or more or less lasting and sustainable. These associations were born out of the spontaneous desire of people to link up with other people. Some of those forms of collaboration may have become labelled as 'Communities of Practice' or 'Communities of interests'. In many cases they have some degree of formality and visibility, or even 'legitimisation' and recognition from management.

COLLABORATIVE SPACES = ORGANISATION

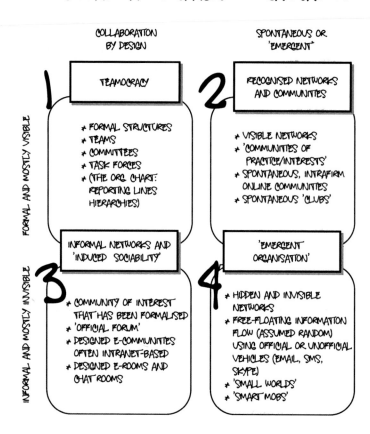

COLLABORATION
BY DESIGN

SPONTANEOUS OR
'EMERGENT'

FORMAL AND MOSTLY VISIBLE

1 TEAMOCRACY

* FORMAL STRUCTURES
* TEAMS
* COMMITTEES
* TASK FORCES
* (THE ORG CHART:
  REPORTING LINES
  HIERARCHIES)

2 RECOGNISED NETWORKS
AND COMMUNITIES

* VISIBLE NETWORKS
* 'COMMUNITIES OF
  PRACTICE/INTERESTS'
* SPONTANEOUS, INTRAFIRM
  ONLINE COMMUNITIES
* SPONTANEOUS 'CLUBS'

INFORMAL AND MOSTLY INVISIBLE

3 INFORMAL NETWORKS AND
'INDUCED SOCIABILITY'

* COMMUNITY OF INTEREST
  THAT HAS BEEN FORMALISED
* 'OFFICIAL FORUM'
* DESIGNED E-COMMUNITIES
  OFTEN INTRANET-BASED
* DESIGNED E-ROOMS AND
  CHAT ROOMS

4 'EMERGENT'
ORGANISATION'

* HIDDEN AND INVISIBLE
  NETWORKS
* FREE-FLOATING INFORMATION
  FLOW (ASSUMED RANDOM)
  USING OFFICIAL OR UNOFFICIAL
  VEHICLES (EMAIL, SMS,
  SKYPE)
* 'SMALL WORLDS'
* 'SMART MOBS'

COLLABORATIVE SPACE 3: DESIGNED BUT SEMI-FORMAL COLLABORATIVE SPACE

It's a designed space but with more informality than the standard teams and committees. Management may decide to 'facilitate discussion' and provide the means and tools for people to discuss or share information. Some e-rooms or dedicated spaces on the company intranet fall into this space. Spaces 2 and 3 have something of a two-way traffic flow depending on the degree of both informality and spontaneity. Many spontaneous clusters of collaboration become formalised, sometimes victims of their own success when the 'designers' (management) absorb the 'good ideas' and 'good works' and prompt: 'let's have a forum for this' or 'we should have a team for this' or 'don't you think we should create a Task Force to explore this?'

COLLABORATIVE SPACE 4: EMERGENT, SPONTANEOUS COLLABORATIVE SPACE

This is the largest and more invisible since it hosts all the informal traffic of connections between individuals, no matter which vehicle they use, from email itself to SMS, Skype, etc. It is a true 'networkracy' at the other end of the spectrum of the 'teamocracy'. Until recently, people were making the following assumptions about this space (even when it had not been identified as such!):

- As said before, most of it is noise, waste or 'normal life' of people (who otherwise may belong to formal teams) doing their jobs.
- We don't know, can't know what's going on in there.

75 %

OF WORK CONVERSATIONS (PEOPLE'S COLLABORATION, INFORMAL PROBLEM SOLVING, KNOWLEDGE TRANSFER, NEW IDEAS, INNOVATION, INFORMATION AND COMMUNICATION FLOW) OCCURS IN THE INVISIBLE, NON-DESIGNED, EMERGENT,

NETWORKRACY,

'SPACE-4' PART OF THE ORGANISATION

25 %

IN TEAMS, COMMITTEES, TASK FORCES AND THE 'PLUMBING SYSTEM' OF THE

TEAMOCRACY

- If it's invisible, I can't manage it, I can't measure it.
- In any case, it could be described as the totally *random* web of connections between people.

Let me pick up on some points. This 'space 4' that hosts all sorts of spontaneous collaborations and the free floating information flow, is very rich in connections (see graph p. 100). What we 'see' happening in formal teams and structured information and knowledge traffic (as captured in meeting minutes, project and document management systems, etc.) is only the tip of the iceberg in terms of human collaboration.

Let's assume a firm of 500 employees and an average of 7 invisible but relatively stable links with other people. Let's assume another modest 7 links which are far more infrequent. Use the calculator.

However, conventional management thinks of this as waste (!) and subsequently, conventional 'change management' ignores all this in favour of the cosier dealing with what is visible and represented in the organisation chart/ plumbing system. In summary, their assumption reads:

CAN'T SEE = CAN'T MEASURE = CAN'T MANAGE

>> BEHIND THE CURTAINS

In order to comprehend those hidden relationships and to establish a sort of 'real organisation chart', many things need to take place. First of all, it is the simple recognition that those networks of social interaction do exist. Second, if there was a way to represent them and capture them, this would be enlightening. Well, there is. It is called Social Network Analysis, the closest thing to an endoscopy, or an MRI, of the organisation! It has been progressively applied to business organisational life.

Social network analysis (SNA) is not new but for many years it has largely been confined to academia in the area of Social Psychology. This is how it works. Via questionnaires and interviews one can map the real connections between people 'outside the organisation chart'.

You could ask people, for example, who they would go to in order to solve a type X problem, or for advice on Y. You could also ask, for example, who they would trust, who they would go to for 'real knowledge of what's going on', etc. If you have been working in a large or semi-large organisation for a while, you may have experienced that there is a sort of group of people or individuals who 'seem to know more than anybody else', better connected and attracting people for multiple reasons, not always represented in the formal hierarchy of the organisation chart.

Many years ago, I found myself discussing this topic with my colleagues and - half seriously, half for fun - we decided to draw our individual 'list of these people' on the back of a napkin in the company cafeteria. When we shared the homework, we discovered that (1) a few names were repeated on all the napkins and (2) there was nobody from 'senior management' on the lists.

The one with more entries on napkins was Joe, and Joe was the man in charge of the post room. Joe had excellent, unwritten, non-hierarchical connections with other 'important nodes' such as somebody in Facilities Management and a junior clerk in HR. We went on, stimulated by our discovery, and ended up with what we called 'the map that mattered'!

Today, Social Network Analysis has gone well beyond the academic exercise that used to live in the psycho-sociology department or classroom. The questionnaire system has become more sophisticated and, of course, we count on software that can map the results and project them in a multicolour web on screen. All very sexy. And colourful. However, it is still a bit 'static'.

Those maps are naturally the result of specific questions. Not surprisingly, because that was the whole idea! If you ask different questions, you get different maps. But they may be old the moment they are drawn up, if for some reason the dynamics between individuals change. Although in our old case there was little chance that our Joe-in-the-post-room web would change overnight, other maps may be different. Today, we have software at our disposal that can 'crawl' inside the document management system or the email traffic of the company and map real-time 'what's going on', provided we give the right permissions and we use a few tricks to protect privacy.

A real-time SNA is possible today, making it the real representation of the 'organisational conversations' and finally sending the old organisation chart to the cupboard as a mere hierarchical Kodak picture with the simple value of describing everyone's boss.

Real-time SNA particularly, but not only, is a good way to understand social capital. It can tell us what the real life groupings of individuals are talking to each other about. Tacit knowledge, the one in people's brains, flows from individual to individual in form of 'those conversations'.

Thomas A Stewart[11] says that one of the reasons for a company to exist is precisely to act as a 'host for those conversations'. In other words, to act as an enabler of that flow of tacit knowledge that constitutes a major part of the total organisational wealth.

Spaces 1 and 3, if you remember, are designed to 'force these conversations'. Spaces 2 and 4 host the spontaneous ones.

SNA allows us to 'see' and 'feel' those invisible conversations. The invisible organisational world may be less invisible after all! We have a way to map that 'hidden organisation' that is not represented in that organisation chart: the network of connections, influences and relationships between people that is not based on hierarchy but on information flow and knowledge, trust and other mechanisms.

>> WHAT THE 'INVISIBLE ORGANISATION' LOOKS LIKE

What the SNA-type of analysis has taught us (whether via the old pen and pencil questionnaires or more sophisticated web-

---

[11] Stewart, Thomas A., 2001, *The Wealth of Knowledge: Intellectual Capital and the Twenty-First Century Organisation*, Currency, New York

based ones, or the hidden crawling of a software that can map connections and relationships) is that 'things inside' are far from random and chaotic. Intuitively, we imagined Space 4 to look something like in the top graph on page 106, but, once the detective-endoscope work is done, it looks more like the bottom graph on page 106.

Our preconceived idea of a network was one of a multitude of nodes linked to each other in a more or less 'equal manner'. But today this is a simplistic way of looking at things. In reality, you should visualise the picture better as a series of clusters linked to each other via some nodes in each cluster.

In other words, in a network, the nodes ('some highly-connected people') play the role of traffic warden, project manager, dating agent, cartographer, matchmaker, and village wise man, all in one! The network is not democratically egalitarian, as we will see soon! The nodes possess a high degree of 'power', simply by exercising that linkage.

In summary, this is what we 'see':

- Some people have lots of connections.

- Some clusters are small, one or more are sometimes bigger.

- This fascinating map or maps have little to do with the organisation chart. In fact, it is telling us that the organisation chart is cheating on us!

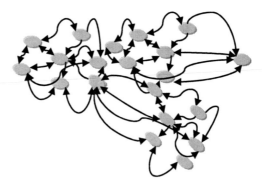

A random network: intuitively we tend to think that this is what
people's connections within the organisation may look like

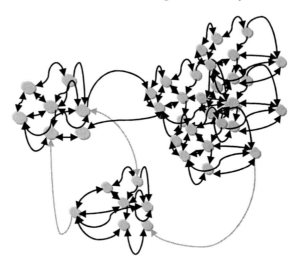

The reality of the internal connections of people inside the
organisation: some people-nodes have more connections than
others. Clusters - some smaller, some bigger - have connections
via some highly linked people

- The degree of power or influence is not distributed in an egalitarian way. It is based upon the power of linkage, not hierarchical power.

- Presumably, 'ideas and/or fashions' travel through these internal networks. If so, these highways are not evenly distributed. It must matter to understand the traffic!

- 75% of the organisation (if you pull together assumptions and data from many sources) looks like a loose-not-so-loose network, feels like a network, smells like a network. In recent years we have gained a great deal of knowledge about networks! It sounds like a good plan to understand the organisation (in perhaps a different way) and the management of change within.

Let's take a further look inside the organisation because we have only just begun to uncover the richness and complexity of 'the real organisation', the one where that 75% of good things happen! If traditional management of change has focused on that 25% (the visible, structured and 'manageable'), VIRAL CHANGE™ focuses on how we can use the 75%, which is hidden and rich in connectedness. The why and how comes next!

(4)

SMALL WORLDS INSIDE

What my colleagues and I suspected many years ago in that cafeteria and - what was recorded for history on those napkins - was true after all. It's a small world inside the organisation! Or better, a series of connected small worlds! Not much different from 'the external world'.

>> DEGREES OF SEPARATION

You're having your second drink at a cocktail party and you meet somebody whose neighbour turns out to be your best friend from high school, somebody you haven't seen for over twenty years. Or somebody who is working with your first boss from many years ago, who, as you now learn, has since moved to places that you didn't know about. Or somebody who is married to somebody you met at a business school reunion. Or somebody who has a holiday home five minutes from yours (and a few thousand miles from here), and who you have never met over there. Or, to be more specific, you meet a complete stranger and after your second drink together you discover that you both have lots of things in common: people you know, places you've been, etc. And you say with surprise: *"It's a small world!"* It seems as if for some reason our 'distance' from others is less than we thought. Or perhaps this is all just coincidence? But we all know that sometimes it seems like too much of a coincidence, especially for such a repeated phenomenon.

There is a lot of literature and experimental sociological data around this phenomenon. Stanley Milgram, a prolific and unconventional American professor, conducted an experiment by sending a series of letters from departure points in Kansas and Nebraska to one of two destinations in Boston. Duncan Watts, author of *Small Worlds* (1999, Princeton University Press) describes it like this:

> "The letters could be sent only to someone whom the current holder knew by first name and who was presumably more likely than the holder to know the person to whom the letter was ultimately addressed. By requiring each intermediary to report their receipt of the letter, Milgram kept track of the letters and the demographic characteristics of their handlers. His results indicated a median chain length of about six, thus supporting the notion of 'six degrees of separation', after which both a play and its movie adaptation have since been named."

And then, there is the Kevin Bacon Game (you need to be a fan of cinema to understand this). Here Duncan Watts again:

> "The Kevin Bacon Game is a curious thing for sure. For those who don't know him, Kevin Bacon is an actor best known for not being the star of many films. But a few years ago, Brett Tjaden - a computer scientist at the University of Virginia - catapulted Bacon to true international recognition with the claim that he was somehow at the centre of the movie universe. This is how the game goes:
> - Think of an actor or actress.
> - If they have ever been in a film with Kevin Bacon, then they have a 'Bacon Number' of one.
> - If they have never been in a film with Kevin Bacon but have been in a film with somebody else who has, then they have a Bacon Number of two, and so on.
>
> The claim is that no one who has been in an American film ever has a Bacon Number of greater than four. Elvis Presley, for example, has a Bacon Number of two. For real enthusiasts, Tjaden created a web site that provides the Bacon Number and shortest path to the great man for the most obscure of choices. In fact, Tjaden later fireproofed his claim by conducting an exhaustive survey of the Internet Movie Database, and determined that the highest finite Bacon Number (for any nationality) is eight. This may seem nothing more than a quirky fact about an already bizarre industry, but in fact it is a particularly clear example of a phenomenon that increasingly pervades our day-to-day existence: something known as the 'small-world' phenomenon."

So here is the working summary:

- In the real world, we are all linked to somebody else (I know, I won't win the Nobel Prize for this).
- We think that we have small worlds around us, and this is both true and false. True, because it's correct that we have connections with a finite universe (family, friends, colleagues...) and it feels 'small'. False, because if you apply the principle of the six degrees of separation, you are closer than you think to anybody you can think of.

>> INSIDE THE ORGANISATION

In the small worlds of the organisation, whether visible (teams) or invisible (clusters within the informal network), the links between people tend to be 'strong'. That's the whole idea. After all, you know these people one way or another. This mini-network-cluster is full of what is called 'strong ties'. This is as opposed to 'weak ties'[12] or connections with distant or semi-unknown people, such as people you may have never met but with whom you have shared some email correspondence for whatever reason, or people you've met once and decided to include them in your Christmas card list

If you have a very thick Rolodex or address book, or a big contact list in your Outlook, chances are that most of the 'connections' are 'weak ties' and only a small number is of the 'strong ties' type.

---

[12] Granovetter, Mark, 1973, The Strength of Weak Ties, *American Journal of Sociology*, Vol. 78, Issue 9, pp. 1360-1380.

What the 'six degrees/small world' would tell you, of course, is that this is only your perception, but that in reality there are many other 'small worlds' inside the contact list, or clusters of people with 'strong ties' (see graph p. 114).

> Within the organisation, when you are in touch with somebody via a 'strong tie', you are likely to be part of the same team(s), or division, or in a close working relationship with that person. You are also likely to be on 'strong ties' terms with other members of that cluster or team. When you are in touch with somebody via a 'weak tie', you are also connecting with that person's own small worlds (and their 'strong ties').

'Weak ties' allow you to connect with a vast (more or less invisible) network. Part of that network will be organised loosely and other parts will be clustered in teams or formal structures.

>> THE INNOVATION PARADOX

Which, incidentally, takes us to other interesting territories. Let's think innovation. Innovation requires (amongst other things) spotting the new idea, the new connection between ideas, mastering the quest for novelty, for alternative ways, out-of-the-box thinking, rule breaking, discovering what one doesn't know, etc. Where do you think we'll find the best kitchen to cook our innovation? Our conventional wisdom says 'in teams, of course'. But, strong-tie-structures (teams)

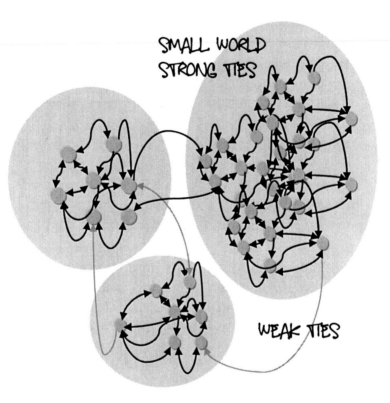

SMALL WORLD
STRONG TIES

WEAK TIES

may not be the best platform for alternative thinking and discovering the unknown. Think of the membership: people you know relatively well, who you work with most of the time and who are used to intellectual interaction with you.

In teams, most of the time, what other members think about an issue is very predictable. You know John's views and you know how Peter reacts. You know Mary's area of expertise and you know what Carol always wants to do.

> The strong-tie-small-world-team is highly predictable. You trade off the unknown for a cosy environment and the supposed power of all brains together. But if you want innovation, and quest for unpredictability, 'novelty' and 'what you don't know', you don't want your team-mates John, Peter, Mary or Carol. They are part of your brain furniture. You want people you don't know yet (although they may be closer than you think, remember the 'six degrees'), or only know 'a little'. You want your 'weak ties'.

This is why Granovetter titled his article *The Strength of Weak Ties*. Incidentally, Granovetter also proved that you are twice as likely to find a new job via the introduction from a 'weak tie' of yours (somebody loosely connected, perhaps via annual Christmas card), than via a 'strong tie'. Although counterintuitive at first, it makes sense: with your 'strong ties', you share the same world and perhaps the same information, so you may know as much as them about opportunities! But your 'weak ties' are in a different world and you are tapping into unexpected sources of choices (and recommendations!).

There seem to be two worlds for different purposes. In one extreme, an over-designed and over-structured organisation which may kill innovation and knowledge flow, but it is a cohesive environment, probably very good for operational achievements. In the other extreme, a loose, ambiguous and rather unstructured organisation which may be unmanageable, if - and here is the trick - you are a manager grown and groomed in the designed part, unable to navigate and lead in that more ambiguous and network-centric organisation. Paradoxically, that 'unmanageable' part may be the source of new ideas, which in some cases may mean your survival!

Heads up: what I have described for 'innovation' also applies to diffusion of new ideas, or diffusion of information, or diffusion of new behaviours.

>> DIGRESSION: SOCIETY AND SMART MOBS

The year is 2000 and the place the Philippines. A million Filipinos are out on the streets, exhibiting a curious behaviour. They are all sending text messages to each other through mobile phones. It looks like an epidemic of mobile phone addiction, but it's not. In fact, they are toppling the government of President Estrada by organising massive demonstrations and moving from one place to another, confusing the police and other government forces as much as they can. The government had succeeded in controlling TV and radio but it didn't think of the cell-phone network. Estrada was history.

In March of the same year in Mumbai, India, in a situation of civil unrest, the authorities were more astute and disabled the SMS service of the mobile telephone network to avoid the organisation of illegal demonstrations and to reduce that social unrest.

When Geneva hosted the G8 summit years ago, the city was expecting up to 300,000 demonstrators. There were plenty of rumours that the cell phone network would be cut off if demonstrators got out of control, as this would be the only way to disrupt their re-grouping and re-organising. The rumour prompted an official pre-emptive response from the network operators saying they had no intention of disabling the network 'unless under direct orders from the police'. Anti-globalisation demonstrations in Seattle followed similar patterns. Still on mobile phones, Japanese teenagers seem to lead the world in fast organisation and reorganisation of 'spontaneous' meetings at the command of text messages.

> Spontaneous association of people relying heavily on communication devices has been described by Howard Rheingold as 'smart mobs'[13] and the term has gained ground as a new buzzword.

Smart mobs as a concept is a cousin of 'swarming', a term borrowed from biology and now applied to many human social areas. According to the Oxford Dictionary, a swarm is a cluster of bees leaving the hive with the queen to establish a new colony. It's also a large number of insects or birds

---

[13] Rheingold, Howard, 2002, *Smart Mobs: The Next Social Revolution*, Perseus Book Group, Cambridge

moving in a cluster and a large group of people moving over or filling a large area. It's often also a synonym for crowded and infested ('the place was swarming with tourists'). 'Swarm' and 'swarming' have left the world of the biology of bees to explain human social phenomena.

Swarming describes the power of spontaneous association of people (from a small group to a crowd), an effect that can easily be multiplied. Kevin Kelly, editor at large of *Wired* magazine and author of the insightful book *Out of Control*[14], says:

> "What emerges from the collective is not a series of critical individual actions, but a multitude of simultaneous actions whose collective pattern is far more important. This is the swarm model".

'Swarming tactics' have been used to describe not only the demonstration activities and 'social unrest' referred to above, but also the collective behaviours of teenagers clubbing on a Saturday night and organised crime in São Paulo. In other words: people talking to each other in real time, heavily using and relaying on technology – including but not limited to mobile telephones – to group, re-group and multiply the sending of instructions. People able to gather fast at a place where the 'meeting' takes place, even if there was no previous idea of where that would be. That's social swarming and they are smart mobs.

---

[14] Kelly, Kevin, 1995, *Out of Control: The New Biology of Machines, Social Systems and the Economic World*, Perseus Book Group, Cambridge

There is also a whole new understanding of warfare using this model. How a network of enemies moving from one place to another (guerrilla tactics or a terrorist organisation) works: all this can be explained via the biology of bees and the social dynamics theory. The RAND corporation has a bunch of public documents on 'new warfare' and 'theory of conflict', based upon these principles. If only the bees could use mobile telephones... God knows what they would do to us!

Of course, mobile communications are getting more and more sophisticated by the day. Networks of people can easily use a 'fast moving' website on which to log data, for example, what's happening in my 'cell territory' ('weblogging') and to retrieve information. If this is done by a big group ('moblogging')' you have a 'permanent' and real time place in cyberspace to refer to. You've seen it on the news, mainly at times of anti-globalisation demonstrations, that the Police monitor 'some specific websites' whose content changes by the minute for indications of social unrest.

Edge (www.edge.org) - an organisation founded *"to promote inquiry into and discussion of intellectual, philosophical, artistic, and literary issues, as well as to work for the intellectual and social achievement of society"*, summarises key aspects of the 'smart mobs' phenomenon as follows on their website:

> "Communication and computing technologies capable of amplifying human cooperation already appear to be both beneficial and destructive, used by some to support democracy and by others to coordinate terrorist attacks. There are both dangers and opportunities posed by this emerging phenomenon.

The people who make up smart mobs cooperate in ways never before possible, because they carry devices that possess both communication and computing capabilities. Their mobile devices connect them with other information devices in the environment as well as with other people's telephones. RAND corporation analysts have pointed out that the Russian mafia and Colombian narcotics trafficking enterprises use 'netwar' methods, combining communication networks, social networks, and networked forms of organisation. Just as medicine only became an effective weapon against illness when science furnished useful knowledge about the nature of diseases, the most effective use of communication and computer technologies could emerge from new scientific understandings of human cooperation. The most powerful opportunities for human progress are rooted not in electronics but in understandings of social practices. Sociologists, political scientists, evolutionary biologists, even nuclear warfare strategists have contributed the first clues that an interdisciplinary science of cooperation might be emerging".

What do teenagers in party mode, anti-globalisation demonstrators, social activists, 21st century terrorism, Colombian cartel-like tactics and the fall of a government in the Philippines have in common, or what can they teach us?

The key combination is one of spontaneous association plus pervasive technology, such as mobile communications and internet. There is very little design in the 'structure' other than the call to arms or mobilisation and the reliance on progressive association (grouping and regrouping) via the information network created by possessing a communications device.

>> SMART MOBS AND SMALL WORLDS INSIDE

The lessons for organisations are multiple, but we have just begun to understand the extrapolations, with not much enthusiasm from traditional academics and consultants.

Business organisations are largely designed. What a statement to make at this stage! However, I think this is an understatement. They are over-designed. That is: we have organisation charts; people in place who report to somebody; groups, divisions, teams and task forces. The idea is to have a rational distribution of labour, accountabilities, and maximisation of the chances of success by having people work with others on a common goal. Fine. But we haven't even started to think about - let alone started to uncover and discover - the power of the non-designed associations within the firm, those hosted by that 'Space 4' that I described in the previous chapter. They often constitute the equivalent of internal 'smart mobs' that get together using the internal (or other) communication channels. And there is plenty of available technology for communication and collaboration inside the average firm. Today, blogs (online diaries and records of conversations) and wikis (websites that anybody can edit) are available everywhere, both for use in the internal organisation and the external world.

I have repeated before that if we could master the incredibly powerful internal dynamics of the more or less spontaneous, hidden, collaborative spaces within the organisation, (and we have seen before how this could be done) we could discover how rich we are! Different evaluations and estimations from different places point to the figures I shared in a previous chapter: up to 75% of the 'real work' done invisibly in the 'networkracy', versus 25% in the visible 'teamocracy' of the teams, task forces, committees and formal reporting lines. But, is mastering the wrong word?

> The trouble with successful, spontaneous associations is that the designed structure of the firm acts as a shark: it tends to swallow them by converting them into teams, communities of practice or something formal. And this is like signing their death certificate. Like the 'smart mobs' on the streets, their internal networks are not interested in being labelled and given a timeframe. The moment spontaneity is compromised, they will go underground. You won't see 'smart mobs' having a workshop to develop their transition to a Task Force!

>> THE CASE FOR VERY, VERY, VERY, VERY LONG COFFEE BREAKS

So what's the answer? My advice: leave them alone! Just watch them, take notes, and interpret what's going on, but don't interfere! Acknowledge their presence and facilitate the connections by allowing the use of technology that is already in the firm. This will not satisfy many. In the classical model of a business organisation there is no room for these 'unmanageable' groupings that don't add value to the bottom line. More on this later.

Actually, there is something fascinating about the differences in the kind of work we do, the language we use and the problem we solve, between collaboration by design, spontaneous collaboration or something in between[15]. The design inevitably constrains us. Many years ago, a clever observation was made: at conferences, meetings, workshops or other forms of structured collaboration, many of the best discussions, interventions and advances are made not in the meeting room and the formal sessions, but during the coffee breaks. If this is so, a big, long, permanent coffee break sounds like a good idea! The 'Open Space' methodology for interventions with big groups was born![16]

The macro-social digression was inserted on purpose. Organisational and business life is very good at fencing itself in from other worlds. It doesn't tend to see a continuum between many aspects of social life and life inside the organisation. Organisational life, however, is pure human collaboration. We can gain tremendous insight if we open the windows to the external world and learn from any other form of human collaboration 'out there'. VIRAL CHANGE™ places great focus on using the conduit of spontaneous internal collaboration to create and spread change. How this is happening inside the firm is not miles away from how it

---

[15] Herrero, Leandro, *Teamocracy and its discontents* (To be published by meetingminds)
[16] Owen, Harrison, 1997, *Open Space Technology: A User's Guide*, Berrett-Koehler, San Fransisco.

happens outside. The key commonality of both is the network and how it works. So coming back from Geneva, Mumbai and Seattle, from teenagers spontaneously getting together or wild groups swarming into places, we need to focus now on the organisational life. And some similarities are striking!

>> CONNECTEDNESS; NETWORK SCIENCES TO THE RESCUE

In recent years we have seen the fascinating convergence of ideas coming from divergent disciplines, from territories as different as mathematics, social psychology, sociology physics, computer sciences and anthropology. Not the usual fellow travellers! The real beneficiaries are the social sciences and there are serious implications for the management of organisations!

One of these, perhaps we should call them 'meta-sciences' is 'Network Theory' or 'Network science'. With a strong foundation in mathematics, this meta-science has expanded well beyond the theoretical world to try to explain 'connectedness'. Since connectedness is a characteristic of both the live and non-live world, it is impossible to ignore what this science has to tell us.

> The core ideas on networks of all kind have not come out of the blue. In fact, Euler fathered 'network theory' in 1780 … but he didn't have the internet, for example, to apply it to the 'real world! Network ideas remained the property of theoretical mathematics for

a long time. The basic concepts,
however, were there.

A network (social, biological, electric, computer information, the internet, etc.) is composed of nodes and connections or links. This was described in 1780 and still remains true today, whether you are thinking about the electricity grid, a terrorist organisation, the internet, the mafia or indeed the connections of individuals inside the organisation.

There was a slight problem, however, with that original thinking. In those early days, the mathematical assumption about the distribution of these nodes and connections in a network didn't seem to work when applied to specific situations such as social connections or the working of the internet. As we said before, when we assess what's going on inside the organisation, we don't see random connections, we see those clusters described before.

Jumping ahead several years and moving several steps away from Euler, we come to today's world and meet Albert-László Barabási. He is a professor of Physics at Notre Dame University in the US and, incidentally, not on the list of management gurus preaching on organisational change. If you wanted to read one book that would take you to this territory of network theory as we know it today, it must be his book *Linked: the new Science of Networks* (2002, Perseus Book Group, Cambridge)[17]. Barabási explores multiple network

---

[17] The other two (non-academic) books that constitute a good reference are:
- Watts, Duncan, 2003, *Six Degrees: The Science of a Connected Age*, W.W.W. Norton and Company, New York
- Johnson, Steven, 2002, *Emergence: The Connected Lives of Ants, Brains, Cities, and Software*, Scribner, New York.

THE NON-EGALITARIAN WORLD OF
THE NETWORK (SOCIAL OR ELECTRONIC)
INCLUDING INTERNAL ORGANISATIONAL
NETWORKS

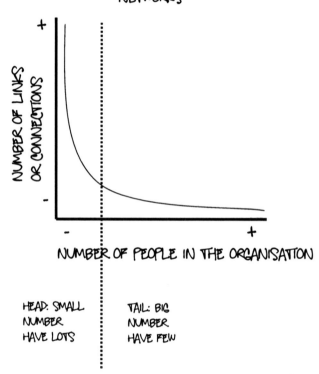

HEAD: SMALL
NUMBER
HAVE LOTS

TAIL: BIG
NUMBER
HAVE FEW

territories, including the internet. Three fascinating findings are crucial for us, for their application to the understanding of the organisation.[18] Management of change will never be the same! Welcome to VIRAL CHANGE™!

(1) THINK 'POWER LAW', NOT THE CONVENTIONAL BELL CURVE

The distribution of links in a network follows a logarithmic power law as the figure on page 126 represents. Few nodes have lots of links, most nodes have few links. This is exactly what we found out in that cafeteria with my colleagues but we never articulated it as such![19] Remember that the historical network-assumption was that nodes and connections were randomly distributed. We still make that same assumption, consciously or unconsciously, about that 'invisible world' in the organisation!

The bell curve of normal distribution is so embedded in our thinking that unconsciously we expect to find it everywhere, in any given population, for example, when mapping IQs or people's performance within the organisation. So, it's only normal that when we get close to understanding that fluid network of connections of individuals inside the firm, we think normal distribution and bell curve. But the network has tricked us. This is simply not true.

---

[18] These three points are clearly summarized by Andreas Ramos on www.andreas.com, a reviewer of Barabási's book. That summary has helped me to simplify these accounts.
[19] In 1900, Pareto, an Italian economist, described a related '80/20' rule: 20% of people own 80% of the land. Conventional wisdom has extended the Pareto-principle to many other areas: 20% of customers account for 80% of queries, or 20% of people in your organisation do 80% of all the work!

- On the internet, for example, a comparative low number of websites have huge links, whilst the vast majority have few. The Google ranking system for web pages follows a network-like power law with logarithmic differences between the positions in the rank; that is: page at the top of the list 10 times more links than the second; 100 times more links than the third, 1000 times more than the fourth, etc. (logarithm law = powers increase by a factor of 10) which makes rankings apparently as 'high' as 10 pretty irrelevant when compared with number one or two.

- The home page of my company's website has a Google ranking of 6 and the 'about us' page has a ranking of 5, all according to Mr Google. That means that the home page is 10 times more 'linked' (here meaning visited, not linked by design with another site) than the page with the addresses (a strong case for my webmaster to bring the addresses to the front!).

- Chris Anderson, editor of *Wired* magazine, is using the power law analogy to describe whole new economic dynamics based upon 'scarcity' (the head) and 'abundance' (the long tail) and he gave his book *The long tail*[20] the subtitle: *why the future of business is selling less of more.*

- The blogging phenomenon also follows power laws, as you would expect from web-based spaces (sites) linked to others. The majority of the blogs are read by their

---

[20] Anderson, Chris, 2006, *The Long Tail: why the future of business is selling less of more,* Hyperion, New York.

writers and their families. But a few blogs have such an enormous linkage that their power/influence is greater than printed media. Blogs are becoming a vehicle of social and political expression with extraordinary power. They are very prominent in American political elections. Technorati, a site that monitors blogs, has shown how a few blogs - probably written by their authors from their kitchen - have more influence (linkage, referrals and readership) than media such as *The Economist*, the *BBC* or *The Washington Post*.

(2) THINK
'MATTHEW EFFECT'

The network is not only non-democratic and non-egalitarian, it is also terribly unfair. I call this the 'Matthew Effect': *"For unto every one that hath shall be given, and he shall have abundance: but from him that hath not shall be taken away even that which he hath." (Matthew, XXV: 29)*. Or in popular translation: *"the rich get richer and the poor get poorer"*. If a node within a network has lots of links (and we just said that there were few of those), it will be reached with greater ease, which will increase its links, etc. The more links you have, the more links you will get...

- In the macro-social world there are plenty of examples of 'Matthew Effects', other than the apparently obvious 'the rich get richer'. This effect has been observed in the scientific literature where a relatively small number of academics are quoted and quoted again, attracting progressively more references. Similar observations have been made in the philosophical world.

129

- The phenomenon is old. The Royal Society was formed in England in 1660 drawing membership from more or less 'secretive or informal societies'. Many years before that, there were already references to 'The Invisible College' or a tight small network with increasing influence and attracting more and more connections.

- In my own professional experience in my previous life as a practicing psychiatrist, we saw a Matthew Effect in the way American Psychiatry took over the world with its new classification of mental disorders that would become known as DSM-III and then DSM-IV. Despite the apparent broad involvement of researchers, academics and clinicians describing the supposedly 'new entities', all could be traced back to a relatively small number of American psychiatrists, really a handful, that were consistently referred to and quoted in the scientific literature.

(3) THINK PHASE TRANSITIONS

The connections in the network experience 'phase transitions'. At some point of a critical threshold, the nodes stop being 'individualistic' and all start behaving like a single entity, adopting a single property, the one of the network. The molecules of water become 'vapor' at a threshold point of heating or 'ice' at a threshold point of freezing.

These three characteristics of the network also explain multiple social phenomena[21]. To name a few:

---

[21] I am borrowing most from the list at www.andreas.com

- How companies with a web of relationships (including suppliers) differ dramatically in performance from those with only a few.

- How a few companies in an industry at some point of their evolution create single standards adopted by all.[22]

- How terrorist organisations function and why conventional frameworks to understand and fight them fail.[23]

- Why attacks on a network (from computer virus to sabotage of the electricity grid) may result in anything from nothing to a disaster, depending on which bits of the network have been attacked (linkage power of the nodes attacked).

We'll bring network theory with us to the next chapters. We now know what's going on inside the organisation and we will use this to understand how real change works. We can create real cultural change by using this knowledge and getting rid of many old ideas about a mechano-hydraulic organisation. We have the knowledge to trigger, spread and create cultural change fast. So, let's take a look at how this may work. And the following is a quick summary preview.

---

[22] Analysis of the dot-com era shows how few survived and consolidated, creating 'new standards'

[23] SNA has been used as a technique to map the connections between terrorist suspects. An Al-Qaeda type of organisation will never be understood by applying rational command and control concepts and extrapolating these to that network. Network science should be at the front of studies in politics, social sciences and military strategy (see: Committee on Network Science for future Army applications, 2006, *Network Science*, The National Academy Press, Washington, D. C.- www.nap.edu/catalog/11516.html. See also Valdis Krebbs' site: www.orgnet.com.)

Power law

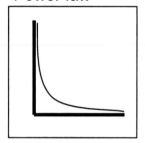

Small group of people inside the organisation has many connections. This small group has great potential to influence the whole (positively or negatively, and by different means). Massive communication and engagement of the whole organisation may not make much sense if a small group has the potential power to spread, infect, influence and trigger change. This small group may be be 'artificially created' as well.

Matthew effect

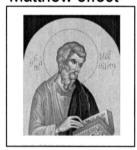

People with more connections will always tend to get more of them. Once their influence has started to show, they will tend to get even more influence (positive or negative). You can reach the entire organisation via a (growing) viral influence of a few. This could be helped or facilitated by choice (management).

Phase transition

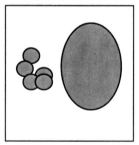

We can expect at some point that clusters of connected people start behaving as more visibly cohesive groups ('let's have a team?') or think suspiciously alike, or with less and less self-criticism ('groupthink'). New ideas, new behaviours, new routines spread via VIRAL CHANGE™ will appear more or less suddenly ('tipping point') after a period of little visibility. Once they appear, they will become 'established' very soon.

THE TSUNAMI AND THE BUTTERFLY

The traditional view of the management of change is simply at odds with what we know today about what's going on inside the organisation, as described in previous chapters. There is a better, more efficient and faster way to create and sustain change in organisations based upon this modern knowledge. In previous chapters, we have been building up a series of differences between a traditional approach to change and the one behind VIRAL CHANGE™. And we have done so on the back of the fascinating new knowledge about how the organisation works, particularly the invisible networkracy, the one where 75% of the good stuff happens!

In this chapter we will put all those things together as a way to map our way towards VIRAL CHANGE™.

(1) CONVENTIONAL MANAGEMENT OF CHANGE IS TSUNAMI CHANGE

I call the conventional way of understanding and practicing 'management of change', the tsunami approach. As a formal process ('change management programmes') it is usually orchestrated and implemented as a vast complex process often of gigantic proportions, very inclusive of all aspects and players of organisational life, usually long, painful, expensive and in many cases looked at with regret and scepticism after a few months of so called 'roll-out'. Of course, this is not always the case, but I am describing a picture that those of you who have been or are connected with this traditional view may recognise.

(2) VIRAL CHANGE™ IS BUTTERFLY CHANGE

A very different approach that obtains fast organisational change by the injection of energy and focus on a few 'levers' or 'hot spots', is what I call the butterfly approach. Remember Capra's outrageous statement? 'Disturb' versus control... This approach is consistent with a view of the organisation as a living network. There is an old saying that the flapping of the wings of a butterfly can create a hurricane miles away. This translates into at least two real-life situations. One, that small actions can create significant effects on a larger scale. The other, there are some computer models for weather forecasting that are so sensitive to initial conditions that the outcome might be changed by the flapping of a butterfly's wings. This is often called the 'butterfly effect'.

This form of 'butterfly management' is the one behind VIRAL CHANGE™. As we have said before and will explore later, its mechanisms of change resemble more the way infections diffuse and fashions appear. Unlike in tsunami programmes, the visibility of a concerted 'butterfly programme' is very often – but not always - low. In the previous chapter, network theory helped us to understand why.

>> WHY WE LIKE TSUNAMI CHANGE SO MUCH

The clue to understanding why we are still stuck with these tsunami-change-management programmes - despite their poor record - lies in two connected phenomena:

(1) TRADITIONAL MANAGEMENT SEEMS TO HAVE AN 'ENGINEER WITHIN'

Our appetite for a rather mechanistic view of the organisation, its composition and dynamics; a sort of 'engineer within' that management, academics and consultants seem to have. We prefer Lego pieces that can be put together, seen and measured.

(2) OUR NEED FOR FINDING LINEAR CAUSE-EFFECT CONNECTIONS

Our psychological need to create apparently rational relationships with cause-effect that 'explain' the why and how of the functioning of the organisation. And both a mechano-hydraulic view of the organisation and its associated 'tsunami change management' are ideal for our desire to connect input and output, push from the top of the organisation and result at the bottom.

>> WE EXPECT PROPORTIONALITY AND LINEARITY, EXCUSE MY LANGUAGE

This input/output linkage is not unique to management thinking! Indeed, there is something about our general education that assumes and seeds two things everywhere:

(a) linear connections and
(b) proportionality and linearity of cause-effect.

After all, ideas such as 'punishment must be proportioned to the crime' are well embedded in our culture! We praise measured responses and balanced reactions. 'Proportional response', for example, is a military term to indicate the degree of force to be used when one has been attacked. Proportional effects to causes, proportional outputs to inputs seem logical. So much of this, will give so much of that. You increase this, you get more of that, the predominant, learnt mental model tells us.

Mathematics and physics calls this *linear* or linear dynamics. We could say that we are educationally, socially and epistemologically (the philosophical theory of knowledge) comfortable with linear systems and linear dynamics, excuse my language.

> Paradoxically, our linearity-comfortable minds are surrounded by a non-linear systems world. In reality we - in organisational life, business life, real life - are prisoners of a particular thinking model in a land where the alternative is the norm!

This paradox has implications not only in the way we manage and lead organisations but also, and I would say, in particular, the way we 'manage' change.

Here is a good distinction between linear and non-linear systems as described by Jeffrey Goldstein in his book *The Unshackled Organisation* (1994, Productivity Press Inc, New York):

> "In linear systems, change is gradual and incremental, whereas in non-linear systems, change can be precipitous and revolutionary. In linear systems the whole is merely the sum of the parts, whereas in non-linear systems, the whole is greater than the sum of the parts. In linear systems interaction is only one-way, whereas in non-linear systems interaction is multidirectional. Linear systems have predictable outcomes, whereas non-linear systems may have unpredictable outcomes."

Test: look around you and see what kind of world you find. If you are like me, I see 'precipitous and revolutionary', 'the whole being greater than the sum of the parts', 'multidirectional interactions', and 'unpredictable outcomes'. That is, a non-linear-system world. I feel cheated by my maths teacher! He told me that 4+4 =8. Not only that, he didn't mention what Albert Einstein said about mathematics:

> "As far as the laws of mathematics refer to reality, they are not certain; and as far as they are certain, they do not refer to reality."[24]

---

[24] Einstein, Albert, 1921, Speech to Prussian Academy of Sciences in Berlin

>> POST HOC ERGO PROPTER HOC MANAGEMENT

In the organisational life, cause and effect language is ubiquitous. We have plenty of input (training programmes, management guidelines, professional education, instructions, etc.) that in our eyes justifies the outputs (good sales, more products on the market, increased quality). If you have a massive training programme for your sales force and this is followed by good sales, I can think of more than one executive in the Training and Sales department who will claim the connection. However, good sales may have come from pathetic competitor activity, or luck, or indeed other efforts made before the training programme.

Philosophy described this a long time ago. It is the 'post hoc fallacy' or 'after this, therefore because of this'. Management is full of management dogma based on quite a lot of thin air or weak evidence.[25] We are fundamentally determinist in our traditional management thinking. Many times we are happy to just be 'fooled by randomness' as a recent book of the same title illustrates[26].

>> WORTH ANOTHER DIGRESSION: ECONOMICS AND THE SOCIAL WORLD

Paul Ormerod did not invent non-linear economics, but he is certainly known as an advocate and a controversial economist.

---

[25] Pfeffer, Jeffrey, Sutton, Robert I, 2006, *Hard Facts, Dangerous Half-Truths and Total Nonsense: profiting from Evidence-based Management*, Harvard Business School Press, Boston.
[26] Taleb, Nassim Nicholas, 2004, *Fooled by Randomness: The Hidden Role of Chance in life and in the markets*, Texere, New York.

Ormerod is saying that traditional linear economics don't work and that the social effect of individuals, copying or learning from others alters the equation.[27] The rational world of traditional economics where 'the rational man' is assumed (when given choices, people will behave in a way that maximises the utility) is shaken, to say the least, by the newest 'Behavioural Economics'. The social factor is a big modifier and, very often, what in traditional economics would be expected, doesn't happen because people behave in a volatile manner.

At first glance, the view from this position is disturbing: things are more unpredictable than you think, surprises occur, swings in the markets are common, traditional forecasting models are weak.

In a recent issue of *Prospect magazine*[28], Bob Rowthorn, professor of Economics at Cambridge (UK), has reviewed some of Ormerod's positions in different areas. Let's read it, because this apparent digression beyond the territory of 'the organisation' and management of change is very helpful for us to extrapolate!

> "Most empirical work in the social sciences is based on the assumption that relationships are linear, so that small changes produce small effects and large changes large effects. However, if relationships are non-linear, the link between cause and effect is more complex. Over a certain range, small changes may produce small

---

[27] Ormerod, Paul, 1997, *The Death of Economics*, John Wiley and Sons, Inc., New York
[28] Rowthorn, Bob, 2005, Review of 'Evolutionary Economics' by Paul Ormerod, *Prospect Magazine*, June 2005, pp. 111.

effects, but at a 'tipping point' a small change may produce a very large effect. Moreover, this very large effect may be extremely hard to reverse".

Mentally bookmark this, please! Rowthorn reminds us that this thinking is behind some underlined assumptions in political systems, very often without politicians knowing it. Again, it is worth the digression here to understand how we are constantly confronted with at least these two different versions of reality: linear and non- linear.

Rowthorn continues, now in the political arena:

"This is the vision that underlies the conservative argument on crime. The extent of criminality in a society, it is argued, is partly a matter of material incentives in the form of rewards and punishments, and partly a matter of socialisation. Consider a society in which the crime rate is initially very low and young people rarely meet criminals who lead them into crime. Suppose that punishments are gradually reduced with the result that crime slowly increases. In itself, this may not be a serious problem.

However, at a certain point the crime rate may suddenly shoot upwards, perhaps stabilising at a new and very high plateau. Policymakers are likely to respond to this development by reverting to the harsher penalties which they had previously abandoned. Unfortunately, such penalties may have only a limited impact on the crime rate because decades of liberal policy have given rise to a criminal underclass which reproduces itself by transmitting its values to young people".

"Conservatives make similar arguments in many other areas, such as divorce law and welfare for lone parents. In each case, they believe that liberal policies set in train social processes that eventually end in disaster and create situations that are very hard to reverse. The liberal response is to dismiss such fears as paranoid and unsupported by the evidence. This is not the place to adjudicate on the issue. The point is that liberals have a rather linear view of social policy in which small changes normally produce small and reversible effects, whereas conservatives have a non-linear view, believing that small changes often give rise to large, unpredictable and irreversible effects. On environmental issues, such as global warming and biodiversity, the positions of these two groups are reversed. Liberals tend to believe that the world is on the brink of disaster and if we do not mend our ways there will be huge and irreversible changes, whereas conservatives take a more relaxed view."

I have taken this long promenade on purpose to stress how adopting a linear or non-linear way of approaching the social, political and economic world makes a lot of difference. I have also mentioned how the pervasive non-linear world around us contrasts with our more linear-thinking education, which in turn forms organisational/business education and practices.

Our choice of glasses through which to look impacts on our relationships with the social world at many levels. On one hand, the 'macro', socio-economic and political level, as has been described above. On the other hand, the 'micro social' life in organisations, their management, and their consequent mechanisms of change.

> Linear vs. non-linear thinking is a dilemma that haunts us in the management of change in organisations. Your style of leadership and you as a driver of change totally depend on what side of the dilemma you are on and what type of 'resolution' you have embraced.

All this has significant implications for the management of organisations and for the management of change.

>> VIRAL CHANGE™ IS NON-LINEAR: HERE IS THE 'SO-WHAT'

(1) SMALL (VIRAL) CHANGES BECOME RADICAL CHANGE

Most, but not all, management thinking is pretty linear...no surprise there. It says that big problems require big solutions; big organisational mess a big shake; big key issues a radical, surgical approach. Goldstein described it well[29]:

> "Conventional approaches to organisational change assume the system is linear. Hence management usually assumes that a major change initiative requires extensive advance planning, that resistance to change must be anticipated, when resistance arises you

---

[29] Goldstein, Jeffrey, 1994, *The Unshackled Organisation*, Productivity Press Inc., New York

overcome it with persistence, determination and skill, and that large change requires large-scale efforts. This approach is based on a number of questionable assumptions, notably that organisations are 'largely predictable enterprises', that do not change naturally and are 'inert masses' which require 'proportionality between effort and results'."

VIRAL CHANGE™ adopts a fundamentally non-linear view of life, in the way this has been described before: small changes can produce revolutionary change via 'butterfly effects'. And we are ready to see how. But before we go there, let's agree that this is very counter-intuitive for traditional management, who will crave a recognised and mechanistic process, theoretically crafted to deliver predictable results.

Some instinctive practices - such as 'let's have small wins' or 'quick wins' - are using de facto non-linear thinking. They are banking on socialisation à la Ormerod.

If you create some change that, even if small, is very visible and people can copy, that small change may trigger big change. It may look, however, like a fortuitous tipping point effect, i.e. not much going on or no visible effect at the beginning but, suddenly, things start to look different and people start to do things in a different way.

Interestingly, the big critics of the initial small change/'small wins' are found in the change management industry (consulting, academic or both). They claim that most of these 'changes' are superficial and don't count as real change. This is very often an over-cautious view and underestimates the power of non-linear intervention. But they do like tsunamis!

There is a solid theoretical basis to support the idea that a small set of 'something' can produce a big impact, or meaningful outcome. Again, biology teaches us about self-generating life starting from a sophisticated code, composed, however, of a finite number of 'units', the DNA, etc. At the other end of the spectrum, computer sciences show us that a small set of rules can generate extraordinary patterns, for example. The entire computer games production is based upon the use of a relatively small set of rules (of the game) conducing to a self-generating world.

(2) CHANGE SPREADS VIA SOCIAL IMITATION

The socialisation aspects of change are well-known. People need to see things happening in order to believe them. Cynicism is a chronic illness in many organisations. People respond in this fashion to many mission and vision statements, lists of 'the seven key values' and 'the ten new commandments'. It is only when leaders start behaving in particular ways that people pay attention. There is a term for it: walk the talk.

> The non-linear aspects of life within organisations tell us that you may not need massive interventions or postures by management, but small, concrete, key and meaningful actions that can be seen, imitated and copied.

(3) VIRAL CHANGE™ (POSITIVE OR NEGATIVE, DESIRABLE OR UNDESIRABLE) WORKS THROUGH TIPPING POINTS

The tipping point effect[30] will spread changes faster than gigantic change management interventions labelled as The Big Change Management Initiative. Tipping point effects are notoriously present in organisational issues such as trust and reputation. Both are gained and lost at different paces that remind us of non-linear mechanisms.

For example, by doing 'small' things to others, such as responding to requests for help, trust appears 'at some point', beyond which it is pretty much established. Inversely, a possible 'small breach of trust' can trigger a cascade effect and destroy years of gains. It sometimes seems irrational to the observer, and it seems so because it is not a 'logical' linear effect. Experts in reputation management see the same all the time: gains and losses often depend on small actions or chains of events.

(4) VIRAL CHANGE™ DOES NOT NEED TO WORRY ABOUT MAJORITIES OR MINORITIES: IT SPREADS BY INFLUENCE AND CONNECTIVITY

Conventional approach to management and management of change will say that in any organisation there are always a few people who are already 'converted to the need to change' and willing to do something about it. It follows that there will always be a pool of people who are very resistant to change and 'may not make it'. In other words, it may be necessary to invite them to leave.

---

[30] Malcolm Gladwell, a staff writer with *The New Yorker Magazine*, popularised this concept through his bestseller *The Tipping point* (2000, Little, Brown and Company, UK)

Consciously or unconsciously, conventional approach focuses on that large majority who are, yes, 'resistant to change' but who can be 'converted'. In other words, forget the hopeless. The good news is that you may have just a few on board. But apply the tsunami effect to the organisation because you have the large bulk in the middle! Incidentally, does this sound like another bell curve to you?

Non-linear, VIRAL CHANGE™ management' is more interested in effective and faster seeding of change. We have just said that it will be looking at how to inject 'small changes' (behavioural changes) that can be amplified. Therefore, in parallel to working with the 'converted', VIRAL CHANGE™ thinking would strongly advocate that key visible and vocal sceptics are identified and worked with. Perhaps some of these may be on the list of 'will-possibly-never-make-it'. Showing the organisation any one visible sceptical person adapting to changes and buying in, is worth 100 already converted people showing compliance. Suddenly, some of the people on your black list may become your assets because of their counter-intuitive power in spreading change fast when 'converted'. More on this later.

The following charts summarise and compare the two approaches before expanding in the next chapter on the interaction of four components: language, behaviours, tipping points and culture/routines. In these graphics, you will find concepts that I have shared with you in previous chapters already, for example, what we have found 'behind the curtains' of the organisation chart and what we know about how networks work. These charts try to put all these things together.

1. IMPLICIT MODEL OF THE ORGANISATION

CONVENTIONAL APPROACH

Organisation as machinery of bits and pieces linked by a sort of mecano-hydraulic dynamics. Information, guidelines, pressures, support or anything that flows inside, does so mainly top-down. Pushed from one side, it will have consequences on the other side. 'Corporate goals are my objectives; my objectives are the basis for yours (direct reports)', etc. Life percolates down the organisation chart or its 'collaboration by design' spaces (mainly teams). The pre-determined 'plumbing system' described in the organisation chart is the communication highway. Influence and power are assumed to flow down the plumbing system.

VIRAL CHANGE™

Organisation is better explained as a living organism sharing many of its characteristics. There is a formal structure of authority (represented by the organisation chart) but, beyond this, there is a multi-directional flow of influences and other dynamics. Self-adaptation and re-configuration are key to survival and grow mechanisms. Managerially, it doesn't discard a structured system of goals, objectives, etc, but it is less concerned with absolute consistency in 'cascades' as long as there are a few overriding strategies and directions. An incredibly rich 'network world', often invisible, coexists with the plumbing system.

2 'STRUCTURES'

CONVENTIONAL APPROACH

Connections are established in a tree-like way. Organisation of 'collaborative spaces' mainly by design: teams, task forces, committees, 'solid lines' and 'dotted lines'. Acknowledgment of the existence of a looser network of connections but mainly seen as noise, or informal communication system impossible to tap into, quantify or manage.

VIRAL CHANGE™

The organisation as a complex system of connections, with high adaptation capabilities. Some of the connections have been formalised by design providing relatively stable platforms of collaboration (teams, etc.) This designed architecture is superimposed to a far bigger and looser, non-designed, ('emergent') network of connections, or structure. A healthy dynamics between the 'designed' and 'emergent' is the key for effectiveness and success.

3. 'DISTRIBUTION OF PEOPLE'

CONVENTIONAL APPROACH

Everything from 'quality of the components' to 'flow' assumes a bell curve distribution. Management practices consistent with this: communication reaches (or has to reach) the majority of people; change practices need to involve the majority under-the-curve acknowledging that there will be sigma deviations at both sides, for example, casualties of people who 'will never change'.

VIRAL CHANGE™

The organisation is a network and follows the power laws of networks where (1) a few people have multiple connections, (2) those with greater connections and perhaps influence will continue to have more and (3) spread of information, communication, influence, new behaviours new habits, etc., happens via 'tipping points'.

4. PROCESSES AND SYSTEMS

CONVENTIONAL APPROACH

Processes and systems inside, well-defined so that the majority in that distribution can repeat them and ensure consistency. Predictability is key.

VIRAL CHANGE™

Acknowledgment of formal processes and systems but management in VIRAL CHANGE™ mode very sensitive to the risk of those processes and systems taking over organisational life. Emphasis on behaviours needed to support processes, versus processes creating behaviours.

5. CAUSE-EFFECT AND INTERVENTIONS

CONVENTIONAL APPROACH

Linear dynamics territory: big problems require big changes and a proportionate change management programme. Change progresses in a steady, measurable way (milestones and calendars). Tsunami effects, and the bigger the tsunami the better. 'We have to catch all at the same time with the same intensity'

VIRAL CHANGE™

Non-linear dynamics view: big changes may require a small set of key and meaningful actions or (new) behaviours. Butterfly management effects. Small initial change in key areas suddenly appears widespread, possibly 'revolutionary' (phase transition and tipping points).

6. FORMAL PROCESS OF 'CHANGE MANAGEMENT PROGRAMMES'

CONVENTIONAL APPROACH

Consistent with the assumed and lived model of the organisation It stresses sequence [create a 'burning platform first, communicate strategy, plan, distribute tasks, train, roll-out, check]. It relies on processes above behaviours

VIRAL CHANGE™

Consistent with the understanding of the organisation as a living, adaptable network. It stresses multi-directional influence and creation of stable change by the combination of four elements: (1) language, (2) behaviours and their reinforcement, (3) creation of tipping points (with emphasis on 'social imitation' and (4) establishment of new routines or 'cultures' (see later). Emphasis on behaviours above processes.

7. CONDUIT OF CHANGE

CONVENTIONAL APPROACH

The management tree/structure represented in the organisation chart is the primary vehicle for the change. VPs fire the shots and take care of directors so they are on board. Directors repeat at their level involving managers and their groups, sections or divisions. Managers take care of their own trees. Change is created by a sequential cascade down via 'the plumbing system' of 'burning platform signals', communications and activities, training and review processes. Buy-in is assumed as rational process. All people equal under the tsunami!

VIRAL CHANGE™

Networks of people are the primary conduit. Signals (language, strategy, 'burning platforms' and directions of change) may have been started at the top, and indeed communicated down via hierarchical 'pipes', but change is created by social imitation in networks of influence and driven by few individuals who act as key nodes. They constitute either an informal, natural network, or they may be aided by a designed network of 'change agents' or 'Change Champions'. Not an egalitarian view: there is no point in communicating to all and cascading down as *the only* mechanism to spreading change.

8. WHAT 'CHANGE MANAGEMENT' LOOKS LIKE

CONVENTIONAL APPROACH

The change management process looks like a massive series of activities: project team meetings, workshops, training sessions, etc. A 'reporting back' mechanism of some sort allows for feedback and checking. Behind those activities there is 'a map' (a plan, a binder, a poster...) with well-defined objectives, timelines, etc. so the change process can be tracked. Consequently, progress assessment relies heavily on a metrics system which will have been created up front and which will contain as many hard measures as possible.

VIRAL CHANGE™

Here, the process looks like a series of induction sessions with top management, identification of a Change Champions network and sessions with this network to provide them with some tools and techniques to spread the change. There is a formal metrics system but only known to the Change Champions network (if there is one, see later chapters) and the key management sponsors. Progress tracking relies heavily on a mixture of semi-hard measures and qualitative data (particularly 'stories' constantly shared across the organisation.

Note that most models of organisation are 'tacit'. Not many people in management and leadership positions declare up front that 'we are a machinery of so and so' or 'we are a living organism of that kind'. What model or version of the organisation is 'live' is something that very often is deducted from seeing how it works, what management styles are prevalent, what the rules of the game are, and, in general, what the daily life looks like.

>> HOW VIRAL CHANGE™ WORKS

VIRAL CHANGE™ is achieved by the complex interaction of the four drivers represented in the figure on page 152. In the next chapters we will describe how these drivers work and interact with each other. The graph is self-explanatory in terms of its components. The next chapters ('In Practice, for the theorists) give an account of how VIRAL CHANGE™ works.

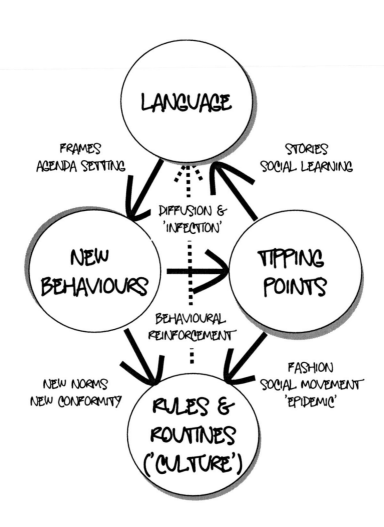

IN PRACTICE,
FOR THE THEORISTS

LANGUAGE

NEW BEHAVIOURS

TIPPING POINTS

'CULTURES'

(6)

LANGUAGE, FRAMES AND CONVERSATIONS

You've heard it all. You have perhaps been involved in a corporate tsunami. Let me guess: a new CRM system, rolling-out of SAP across the world, cost-cutting/re-structuring, re-engineering, merger, expansion, contraction, rightsizing, downsizing. Perhaps the change was not a tsunami but a progressive elevation of water levels followed by a hurricane. In any instance, you have either been at the receiving end of a 'communication plan' or perhaps at the helm, or perhaps somewhere in between.

And you will recognise this. Organisations spend a lot of time 'telling people' that they have to change, find a new mindset, have a new attitude, or get ready for an incredibly competitive environment. The language used belongs to a spectrum that

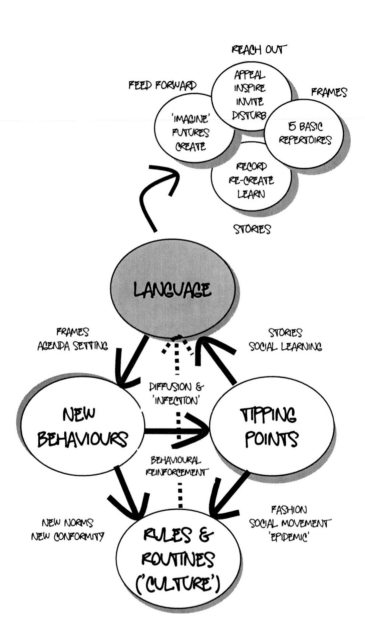

contains excitement, terror, logical and rational appeals and/or 'numbers' (sometimes lots of numbers) or combinations thereof! There is no shortage of words in the corporate supermarket.

Each organisation has its own language. It may or may not be obvious or clearly written on the posters hung on the walls, but it is certainly there, alive, in conversations. Their visible and anecdotal bit is often the jargon. Sometimes it is the generic, most likely Anglo-Saxon or Anglo-Saxon-recycled corporate vocabulary, filled with 'empowerment', 'being on the same page', 'bottom-line', 'net-net' or 'customer-driven-centric' stuff. Other times it is the distinct, home-grown, customised, indigenous and repetitious buzzwords that strike you.

In any case, language is the first dimension in VIRAL CHANGE™. In this process, language plays four overlapping roles (see the figure on page 158):

1. The (obvious) vehicle for reaching out to people.

2. The tool to imagine futures and visualise the changes, the benefits of doing it and the cost of not doing it.

3. Framing: the construction of a mental and social reference that acts as provider of 'the borders' and 'the maps' for the changes.

4. The core of one of the best mechanisms of social learning: stories.

(1) REACHING OUT   Language is the obvious vehicle for communication! We have said several times that communication is seen by the traditional change management as a key component of change, if not the key component. Effectively, however, we encounter the following traps:

COMMUNICATION (+ TRAINING) = 'CHANGE MANAGEMENT'

It has always surprised me how widespread this reductionism is. There are significant numbers of consulting groups, for example, that would not hesitate to label their services as 'change management' when what they do is communication stuff, from sophisticated broadcasting of ideas to serial-killer-workshops focused on, well, err, communication of the messages.

COMMUNICATION = PR DEPARTMENT = CORPORATE
COMMUNICATION = CHANGE

This is a version of the above where communication has become 'functionalised' and delegated to 'the professionals'. Beware of the myriad of booklets/DVDs/packages coming down soon!

COMMUNICATION = CONTENT = CHANGE MANAGEMENT

This is: standard PowerPoint packages that can be used in a cascade-down effect. It is likely that traditional management feels uncomfortable if the messages are not exactly the same all the way down the plumbing system. Therefore, 'the standard package' has arrived in town (and incidentally, they may need a good 'communication company' to create meaningful stuff!)

COMMUNICATION = 'EVENTS' TO COMMUNICATE = CHANGE

This is the same mental muddle which is behind, for example, 'team equals team meeting'. Whilst teamwork and team life are supposed to be a 365-day affair, we have grown up with a progressive mental association of *team* and *meeting*. Here it's the same; communication becomes 'the events': the country-house retreat, the workshops and the Town Hall meetings.

DELIVERING MESSAGES = MESSAGES ARE UNDERSTOOD AND/OR INTERNALISED EMOTIONALLY

Although not many smart people would support this naïve interpretation, the reality is that many organisations act in this way. Delivery is certainly not a good guarantee for understanding, let alone internalising or assuming the need for change emotionally.

In my consulting work on VIRAL CHANGE™ within organisations, we use language as a 'reach-out' mechanism most commonly to cover four aims:

- **Appeal**. This is *mainly* a rational mechanism with the subsequent hope that it will work. It is 'the standard' influence mechanism. It is in itself thoroughly insufficient but in any case necessary. The appeal to others for change comes in different shapes:

- o *Rational*: B is going to be better than A, we need to go to B, these are the reasons.
- o *Emotional*: B is far more attractive, exciting and meaningful than A. Let's stop being miserable, trapped in the past, etc.

- **Inspire**. Inspiration, often coming from charismatic leaders, belongs to that murky area that sometimes seems to have fallen from grace. In my experience, inspirational language is vital. Again, in itself, by itself, thoroughly insufficient.

- **Invite**. In my book *The Leader with Seven Faces* (2006, meetingminds) I refer to the 'invitational' language that leaders should consider. We often have PowerPoint factual toxicity with plenty of bullet points to shoot at people. We have plenty of these, but not enough 'come with me', 'let's do it', 'join me in this', etc. Invitational language is vital to the spread of change.

- **Disturb**. Let me use this generic term to describe the injection of some degree of restlessness or unsettlement via this language. For example, using language that is powerful in describing the possible environmental threats and the liabilities associated with 'no change'.

These four dimensions are interconnected. In my experience, this is a good summary of what language is supposed to do to reach-out. I personally tend to focus on these four pragmatic dimensions as opposed to the dozens or even hundreds of others that anybody could legitimately have chosen.

(2) FEED FORWARD   Organisations have glorified feedback (adjustments, 360° input back from colleagues, customers, etc.). Feedback is a necessary mechanism for adjustment and learning, No question about that. But in the process of spending most of the time on the feedback side, we have forgotten that, as living organisms 'with a mind', feed-forward is a more creative and progressive mechanism.

> Feed forward means visualising the future and imagining it. It is to reverse-engineer the future by imagining it, theoretically and in its reality. It is imagining ourselves in that future and visualising our actions, making judgement on them and adjusting current behaviours accordingly. Imagination is a key component of change. If organisations can't properly visualise futures, they will spend most of the time fixing today's problems.

The language of 'imagine that' is incredible creative and illuminating:

- Imagine that behaviour X is widespread, that all of us do things in that way...
- Imagine that we get rid of behaviour B, that it is no longer part of our behavioural furniture...
- Imagine that our management team is at stage C at a certain future time, that we achieve that level of leadership...

- Imagine that in year Y we attract this kind of people to our organisation…

(3) FRAMES Language constructs 'mental and social frames'. This is an old sociological concept described as 'an interpretative scheme that simplifies and condenses the 'world out there' by punctuating and encoding objects, situations, events, experiences and sequence to actions'[31]

> Frames are extremely powerful. They create the borders of the change, its philosophy, somehow the expected outcomes and the rules of the game. Each frame has its associated repertoire of routines. Pick your frame, before the frame picks you! If you don't make a conscious effort to define the frame (which your language is going to translate), events will take over and will soon define 'the frame' by themselves, whether you like it or not.

If a change programme is 'framed' as part of the quest for innovation, for example, it is likely to carry expectations, language, initiatives and processes addressing current practices, the way things are done today and the need to do things differently. If it is framed as 'efficiency', chances are there will be some level of reorganisation and perhaps cost-cutting, etc.

---

[31] Strang, David, Soule, Sarah, 1998, *Annual Review of Sociology*, Diffusion in organisations and social movements: From hybrid corn to poison pills, 24, pp. 265-290.

164

Decide your frame (as in 'frame of mind'!) because your choice has consequences!

FRAME = (1) LANGUAGE + (2) EXPECTATIONS (OF BEHAVIOURS, OF OUTCOMES) + (3) TYPE OF PLAYERS INVOLVED (INCLUDING EXTERNAL CONSULTANTS!)

In my experience, the 15 frame-modes most frequently used in the management of change are described below, each with their associated furniture.

FRAME	WHAT'S INSIDE
1 PROBLEM SOLVING	In the problem solving frame, it is often clear what to expect. The immediate assumption is that something is wrong. The obvious expectation is to fix it! Problem solving mode will not necessarily lead you to anything beyond the solution. Problem solved, objectives achieved, change done! Don't ask for innovation on top of it! If your language is one of 'problems', everything you do will look like 'solutions'. Make sure that what you call 'problems' are indeed exactly that.

2	CREATING AND BUILDING	In this frame, the focus is one of improvement, exploration and building something new or better. Building mode and the above mentioned 'problem solving' mode are two very different things! There are managers very good at problem solving but not necessarily equally good as architects or builders. Experience as a 'fixer' does not guarantee success as a builder.
3	EFFICIENCY, EFFICACY, AGILITY, ETC.	This frame and its associated deployment, invariably forces you to look at 'better ways', perhaps even less costly. Many (but not all) 'organisational effectiveness' initiatives de facto hide a desire to minimise cost, streamline and re-structure.
4	RE-STRUCTURING, STREAMLINING, COST-CUTTING	Though very similar to the above, this frame is, however, far more explicit. Change management deployment within this frame means disruption of the status quo and, as we all know, some associated pain. Re-structuring means job losses in people's minds. Managers who don't want to articulate it like this often use 'streamlining' or other language. Beware of 'unspeak'. Call a spade a spade!

5	REACTING TO EMPLOYEE SURVEY	This frame is mainly a 'fixing frame'. Changes of any magnitude come about as a result of employee (satisfaction, effectiveness) surveys. The highest risk of change management within this frame is a tendency to 'please' and show that changes are a result of the feedback. Very often, I find weak management judgement in the decisions for the change, as if the 'doing something' takes priority. Reacting to surveys, and being seen to react, is often used by management as a sign of responsiveness and listening. That may be so in some cases, but management is still paid to make judgements and, in many cases, the preferred outcome may be not to react!
6	CHANGE THE OIL	I call this frame like this to describe management of change, often of great magnitude, that in reality is going to keep the same 'machinery' intact but with new oil. Some 'time-to-market' (for product development) change programmes may end up delivering the same garbage to the market faster.

7	COMPETITIVE MINDSET	This frame contains a high degree of (management) restlessness and often concessions to the idea that complacency of some degree has reigned so far. They contain many initiatives focused on 'mindset setting'. They are largely in great need of translation into 'behavioural change', since 'change of mindset' is not a terribly operational currency (see later).
8	BENCHMARKING MODE	You will recognise change management programmes, whether they are labelled like that or not, where the goal is clearly and numerically defined: become number 1 on X by year Y. Numbers are the anchors and the language used follows this. It's a race language, which very often is simply prostituted as jargon. In my experience, this frame is not terribly inspirational.
9	IMAGINE	'Imagine frames' are usually found in broad spectrum programmes that contain a high degree of soul-searching followed by 'building'. In this frame the emphasis is on mapping possibilities and making choices. In my experience, this future-driven, heavy use of 'imagination lexicon' is very rich and powerful.

10	CHANGE OR DIE	This 'the-sky-is-falling' frame is the host for the famous 'burning platform' and all the 'warning/fear' stuff. In my experience, 50% of the time re-structuring is disguised as change, the other 50% is portrayed as adapting to new environment (or post-loss of market share or competitive position reaction).
11	IS THERE A BETTER WAY?	This frame is often one of 'tiredness' and realisation that the organisation has been doing the same thing for a long time. There may or may not be genuine fear of loss of control but it involves some mixture of quest for innovation and the above 'change or… we are getting too old'.
12	CUSTOMER-CENTRISM	A change management frame that exhibits a lot of customer-driven or customer-centrism music smells suspiciously of disguised re-structuring, which, incidentally, may be needed for very good reasons. Very often management with a good-reason-re-structuring agenda may prefer to re-frame it on the back of the need to mirror customer needs. And what a fantastic reason this is for doing almost anything you want to do or change!

13	INNOVATION	This frame may contain genuine innovation, but innovation is often used as surrogate (re-framing) for productivity. The two things are completely different. But in many cases the 'need for innovation' type of management of change is simply presenting a more acceptable face for 'our poor productivity'.
14	MERGER, ACQUISITION, RE-ORGANISATION	This is straightforward. The reason to declare it as 'frame' in itself is the associated paraphernalia expected in the conventional management of a merger, very often top-down re-plumbing (system) of a new (combined) organisation in which efficiencies (read: redundancies) are expected. The importance of the frame is embedded in the assumed: 'if this is M&A, expect pain and job losses'.
15	BIG NEW IT ('BECAUSE WE'RE WORTH IT')	This frame links all things almost invariably associated with tsunamis to the implementation of a big, expensive, and 'extremely ROI-positive' implementation of new processes and systems for which an IT software architecture has been invented.

The figure on page 172 articulates a simplified version of frames which I use to prompt management choice.

(4) STORIES

Stories are one of the best vehicles for the sharing of information and organisational learning. People who may not remember the 35 strategic points, the 7 value criteria and the 20 drivers for change, may remember the story of the team that did so and so or the colleague who managed to do such and such. There is now a vast literature on the role of storytelling in the creation of learning, not so much in the creation of change. We use story-telling as a key feature of VIRAL CHANGE™.

Stories of successful (and unsuccessful) change travel faster than Key Performance Indicators. Stories are powerful socio-behavioural reinforcement mechanisms. For the management of change, you need to create a powerful and visible mechanism for the collective sharing of stories. If 'a picture is worth 1,000 words', a story is worth 1,000 parameters in the best score-card system. Invest in story-recording and story-telling as a *primary* way to spread success of change, or its challenges, or any form of progress that needs to be evaluated.

4 MAIN FRAMES AND SOME EXAMPLES OF CONSEQUENT QUESTIONS

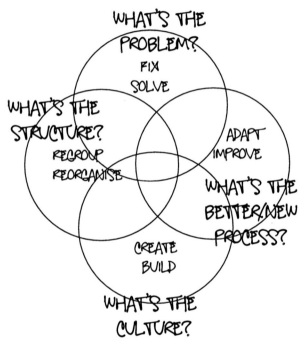

WHAT'S THE PROBLEM?
FIX
SOLVE

WHAT'S THE STRUCTURE?
REGROUP
REORGANISE

ADAPT
IMPROVE

WHAT'S THE BETTER/NEW PROCESS?

CREATE
BUILD

WHAT'S THE CULTURE?

IMPLICATIONS
- LANGUAGE, COMMUNICATIONS
- 'MINDSET', MENTAL MODELS
- EXPECTATIONS
- TYPE OF PEOPLE INVOLVED INCLUDING EXTERNAL HELP
- VIEW OF THE FUTURE
- ?

→ PICK YOUR MODEL - BEFORE THE MODEL PICKS YOU!

LANGUAGE 10

1   DECIDE YOUR FRAME. KNOW WHY YOU
    ARE MAKING CHANGES AND FIND A
    CONSEQUENT FRAME.

2   TEST THE FRAME BY IMAGINING WHAT
    YOUR MANAGEMENT OF CHANGE WOULD
    LOOK LIKE IF YOU USED A DIFFERENT
    ONE. FOR EXAMPLE, IF INSTEAD OF A
    'SOLVING PROBLEM' MODE YOU WOULD
    GO INTO 'BUILDING MODE', WHAT
    DIFFERENCE WOULD THAT MAKE?

3   WATCH YOUR LANGUAGE FOR 'UNSPEAK'.
    AIM AT CLARITY. EUPHEMISMS WILL
    HUNT YOU DOWN SOONER OR LATER

4   INVITE, DISTURB, INSPIRE, APPEAL.
    CHOOSE YOUR ORDER

5   USE LANGUAGE TO 'REVERSE-ENGINEER'
    THE FUTURE, IMAGINE IT AND FEED-
    FORWARD. WHAT WOULD THE
    ORGANISATION LOOK LIKE IF...?

6   CLEAN UP YOUR LEXICON. USE PLAIN LANGUAGE

7   SPOT COMMUNICATION FLAWS (1): COMMUNICATION AS 'THE EVENTS' OR 'ACTIVITIES'.

8   SPOT COMMUNICATION FLAWS (2): IT HAS BEEN COMMUNICATED; ERGO IT HAS BEEN UNDERSTOOD AND/OR INTERNALISED.

9   CHOSE EXTERNAL HELP SPEAKING YOUR SAME LANGUAGE!

10   CREATE AND BROADCAST STORIES. THIS IS YOUR COMMUNICATION CURRENCY.

LANGUAGE

NEW BEHAVIOURS

TIPPING POINTS

'CULTURES'

(7)

CAN'T CHANGE MINDSET: CAN'T FIND IT

At her latest Advanced Sales Training course, Monique has been given very clear messages. Things need to change! She has been with this pharmaceutical company for almost five years during which she has worked as a medical representative in a specialist niche market where the company had leading market share. One of the reasons for the advanced course is the rapid change in the competitive forces in that market. New entrants from companies of significantly greater critical mass have seriously destabilised the old dominant position of Monique's firm. The 'old ways' of doing things need to be replaced with 'new ways'. This is a clear message.

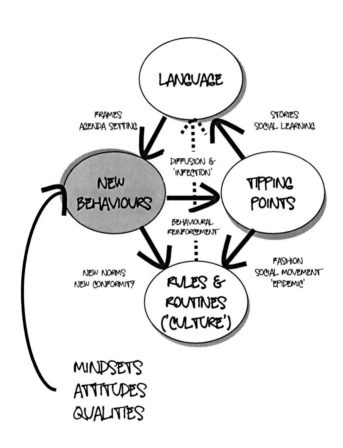

FRAMES
AGENDA SETTING

STORIES
SOCIAL LEARNING

LANGUAGE

DIFFUSION &
'INFECTION'

NEW
BEHAVIOURS

TIPPING
POINTS

BEHAVIOURAL
REINFORCEMENT

NEW NORMS
NEW CONFORMITY

RULES &
ROUTINES
('CULTURE')

FASHION
SOCIAL MOVEMENT
'EPIDEMIC'

MINDSETS
ATTITUDES
QUALITIES

The company is investing heavily in a massive re-training of its sales force with the objective of creating what they call 'a whole new mindset'. In a series of modules and sessions spread over an intensive week, Monique has been told that they all now need to change and adapt to the new competitive environment. Today we need - Monique's notes said - a different attitude. Complacency is gone; a sense of urgency is required, big time! We need a 'will to achieve', 'will to surprise' and 'will to succeed'. What is now needed more than anything else - Monique's notes continued - is an 'esprit conquérant", as the French affiliate says, a 'spirit of conquest' coupled with more confidence in dealing with the customers, which for this Sales Force means mainly physicians and pharmacists.

Also, more than ever, one of the company's old values, 'entrepreneurship', is required and needs to be revived. Entrepreneurial spirit is key, particularly at local district level where they have now been given more flexibility in the use of resources. In this 'new mindset', conviction and confidence 'should be seen' - Monique had highlighted it on her notepad.

The main theme in the second week of the Advance Sales Training course was 'culture'. Monique's bundle of notes grew bigger and bigger. There was more group work this time. A consolidated output of many hours of work with colleagues, some of them more experienced than her, pointed to very clear directions. Monique's accurate notes read: we need to create a solid 'winning culture', where dynamism, creativity, optimism and confidence in the future are in everybody's mindset. We need to project a new image, living the values of the company: integrity, excellence and customer-centric mentality. This new mindset of self-belief, 'conquering spirit' customer effectiveness and entrepreneurship - Monique wrote down - is the key to the new culture, the only way to face the significant new challenges.

Monique was very excited. She said the course was excellent and that it lifted everybody's spirits, which had, quite frankly, been a bit down after having been confronted with the new hard realities. A couple of weeks later, her district manager held a regular meeting with his small group of sales representative specialists. This was a routine meeting but an important one because a new electronic Territory Management System (TMS) had been recently introduced and they were all trying to make the most of the new tool on their personal laptops. HQ had just released the new benchmarking and market data as well. There were new updated lists of 'A' and 'B' doctors, and quite a lot of new information on local hospitals, where many of the sales visits take place.

During the meeting, Monique and her colleagues looked at sales targets, individually and as a district, 'call rates', efficiency ratios, completion of input/feedback into the TMS and some competitive benchmarking data. They all had clear goals to improve rates of customer visits by 15% for the current six month period and to cover 95% of assigned hospital pharmacists. Overall, Monique's district was achieving 85% of sales targets so far and, seeing what was happening in other districts, it wasn't bad at all!

The meeting ended and Monique drove back home, stopping for an extra visit to the local hospital. She had promised to bring some scientific papers on new drugs to the head pharmacist and she thought she would do that. In the waiting room of the hospital pharmacy, she had a sudden revelation, thanks to the peace and quiet of the place and to the unexpected delay in the pharmacist's availability. What was *the connection* between the two-week Advanced Sales Training and this morning's District meeting?

She struggled for a bit until her mind reassured her (the mind is wonderful at comforting us). "*It's all there,*" she thought, "*in the background, in the mindset*", as the sales trainer had insisted. 'Change your mindsets' seemed to be the unofficial summary of that training! The waiting continued, apologies were given. Monique secretly welcomed the delay because it was rare that she could 'stop and think', as she liked to put it. But restless 'revelations' seemed to come in waves, like a psychological migraine. *"What is the mindset? What kind of mindset do I have? Where is the mindset?"* She found it silly at first, but all sorts of other questions started to bombard her, all about the same mindset-thing. And back to "*Where is the connection?*"

She had her old training notes in her laptop. She went through all of them quickly: esprit conquérant, will to succeed, confidence, conviction... She then opened the TMS by mistake: sales targets, call rates and class 'A' physicians were all there in front of her. "*Where is the connection? Where is the connection?*"

Monique's anxiety was put to rest by the sudden appearance of the hospital pharmacist who went on and on about the ridiculously long and boring management committee meeting she had just attended.

Monique is not unique as a sales force representative of the company. Not too junior, not too senior, she has been around long enough to get through recurrent training programmes, most of them around product knowledge and some on selling skills. But this Advanced Course was a bit different because it focused on a series of *qualities* that were required for success. Like her colleagues, Monique thought highly of the course. It all seemed to make sense but she kept trying to understand 'the connection' (as she put it) between the training and its language and the operational targets in front of her. On reflection, Monique thought that 'the connection' would have been provided by the District Manager, but the reality is that they spent the time on 'numbers', sales targets, sales planning and review of the benchmarking data.

If you work in sales, you may perhaps relate to the above scenario! If you don't, please bear with me because the problems described are universal and embedded in the majority of 'change programmes', whether formal or informal. There are two fundamental, and if I may say so colossal, flaws in this very real life scenario:

(1) 'THE CONNECTIONS'

Monique is quite right that she has not been given 'the connections'. First of all, her annual performance related compensation, incentives and bonus system are mainly focused on sales targets and call rates and efficiency indicators. And these are the themes that occupy air time at the reviews with her boss, a District Manager. None of the new list of *qualities* in her notepad has been *connected* with rewards or recognition. 'New mindset', 'will to succeed', 'entrepreneurial spirit' and others are left somewhere in the background in the weekly conversations. The TMS system hasn't got any line on 'mindset'. Monique and her boss 'talk numbers'.

(2) THE INTANGIBLES The Advanced Training Course contained a rich, comprehensive, beautifully crafted, inspiring, energising and skilfully organised framework of otherwise close-to-useless *non-operational* concepts. Mindset, attitude, complacency, sense of urgency, 'will to achieve', 'will to surprise', 'will to succeed', 'esprit conquérant", confidence, entrepreneurial spirit, conviction, 'winning culture', dynamism, creativity, optimism, 'project a new image', 'living the values', integrity, excellence, customer-centric mentality, self-belief, and customer effectiveness may have come from a company-wide, undoubtedly expensive 'research on behaviours' and development of a Training Programme but they all share the same problem: negligible *predictive value* in operational terms.

To put it more bluntly, the word *behaviours* appears in Monique's training binder, but there are no behaviours in it. The rich list above contains none. It is impossible to know, to extrapolate or infer from the list what it is that a medical representative has to do or not do, do differently, stop doing, do more or do less of, so that the famous 'new mindset' shows.

People don't have a mindset in the same way as they have a car, a pair of eyes or pneumonia. Monique can't find 'her mindset' but she has no trouble in finding her call/frequency rate data, the benchmarking numbers in her spreadsheets and any other day-to-day 'hard indicator' of performance.

183

And inevitably, she is going to focus on
what she can find.

Monique hasn't been given any 'translation' of the
comprehensive *quality-based framework* into her real life.
There is a gulf between 'all these things there in the
background' ('the new mindset') and what she perhaps has to
do differently. Not all is lost from that training, though. In the
absence of that behavioural bridge, Monique would probably
unconsciously apply the energy and excitement of the course
to her relationship with the customer. She was, after all, very
excited and enjoyed it thoroughly. And that 'application'
may result in a more-of-the-same-otherwise-more-energised
way of doing things.

If she is successful in the new
competitive conditions, she will
probably be told that 'the new mindset
works', even if nobody in the District
would have ever seen such a mindset. If
collectively they do well, they will
probably be told that the new culture is
paying off, even if nobody has ever
described in behavioural terms what the
new culture should be.

Like many companies I know, Monique's sales operations
management system (i.e. the day-to-day tools and metrics)
falls short of what I have been calling a behavioural-based
framework. Like many companies I know, they say they have
one. The process of translating 'qualities' into 'behaviours' is
not necessarily complex but needs to be done professionally.
Concepts such as 'will to succeed' or 'entrepreneurial

mindset' need to be made operational and the only way to do it is through a true behavioural framework.

Why all this? Because it is the only way to come to an agreement on what is needed and what's not. Monique's boss needs to know what is expected of Monique and the way she does things that would be qualified for the label 'good mindset' - since no complex neurosurgery in Monique's brain will ever find that mindset. Monique needs to know what exactly needs to change, but this has to be concrete and visible, even to her.

Once a, perhaps simple, set of let's call them 'desired behaviours' is in place (to do, not to do, flexible or 'non-negotiable', in situations such as A, B and C), then the famous 'connections' would have been established. Once this well-defined, operational level has been clarified, the label automatically becomes less relevant. Whether or not you would still call it 'entrepreneurial mindset' (you may prefer to call it 'winning attitude'), it is not going to change the fact that Monique will know what to do and her District manager will know what to look for, measure and reward. So, we are in business.

Monique did very well that year. She managed to get to the top of the sales target ranking at district level and won the rep-of-the-year President's award. Following a long standing sales management tradition of withdrawing the best reps from the field, she has been promoted to a new position in a new Sales Force Effectiveness Unit where she will be in charge of training programmes and in particular the roll-out of a new corporate initiative titled 'Leadership Excellence'.

If you recall the case of our accidental change manager Andrew, the CEO, you will grasp an interesting paradox. In Andrew's company there was not a lot of 'talking' about change. Change happened. And you saw how. Monique, however, went through (designed) 'loads of talking' but whether she will change or not doesn't seem to depend upon any real practical 'translation' of that talking into day-to-day life.

It is, of course, absolutely possible that Monique had been energised by the training and that intellectually, even emotionally, she had internalised the supposed meaning behind 'the mindset thing'. But, let's at least accept that the jury is still out on that. If Monique is not unique and if she is more or less representative of her other 500 colleagues in the sales force, then a lot of juries are still out and there's lots of hope. Surely there must be a better way to spend money and energy other than relying on what could easily have been a non-specific motivational process injecting lots of hope and enthusiasm.

>> FROM QUALITIES TO BEHAVIOURS

> The bad news is that most of the very rich vocabulary that we use in day-to-day management, including management of change, doesn't give us much idea of what do with it, other than enjoy it in conversations. The good news is that if we translate it into behaviours, then we do know a lot more about what to do (do = expect = manage = measure = progress).

I also mentioned in the introduction that it's not because an organisation uses the language of behaviours that it constitutes a guarantee that we are talking about real behaviours. Unlike the Social Sciences territory, where 'behaviours' have a rather stable and specific meaning, in day-to-day 'Management' - and, sadly, in a lot of Human Resources and/or Organisational Development 'practices' - the word behaviour is often used in a very loose way.

In many cases, HR language has simply undergone plastic surgery and the old 'people stuff' has been replaced by 'behaviour stuff'.

This is not a trivial matter, but being a 'practitioner' whose company calls itself 'organisational architects', and with you probably being a practitioner of some sort as well in any organisation, we may just share some aversion to endless semantic wars. So this is my working definition of behaviours at the core of my consulting practice:

BEHAVIOURS ARE UNITS OF ACTIONS THAT CAN BE ATTRIBUTED TO AN AGENT. WHEN DESCRIBED, THEIR MEANING IS UNEQUIVOCAL FOR THE PEOPLE WHO ARE REFERRING TO THEM.

And this is as complex as semantics get in this book. Let's dissect the definition:

(1) UNITS OF ACTIONS There may be 'small units' or 'bigger units' (more on this later) but we are talking here about things that people do or don't do. As simple as that. There is also an assumption of visibility of these actions.

(2) THEY CAN BE ATTRIBUTED TO AN AGENT

'Agent' is part of the jargon of social sciences. For you and me it means people. Sometimes we hear or read about 'the behaviours of the market', for example, but that won't do it for us!

(3) UNEQUIVOCAL MEANING

You and I, or our team, will have the same understanding of what we are referring to. And we'll make a concerted effort to make sure that we double-check! Rule number one is not to assume that the name given to the behaviour means the same for all us!

Most of the problems come from number 3. The 'unequivocal, shared meaning' is the real acid test.

Take a look at the list below and see how many of these terms and expressions - many of them perhaps sitting comfortably in your own corporate training binder, or value statement, or any operational framework under the label 'behaviours' - would pass the acid test of the 'unequivocal meaning'- unless, of course, an effort is made to agree on one.

- HONESTY, BEING HONEST
- HAVING INTEGRITY
- ASSERTIVENESS
- BEING INSPIRING
- MINDSET
- TRUST, TRUSTWORTHY
- HAVING A WILL TO SUCCEED
- TEAM PLAYER
- COMMITTED
- UNRELIABLE
- COMPLACENCY
- RESISTANT (TO CHANGE)
- GOOD/BAD ATTITUDE
- COURAGE
- RESILIENCE, RESILIENT
- HIGHLY ACCOUNTABLE
- FLEXIBLE
- ALIGNED, ALIGNMENT
- ENGAGING
- AGILITY, AGILE

You would probably have discarded most of them as 'highly equivocal' and in need of 'agreement' of what it is that we are talking about. Some of them, perhaps the ones that we use more (!), may seem less equivocal at first. For example, we all have a mental model of what a 'team player' is.

That's also part of the problem, the familiarity of the term. We could create a whole project to increase 'team player-ship' in the company without having had any 'time out' to discuss and agree on the 'content' we were going to attribute to the term.

Behaviours require little contamination from interpretation. Let's have another very simple example:

REALITY/ FACT	8 DIFFERENT INTERPRETATIONS AND DESCRIPTIONS FROM HER COLLEAGUES
Project Leader Alice always arrives on time and is always well-prepared for meetings	- Because she _is_ a good **team player** - She _shows_ **consideration** for the members of her team - She _is_ **rigid** and **obsessive** - She _is_ **efficient** and **reliable** - She _has_ **commitment** - She _is_ very **competitive**, needs to show off - She _has_ **good time management** - Because she _is_ **punctual**

189

The only behaviour here is Alice's arriving on time for meetings (even 'well-prepared' may need some elaboration!) Everything else is a mixture of attributes or qualities as seen by different people using different glasses.

Note that if we use the 'is' word, usually we are referring to a quality or attribute, which as we said clearly needs 'behavioural translation'. Our language sometimes tricks us even further when we use the term 'has' or 'have', creating real problems of personal inventory! We simply do *not* have good time management or *do* have commitment in the same way as we have money or a girlfriend! From the eight descriptions, 'punctual' is probably the one that is closer to zero meaning. It is a pure label for people 'always arriving on time' and nothing more than a shorter way of saying so.

> In the day-to-day management, and in management of change initiatives, we constantly use labels and language that have poor value in terms of getting us all together on the same unequivocal path. If you are interested in creating change, you'll need to make sure that you clean up the vocabulary first.

Let me give you a final example. Imagine that the following question comes up: *"What's special about 'winners' in the team, or in the sales force? What differentiates these people from the rest?"* The informal brainstorm group that you have gathered answers:

- They certainly seem to have a different mindset, says one.

- Yes, it is a question of attitude. They have the right attitude and it shows, says another
- In my experience – says a third - they grow and thrive in winning cultures
- In my case – the fourth *brainstormer* says – in my team, they are basically resilient, persistent and often slightly aggressive in the eyes of colleagues. It's this constant 'will to succeed' that shows above all.

Unfortunately, so far, other than filling white flipcharts fast, and perhaps make the group feel that they are using their time well, we haven't advanced a bit.

(A) There is no way of knowing what a different mindset, attitude, a winning culture, resilience, persistent, aggressive and 'will to succeed' mean,
(B) let alone explaining what it is exactly that makes these people different and
(C) what to do/not to do to create or promote 'winners'.

It may seem like a caricature to you but we have plenty of these beautiful descriptions that certainly make for good management conversations We often base entire projects, programmes, initiatives, and new strategies upon lots of terms with the conceptual strength of a cream cake.

In the above case, it is not until we define what people who we are happy to label as 'winners' <u>do</u>, that we are in a position to move forward: understand, differentiate, act upon and manage.

Our language is rich. It is full of possibilities and nuances to describe the reality around us. I am not suggesting we should get rid of all the 'quality language' altogether. It is part of our conversations with the world but if we want to act (manage, create change, lead) we need to describe what these things mean for us, for others.

- How can I see 'a good attitude'?
- What does 'a new mindset' look like?
- If somebody is inspiring, what does he do so that others call him inspiring?
- What does 'motivated' mean (it doesn't mean 'to have motivation'!) so that you and I can label people that way?

It may not always be possible to define things with the same level of precision as Alice-arriving-on-time-for-meetings. Indeed, it may be useful to allow different degrees or levels of descriptions. See the following example, illustrated in the figure on page 194.

Let's say that we need to 'create collaboration', a broad concept that may mean different things for you and me. We need to make it operational. I say to you that for me, today, in my teams, for my needs, it is very clear: I need people to share information on competitor activity because many of them have access to this information but they don't talk to each other about it. If they did, we would have a great advantage. So, for me, this is 'the collaboration' I need. I accept there may be other angles, but I am happy to restrict or reduce 'collaboration' in a very specific way.

You say to me that collaboration for you is clearly linked to the need to share resources as opposed to each of us being protective of our own. You also have other angles but this is a big thing. If we could get this right, things would be so different! We both agree to leave aside hundreds of other potential expressions of collaboration and choose (and this is a very important word) these two.

Members of our teams listening to this conversation then jump in: *"This is all very well, but how are we expected to 'share competitor information'? When? What are we supposed to do?"* The discussion again explores many things, only to reach a consensus on the activities/actions/behaviours shown on the lines below 'share competitive information' in the graph on page 194. We extend the same discussion to 'share resources with other teams' and we come up with the two other lower lines in the graph.

Peter, a colleague on our management team who could not attend the original discussions, then walks in the room: *"Peter, we have defined 'collaboration'."* Peter looks at the flipcharts and the one that is on top contains the bullet point text of the lower levels shown in the figure on page 194. He says:

> "So, we are going to have people sending an email to all once a month, fill in the weekly sheet, immediately talk to marketing in some circumstances, move resources around on the spot without asking permission and routinely cover for each other's absence as a norm... Is that it? Is that the best we can do to create collaboration around here? Collaboration which we pretty much needed by... yesterday? Forgive me, but if I may say so, it seems a bit trivial to me!"

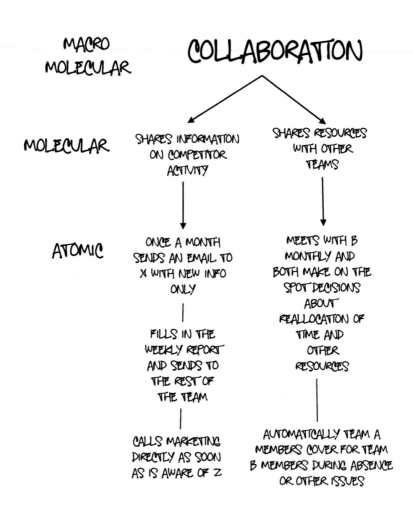

MACRO
MOLECULAR

COLLABORATION

MOLECULAR

SHARES INFORMATION
ON COMPETITOR
ACTIVITY

SHARES RESOURCES
WITH OTHER
TEAMS

ATOMIC

ONCE A MONTH
SENDS AN EMAIL TO
X WITH NEW INFO
ONLY

MEETS WITH B
MONTHLY AND
BOTH MAKE ON THE
SPOT DECISIONS
ABOUT
REALLOCATION OF
TIME AND
OTHER
RESOURCES

FILLS IN THE
WEEKLY REPORT
AND SENDS TO
THE REST OF
THE TEAM

CALLS MARKETING
DIRECTLY AS SOON
AS IS AWARE OF Z

AUTOMATICALLY TEAM A
MEMBERS COVER FOR TEAM
B MEMBERS DURING ABSENCE
OR OTHER ISSUES

Perhaps Peter's idea of collaboration was something that may have looked like this:

- Help each other when needed
- Be sensitive to other's people needs
- Share responsibilities with members of other teams
- Become more aware of the importance of working together
- Create team spirit

And so on. Even if the above list had been considered, still those concepts would have to be translated into specific behaviours. To pick up on one, 'creating team spirit' would need a more detailed agenda and, again, there are potentially two tracks:

POSSIBLY PETER'S WAY: CREATING TEAM SPIRIT	BEHAVIOURAL APPROACH: CREATING TEAM SPIRIT
Create awareness of the importance of team work	Mary and Joanne do X together from now on
Share responsibilities between members	We put any progress data in a shared e-room or server drive or other common place. Not doing so is simply not negotiable
Help each other	Decisions below a particular threshold, are only made by all at the team meeting
See winning as a collective affair	Any member of the team speaks for the entire team at review committee time
Stop being an individualist, Put the team first	Reward and recognition come first for the team, individual contributions second

>> IMAGINE...

The answer to Peter's way (I am attributing to Peter a natural inclination to speak the language of qualities, traditional management concepts and a mindset-like type of approach) is as follows:

(1) IMAGINE ALL THOSE 'TRIVIAL BEHAVIOURS' IN PLACE...

The atomic levels may look trivial sometimes, but just imagine your organisation with all your people sending *that* monthly email to the ones needing particular information, just when they need it, without having to ask; always having an updated database on competitor activity (assuming that this is a big thing for your daily life) because the majority of people religiously input that data; automatically involving another department (as an example) when something requires their attention (no call for meetings, no permissions, get *them*); re-allocating specific resources on the spot without much discussions and permissions from the boss (certainly no meetings to discuss the possibility of sharing resources and how wonderful that would be) and automatically covering for each other's absence (Sales territory? Team membership? Customer interaction?) without any intervention by management, it just happens.

Imagine that these five 'trivial' atomic things happen as a habit, that these five behaviours of people become established:

- Would you be happy to call it 'collaboration'?
- Would you be happier to call it something else, but still acknowledge that it would be pretty good for you?

- If that atmosphere/way of working was 180 degrees from what it used to be, would you accept that you would have created a significant 'cultural change'?

Imagine must become a routine exercise with your people!

(2) THE LABEL PROGRESSIVELY BECOMES LESS RELEVANT

Once the new patterns of behaviours are established, the label that originated the change becomes less relevant. The 'package' of new behaviours that have become routine could now easily now be called:

- Team based approach to…
- Empowerment of …
- New competitive mindset…
- Organisational effectiveness improvement…

And it would still hold water. If you start top-down, preaching collaboration and designing a collaboration-creating programme, chances are you'll find things to fit into the label. If you keep the label as a good starting point, but go down the route of translating it into behaviours, you may find some that you desperately need but that you have unconsciously 'repressed' because they may have felt 'trivial' or 'minor' in comparison with the more grandiose aim of 'establishing collaboration' or 'creating a collaborative culture'. In the process, you may need to revisit the label but, you may even enjoy finding a better one!

(3) PASS THE ACID TESTS FOR BEHAVIOURS?

In doubt of 'what to put into the pot' to cook, go back to the 'behaviour criteria':

- Are these discrete *units* that I can 'see'?
- Could I identify the *agents*?
- And above all: will this have an *unequivocal* meaning for anybody involved?

MINDSET 10

1 MAKE YOURSELF COMFORTABLE NAVIGATING FROM 'QUALITIES' TO 'BEHAVIOURS'.

2 YOU DON'T NEED TO GET RID OF THE LANGUAGE OF 'QUALITY' ('HAVING A GOOD ATTITUDE OR THE RIGHT MINDSET'), BUT DON'T STOP THERE: TRANSLATE IT INTO BEHAVIOURS.

3 YOU NEED TO BE FAR FROM APOLOGETIC ABOUT FOCUSING ON A SMALL SET OF DOWN-TO-EARTH VISIBLE BEHAVIOURS.

4 'SPEAK QUALITY, MANAGE BEHAVIOURS' (THIS IS A SLOGAN I OFTEN USE WITH MY CLIENTS).

5 BE COMFORTABLE WITH HAVING CONVERSATIONS (DISCUSSIONS, PLANNING, SHARING OF IDEAS) WHERE THE BEHAVIOURAL 'CONTENT' IS A MIXTURE OF 'MACROMOLECULAR', 'MOLECULAR' AND 'ATOMIC'.

6 THE ATOMIC LEVEL WILL GIVE YOU A BETTER CHANCE OF REINFORCING BEHAVIOURS, BUT THERE IS NOTHING WRONG WITH EXPLORING THE THREE LEVELS AT THE SAME TIME.

7 BE PREPARED TO EXPLAIN TO OTHERS WHO ARE NOT CLOSELY INVOLVED WITH YOUR TACTICS THAT A SMALL SET OF (ATOMIC-LIKE) BEHAVIOURS HAVE CAPACITY FOR A BIG SPLASH AND THAT THIS IS A CONSCIOUS APPROACH, NOT RANDOM OR A SIGN OF TRIVIALISATION OF THE MATTER

8 CHECK FOR LANGUAGE OF 'BEHAVIOURS' TO SEE IF THOSE WOULD PASS THE ACID TEST OF THE DEFINITION.

9 DON'T ABANDON VALUES AND BELIEFS! ON THE CONTRARY, ADOPT THEM FULLY, BUT MAKE SURE THAT YOU HAVE GOOD 'TRANSLATIONS' INTO BEHAVIOURS OR THEY WILL REMAIN 'UNMANAGEABLE'.

10 IN GENERAL, BE OBSESSIVE ABOUT REACHING UNEQUIVOCAL, SHARED MEANING FOR THE CONCEPTS THAT YOU USE EITHER IN DAY-TO-DAY MANAGEMENT OR THE MANAGEMENT OF A SPECIFIC CHANGE. TRANSLATE, TRANSLATE, TRANSLATE.

(8)

WHY WE DO THINGS THE WAY WE DO

Our behaviours in the organisation are shaped and triggered by multiple things. Some of them are contextual such as the environment we work in, the people we interact with or 'the culture' of the organisation with its declared and non-declared expectations. Others are more individual and have to do with us as people. These include our own values and beliefs, our emotions and how we manage them or the hierarchy of our needs. This list still only represents a fraction of the driver behind our behaviours! You could compile your own list and still there would be many things left out; things that you didn't even know were shaping your behaviours. Intuitively, we know that a combination of things influence us and shape 'the way we do things' and trigger our behaviours. Also, by simple observation, we know that some of these behaviours seem to

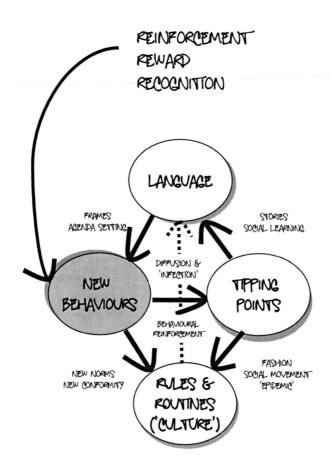

REINFORCEMENT
REWARD
RECOGNITION

LANGUAGE

FRAMES
AGENDA SETTING

STORIES
SOCIAL LEARNING

NEW
BEHAVIOURS

DIFFUSION &
'INFECTION'

TIPPING
POINTS

BEHAVIOURAL
REINFORCEMENT

NEW NORMS
NEW CONFORMITY

RULES &
ROUTINES
('CULTURE')

FASHION
SOCIAL MOVEMENT
'EPIDEMIC'

be pretty stable whilst others may fade over time. To tell the truth, we have lots of stereotypes that we use about 'why we do things the way we do'. The same stereotypes that apply to our behaviours in our personal life seem to be present in our organisational and business life. Here are three of the most common assumptions and their challenges:

ASSUMPTION	REALITY
1 OUR PERSONALITY DICTATES HOW WE BEHAVE AT WORK.	THE WAY WE MAKE DECISIONS, USE INFORMATION AND SOME OTHER DIMENSIONS ARE OFTEN DIFFERENT AT WORK.
2 BEHAVIOURS ARE A CONSEQUENCE OF OUR MINDSETS AND ATTITUDES.	WHAT'S A MINDSET? I HAVEN'T SEEN ANY. ATTITUDES? DITTO.
3 WE NEED TO KNOW THE CAUSE OF OUR BEHAVIOURS TO BE ABLE TO CHANGE THEM. (SEE GRAPH P. 204)	(A) WE CAN INTERPRET THE REASONS BUT IT WILL BE DIFFICULT TO BE SURE. (B) EVEN IF WE COULD BE SURE, THERE IS NO GUARANTEE THAT THE KNOWLEDGE WILL TRIGGER ANY CHANGE IN BEHAVIOUR

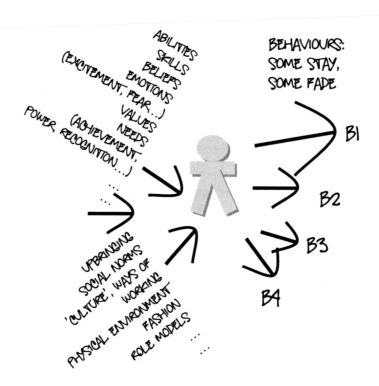

Questions:
1.   Can we find the connections?
2.   If we could, how can we be sure that there is a connection?
3.   If (1) and (2) are possible, how relevant is that in order to change a behaviour?

- To talk about personalities is of limited value. There is a substantial amount of data showing that the way we deal with things and the way we behave in organisational life may be different from our broad-spectrum, all-encompassing 'personality' (which assumes a continuum between business life, personal life, family and social life).

- We have dealt with mindsets in the previous chapter and we said goodbye to Monique when she was still looking for hers.

- It's time to deal with what we know about behaviours and how to change them. And here it is: the shortest PhD in Psychology ever! Just a few pages is about all you need to know!

>> DIGGING

A significant proportion of psychology as a discipline - including its applied versions of clinical psychology and abnormal psychology - has historically been based on the idea that if we dig deep into our history, and in particular into the early days of childhood:

> (1) we will find 'the reasons for how we are today'.
> (2) we will have taken the first step, if not all the steps, to solving either the mystery of knowledge itself (why we are like that!) or 'that anomaly' of our behaviour, or the problems we have.

Psychoanalysis, psychodynamics and other similar disciplines are based upon that past-explains-today-explains-future framework. Psychoanalysis has lots of things in common with archaeology and speleology. It likes digging. Unfortunately, it is well known that the digging does not result in solutions. It is absolutely legitimate, reasonable, commendable, humane and 'meaningful' to try to understand 'the causes' as a way to understand either 'us' or 'our behaviours'. However, like many other legitimate, reasonable, commendable, humane and 'meaningful' things, they are not necessarily effective. How we behave today is probably linked to how we were brought up and the kind of early environment we were in, but we do not really know the nature of the linkage. People brought up in similar conditions often end up behaving in very different ways. And, vice versa, we see similar abnormal behaviour in people with many different biographical pathways.

>> THE ART OF THE 'WHY' QUESTION

The supporters of biographical digging do not like this criticism, of course. Usually they do not like scientific scrutiny either. There are numerous professionals who are genuinely interested in helping people with their problems and use the digging as a tool. Many of those people are undoubtedly helped by the approach. There are unfortunately other sectors of professionals who utilise the non-scientific-digging as a way to make money. I won't comment on them. That people are helped by many 'psychological interventions' is not proof of sound principles behind them. It is a fascinating area for a long, long conversation, and, as you can imagine my psychiatric background is tempting me to expand on this here. However, my interest here is in our behaviours in organisational life. And the message I'd like to leave with you is simple: by all means, if you wish, try to explain WHY a particular behaviour is there. It is going to be almost inevitable that you do so, because our own education has taught us to try to connect A to B, to establish linear chains of cause and effect as I described before. Example: why is Peter consistently jeopardising the efforts of the team?

- Because his previous manager was a difficult person and he learnt to be defensive.
- Because he has a difficult personality.
- Because he has problems at home.
- Because he lost his child in an accident.
- Because he wants to show off.
- Because he has tried hard since childhood to overcome a poor upbringing.
- Because his wife dominates him at home and he compensates for that in the office.
- Because his father left them when he was five.
- Because he wasn't promoted at the last round.
- Because he is getting older.
- Because he 'has an attitude'.
- Because he was used to fighting with his small brothers all the time.
- Because he used to drink.
- Because he has moved around too much when he was a child.
- Because his mother remarried and lost interest in him.

There is not going to be a shortage of explanations. And most likely, many of them are plausible and possible. However, the real questions are:

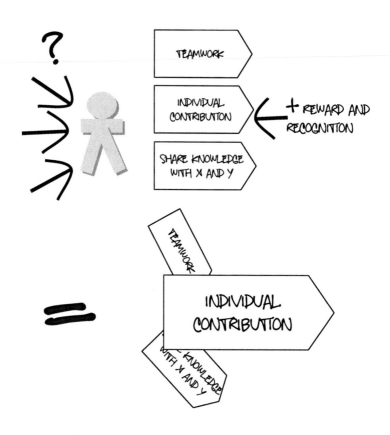

Regardless of the causes that triggered doing good teamwork, delivering personal results and sharing knowledge with others, if individual contribution is the only behaviour of the three that is rewarded or recognised, anything else will tend to fade in favour of the individualistic behaviours.

- Which explanation is right?
- How do we know?
- Is Peter going to stop consistently jeopardising the efforts of the team once 'he knows'?

And the answer to all them is: err, hmmm, errr... well....

There is another way of trying to do something for Peter, if this is what you want. We may not be able to know whether Peter's behaviours were shaped by causes A, B, C, etc., but what we do know today, is that, if Peter behaves like that, it's because his behaviour is being reinforced.

Under reinforcement you need to understand anything that is associated with Peter's behaviour and that, by this association, increases the behaviours further. Peter is rewarded (I will make a distinction between words later) for his behaviour. There is no doubt abut that. It may be very obvious or not that obvious at all, but he is. Maybe if you are Peter's manager you are the main source of this reinforcement.

Here are some possibilities: Peter gets away with murder. He jeopardises the team, but there is no negative consequence for him. So his behaviour is reinforced every time by what feels like a positive outcome. He exercises power and this is tolerated. He is seen as 'difficult', which differentiates him and gives him more attention. When he acts that way, his boss has long discussions with him and he then comes up with several reasons why the team is going in the wrong direction. Recently, he was put in charge of a Task Force to look at the overall efficiency of the project management teams (see another example in the graph on p. 208).

WHY IS 'B' HAPPENING?

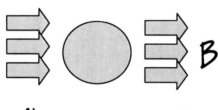

B

(1)

BECAUSE LAST YEAR
WAS DIFFICULT, MANAGEMENT
WAS UNDER PRESSURE AND
ISSUES WERE NOT TACKLED,
CREATING BAD ATTITUDES AND
A VERY CHAOTIC ENVIRONMENT.
ALSO, PEOPLE WERE FRUSTRATED
AND DE-MOTIVATED.

(2)

BECAUSE
SOMEBODY,
SOMEWHERE
SOMEHOW,
TODAY, IS
REINFORCING B

AND THE ONE WE
CAN DO SOMETHING
ABOUT IS

> There is something in Peter's current behavioural pattern that is positive and rewarding for him. This is what is sustaining Peter's behaviour TODAY (even if he learnt to be defensive and 'difficult' when fighting with his brothers as a child!)

So, we have a choice:

(A) Dig in Peter's biography until we establish a link between his childhood and his consistent torpedo behaviours of today.

(B) Try to find out what is reinforcing Peter's behaviours today and stop that reinforcement. Or, even better in behavioural terms, find ways to reward alternative-non-torpedo behaviours (see graph p. 210)!

I am deliberately painting a simplistic picture in the hope of establishing this point:

BEHAVIOURS MAY BE TRIGGERED BY MULTIPLE 'CAUSES' BUT ARE SUSTAINED OR CONTROLLED BY THEIR CURRENT CONSEQUENCES, BY HOW THEY ARE OR AREN'T REINFORCED.

People sometimes use the generic term of 'rewards', although these tend to be mentally associated with 'monetary rewards'. In reality, reinforcement and reward are not the same. A reward is something that I, the manager, have decided is going to be good for you and therefore I expect that it will reinforce your associated behaviour accordingly. But I may get some surprises!

>> NOT ALL REWARDS REWARD OR REINFORCE BEHAVIOURS

If somebody gives you $5 or $10 for something as a reward but you were expecting $500, it becomes far from a reward and far from a reinforcement. If you feel insulted by money altogether, even worse. Thinking that he is rewarding you, what this person is really doing, is putting you off.

Since any PhD worth its name must have case studies, here are a few one-minute vignettes:

(1) PUNISHMENT IS BOTH ATTRACTIVE AND A GOOD INCENTIVE

Parents arrive consistently late to pick up children from the kindergarten in the afternoon. Management is frustrated and introduces a fine of a $5 for every time the parents arrive late. Outcome: significant increase in late arrivals across the board. $5 was a penalty worth paying for having the flexibility of arriving late.[32]

(2) REWARD IS A PUNISHMENT

Joe has managed to achieve maximum, outstanding results during the past year. At the Town Hall, Joe is praised publicly and he is brought to the front to be greeted by the CEO. Joe is a naturally shy chap who hates visibility. Joe felt punished by his manager in the worst possible way.

---

[32] Levitt, Steven D., Dubner, Stephen J., 2002, *Freakonomics: A Rogue Economist explores the hidden Side of Everything*, Allen Lane, UK

(3) REWARD NOT PERCEIVED AS REINFORCEMENT

A stock options scheme is implemented across the board following a review by an external company. It is segmented according to grades and years in the company. Salaries are increased at inflation rate. Expectation of universal joy! Some employees expressed high dissatisfaction. Nobody has actually asked them if they want stock options, with all the associated administrative and tax implications. They would have been extremely happy with a modest pay raise.

(4) FORCE RANKING DEMOTIVATES INSTEAD OF ATTRACTS HIGHER PERFORMANCE

A forced ranking scheme has been implemented. Top 10% of achievers get 120% bonus, the next tier 100%, the next 90% and so on. The following year, more people than expected remain in the second and third tiers. Fewer reached the designed top 10% in the metrics. People are in fact very content with the 90% compensation they are getting. The extraordinary effort needed to achieve the top is not worth it. As described before, the incremental gain is not a reinforcement for their behaviours, but an encouragement to make less effort. I have chosen vignettes on the fiasco side to illustrate how many times rewards backfire!

Part 2 of our fastest ever, Guinness Record PhD in Psychology contains three things that you need to remember:

- The four types of associations that behaviours can get and their consequences
- When to reinforce behaviours
- The business of motivation…

>> BEHAVIOURS + TYPE OF REINFORCEMENT → CONSEQUENCES

There are not a million things that 'can happen' to behaviours:

(1) POSITIVE REINFORCEMENT

They can be associated with a positive reinforcement; i.e. something good, pleasant, positive, a 'reward' (if it really is one), etc. In this case, the behaviour, whether good or bad, desirable or undesirable, will increase. Types of positive reinforcement include monetary ones (such as salary, bonus, financial incentives, etc.) and non-monetary ones (such as gratitude, praise, acknowledgement, (private and public) attention and air time).

(2) NEGATIVE REINFORCEMENT

Behaviours can be 'rewarded' with the withdrawal or suppression of some form of pain that was associated with them. If people were required to write ten-page monthly reports and submit them exactly on a particular day and, now the report has been converted into a half-page, electronic one to be submitted at any time during a one-week period, monthly report compliance will increase! The withdrawal of pain (or simplification of painful processes and procedures in organisations) and its use as a behavioural reinforcement is one of the best hidden assets we have!

(3) PUNISHMENT

Behaviours can be punished by applying pain: psychological, moral, material! Hardly a need to describe what punishment is! Punishments are effective as shock treatment but are very ineffective as modifiers of behaviours in the long run.

Remember that this applies all the time, whether you are punishing an undesirable behaviour or a desired one!

(4) 'EXTINCTION' A reinforcement that was present and associated with a certain behaviour is now withdrawn. The behaviours - whether positive or negative, desirable or undesirable - will tend to fade. One of the areas where this trick is present is in the assumption by managers that established behaviours don't need reinforcement. *"Paul is dong his job. Why do I have to reward or reinforce? It is his job! I understand reinforcing Mary's extra-mile efforts, but not Paul's expected performance"*. Psychology is blind as to whether it was expected or unexpected by David-the-Manager, or whether it was in Paul's job description or not. It doesn't consult with David. But, if Paul's - or anybody else's - behaviours are not reinforced, they will tend to fade! That's why many good performances become less good...

>> WHAT YOU REINFORCE IS WHAT YOU GET

So, make sure you know what you are doing! Behaviours are always competing for reinforcement, for air time. Reinforcing competing and incompatible behaviours is of course possible, but at a cost! To be frank, most of the problems I see come from 'disconnects' between what management preaches and what management reinforces, rewards or recognises:

IN THE TERMS OF THE TRADITIONAL MANAGERIAL PROCESS MODEL: IF YOU PUSH INPUT YOU GET OUTPUT

INPUT
EFFORT
PLANNING ACTIVITIES
USE OF TOOLS
PROCESSES

OUTPUT
PRODUCTIVITY
INNOVATION
(R&D, SALES)

IN BEHAVIOURAL TERMS, IF YOU REINFORCE INPUT YOU DON'T GET OUTPUT, YOU GET... MORE INPUT

- Preach teamwork but reward individual contributions.
- Preach 'helicopter view' but reward people with great focus and narrow views.
- Preach productivity outputs but reward efforts made.
- Preach reflection and thoughtful processes but reward speed and those who come first.
- Preach customer-centric activity but reward those who spend their life managing internal processes and never see a client.

Let's take one of the list as a showcase example. People put some effort into preparing, planning or using processes and tools in order to achieve results. It is assumed that those processes are necessary to achieve the outcomes. The graph on page 216 illustrates how the behavioural model and the traditional managerial-process-driven model are sometimes pulling in different directions. In managerial terms, efforts lead to outputs, so paying attention to efforts (promoting, praising, discussing them) would lead, or so the assumption goes, to better or greater outputs. However, in behavioural terms, spending most of management time discussing, promoting, supporting, refining, querying or enhancing inputs/efforts is effectively a form of reinforcement.

If you reinforce mainly inputs, you won't necessarily get outputs; you'll get more and greater inputs. Since the industry of tooling is well developed (vendors sell project management, market segmentations, automatic sales territory management systems, simulation tools, training, databases, 'best practices',

benchmarking) there is no shortage of
potential refinement of the machinery or
the ever-increasing quest for a better
oil for it.

Management in organisations sometimes spend an obscene
percentage of time managing internal processes, 'inputs'. This
is what is reinforced, and this is what becomes 'the business'.
The situation is similar to this conversation:

- I want a power drill.
- Why do you want a power drill?
- I need a power drill.
- Why do you need it?
- I need to hang a picture on the wall.
- Do you have the picture?
- Yes, and the nail; I want a power drill.
- No, you want a hole.

The hole is what is needed, the power drill is secondary. If the
hole could be made in any different way, or somebody would
do it for you, the power drill would be irrelevant. People in
management spend most of the time talking about power drills
and very little about what the real purpose is: the holes.

DO YOU WANT A POWER DRILL OR A HOLE?

>> WHEN?

Behaviours that are 'new', introduced, for example, as a result of a change programme, need to be reinforced constantly when they are present. Behaviours that have been established for a while need to be reinforced intermittently or from time to time.

Picture this: it is Friday afternoon and you receive an email from your boss saying that he has heard about your great contribution during the week and he just wants to say thanks. You are delighted. You are reinforced in your behaviours. Next Friday at the same time, a similar email arrives. You think your boss is really sensitive to people's efforts and you go home quite 'motivated'. The following Friday, at the same time, a similar email arrives and you... smile. Here he goes again, oh well. You start to suspect that something automatic may be going on. A couple more Fridays and you are thoroughly disappointed. When reinforcements become predictable, they lose their power. Random or intermittent reward and recognition is far more effective.

>> MOTIVATION WARS

Finally, you are about to complete your PhD. You need to know about 'intrinsic' vs. 'extrinsic' motivation. There is a lot of long standing controversy about the merits of one versus the other. Extrinsic motivation has to do with all the external types of rewards and recognition people can get, from money to praise. Intrinsic motivation means doing your job because it is fulfilling in itself, not because you'll be paid or recognised. Psychology wars are constant. You'll find both sides arguing.

A fraction of the disputes are worth the attention. Suffice it to say that many theorists settle for accepting that creating good environmental conditions for the job eventually plays the so-called intrinsic motivation card. It would at least enhance confidence, self-fulfilment, and a sense of worthiness to those for whom doing the job in itself is the motivation. As a practitioner, I do not see any contradiction between the two but I suspect that the war between the intrinsic and extrinsic camps will continue.

BEHAVIOURAL RULES 10 (SHORTEST EVER PHD IN PSYCHOLOGY)

1 CONSTANTLY REWARD NEW BEHAVIOURS IN THE CHANGE MANAGEMENT PROGRAMME; REWARD INTERMITTENTLY ONCE THEY HAVE BEEN ESTABLISHED.

2 CHECK IF YOUR REWARDS ARE GOING TO REINFORCE... DO THE HOMEWORK IN YOUR ORGANISATION. 'ASK' WHAT KIND OF REWARDS AND RECOGNITION ARE GOING TO HAVE POWER

3 CHOOSE BETWEEN POWER DRILLS AND HOLES AND DECIDE WHAT IT IS THAT YOU REALLY NEED. IF YOU REWARD INPUT, YOU'LL GET INPUT, NOT OUTPUT.

4 WHEN YOU DECIDE TO REINFORCE BEHAVIOUR A, LOOK FOR THE BEHAVIOURS B, C, D THAT YOU MAY NEED TO STOP REINFORCING BECAUSE THEY COMPETE WITH OR ARE INCOMPATIBLE WITH A.

5 DIVIDE YOUR BEHAVIOURAL PLAN INTO PIECES. REINFORCE BEHAVIOURAL STEPS; DON'T WAIT UNTIL THE END BEHAVIOUR HAS APPEARED.

6 CHECK FOR DISCONNECTS BETWEEN WHAT YOU SAY YOU WANT TO REINFORCE, AND WHAT YOU ARE ACTUALLY REINFORCING.

7 OBSESSIVELY PRACTICE THE 'WHY?' IN THE WAY OF: IF A IS HERE, IS IT BECAUSE IT'S BEING REINFORCED? 'WHAT IS REINFORCING A' IS A FAR BETTER QUESTION THAN 'WHY DO WE HAVE A?'

8 IF OUTPUTS ARE WELL-DEFINED (INNOVATION, PRODUCTIVITY, ETC.) REWARD OUTPUT-BEHAVIOUR OVER INPUTS OR EFFORTS TO GET THERE.

9 LOOK FOR THE HIDDEN ASSETS OF 'NEGATIVE REINFORCEMENTS' THAT IS, THE WITHDRAWAL OF PAINFUL PROCESSES AND THE FACILITATION OF TASKS.

10 COMBINE EXTERNAL OR EXTRINSIC REWARDS ('EXTRINSIC MOTIVATION') WITH IMPROVED ENVIRONMENTAL CONDITIONS THAT SUPPORT SO-CALLED 'INTRINSIC MOTIVATION'.

NON-NEGOTIABLE BEHAVIOURS

As we have emphasised before, 'if you want to change culture, change behaviours'. Behaviours have an enormous capacity to trigger and create organisational change because:

- They are observable and we can agree on an unequivocal meaning.
- We know how and why behaviours tend to stay or fade. We can manage them.
- A small non-negotiable set of them can deal with multiple issues, needs, desired changes, actions or objectives.

225

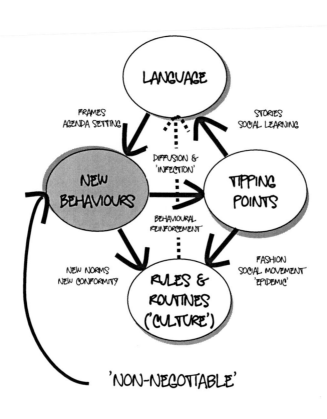

This chapter deals with the identification of the behaviours needed to launch, create and sustain change. We will also cover the mechanisms needed to make them (1) visible, and then therefore (2) susceptible of being spread until tipping points have been created and those new behaviours have become 'the norm'.

We saw previously how behaviours are triggered by multiple causes but are controlled by the specific consequences of each of them. We also saw how they can be reinforced to make them sustainable.

The following map will help us describe a process to 'uncover' which behaviours are needed and how to make them, let's say 'available' to the organisation.

1. DEFINING A FUTURE

Perhaps management or somebody else has already identified the issues that require change. Perhaps this has been done in a detailed way or just in broad terms. It is likely that a list of these issues has been made. It may contain topics such as

- Poor execution
- Very slow decision making
- Not responsive to customers
- Silos and poor collaboration
- Need to improve productivity
- Unacceptable quality
- Overall poor performance
- Need to create/boost team activity
- Sloppy product development process

8 SUSTAINING APPLYING BEHAVIOURAL METHODS TO MAKE BEHAVIOURS SUSTAINABLE

1 DESIGNING A FUTURE DEFINE AND MAP THE PICTURE OF SUCCESS AND FAILURE

5 REINFORCING APPLY BEHAVIOURAL METHODOLOGY TO REINFORCE CURRENT ENABLING BEHAVIOURS

7 LIVING NEW CONDITIONS BEHAVIOURS ARE 'LIVE', SPREAD BY IMITATION AND OTHER SOCIAL FORMS OF 'DIFFUSION'

2 TRANSLATING INTO INDIVIDUAL, GROUP AND MANAGEMENT BEHAVIOURS

3 AUDITING YOUR CURRENT ORGANISATIONAL FABRIC, YOUR PATTERNS OR ENABLING/ BLOCKING BEHAVIOURS

4 MAPPING CREATE A BEHAVIOURAL PLAN INCLUDING NON-NEGOTIABLE BEHAVIOURS

6 SEEDING: DESIGN AND ENGINEER INITIATIVES THAT DE FACTO GENERATE NEW DESIRABLE BEHAVIOURS

- Too heavy structure and set up
- Need to improve 'competitive mindset'
- Overall culture of complacency

And so on. No matter how well-defined an initial list of issues, targets, objectives or areas of focus is, I always try to step back, to imagine and define what *success and failure exactly look like* in a particular time-frame. A group of people, perhaps an extended senior management group, can perhaps gather for a couple of days and brainstorm first - with or without external facilitation - on what those scenarios, success and failure, look like.

A way to start is as follows. Imagine that one year (two? three years?) from now, we are standing here in front of the Board (or other members of senior management) and we concede: 'we have failed'. What does it mean? Can we write 'the script' that led us here? Another parallel group can do the same on the scenario: 'we have succeeded'. This is always a very useful exercise that tries to uncover the true meaning of 'success' and 'failure' beyond the possible initial pavlovian reaction of the type: *"Oh, we know that, success is meeting all the objectives of the strategic plan"*.

When confronted with the task of 'writing the script' as if we were literally writing a movie plot, managers usually have little problem in identifying the characters of the plot! In my experience, the first pass of the exercise is always strongly biased towards 'process description': 'prototypes were not ready in time, project management did a lousy job, we didn't recruit fast enough to get the critical mass, our quality process didn't spot so and so'.

Also in my experience, the group dealing with 'failure' have an easier ride. It seems easier to 'visualise' what could go wrong! Once this is done, we can match the mirror scenarios and see if they contain mirror processes. Then we can see whether we have a generic, consistent 'success and failure' scenario and whether the mechanisms behind them have been identified.

2 TRANSLATING INTO BEHAVIOURS

The next step is the challenge of *extracting behaviours* behind the success and failure scenarios. Here, for example, 'we didn't recruit fast enough' needs to be translated into things that people did or didn't do. It may be that the HR department was slow, or that management was not proactive enough to define their needs, etc. The goal of this part of the process is to 'talk behaviours'. At some point, a good list of those behaviours will be uncovered and available and, again, with or without facilitation, the trick is to see if there are patterns of these behaviours that can either be labelled as *enablers* or *blockers* of the desired success. A simple picture at this stage may look like this real life case study:

> To achieve success as defined by A [or avoid the failure described as B], these key behavioural patterns seem to be behind the processes needed for change:
>
> [1] **Collaboration** between team members in divisions X and Y. There is a strong 'silo mentality' amongst us that has the potential for slowing down any common process. This seems to be an important blocking mechanism across the organisation.

[2] A significant change in **the way we tackle problems** in general. We allow everybody to describe what's wrong and we disseminate this knowledge well. But we don't seem to have a culture of 'solutions' where people routinely go beyond the description of the problem and do something about it.

[3] **Decision making**, speed and implementation. We consistently spend unnecessary time making decisions. We believe that part of the problem is our culture of over-inclusiveness, where we tend to involve a significant number of people in any decision. Also, once the decision is made, people seem to 'wait and see if the decision sticks', because it's very normal to have decisions reversed very soon after they were made and communicated.

In this particular case, the team dealing with this 'uncovering process' mapped many other behaviours that were behind concepts such as 'need for entrepreneurial spirit', 'empowerment of people', 'communicating between cultures' and another dozen or so behavioural patterns that they thought relevant. But the behavioural facilitator had asked them to choose.

The traditional management approach would often ask you to brainstorm and list the problems, group them and define them, then apply solutions *to each of them*. Although not always the case, people participating in these kind of exercises usually end up with a list of fifty or so actions that match an equally long list of identified issues. It is pretty much what we have described before as the 'big problems, big solutions' model, or the 'big list of issues, big list of actions' model. Unfortunately, many times this is just an exercise that makes people happy by being able to produce activity lists that give them a false sense of control and a deluded sense of scientific process.

> Seen through non-linear glasses, only very few actions may have the power of producing the desired change and these are the ones to focus on, making sure that they will be very visible.

I can hear some people saying: "*We do this already, we prioritise, we don't go for everything at the same time!*" However, most of these so-called prioritisation exercises are usually based on pure resource parameters, i.e. this is too much to do, let's try the things that are doable, concrete, focused, etc. Prioritisation in that scenario is pure pragmatism with not much extra thinking. The kind of 'prioritisation' I am talking about is very different: it is the search for those actions that can trigger butterfly effects, regardless of any other judgements about resources needed or complexity.

The same applies to 'behaviours'. For example, ensuring collaboration between the teams in divisions X and Y (and we haven't yet gone into the how of this) may deal with a list of 'issues' such as the ones described in this real case scenario:

- Competitor information is not shared. Processes to obtain this information are systematically duplicated and wasted.

- Nobody seems accountable for sharing the knowledge acquired in the day-to-day dealing with external customers.

- The Customer Relationship Management (CRM) system installed has a poor usage record of 45% with many people in many functions simply not using it.

The traditional approach would be tempted to:

- tell people that not sharing competitor information is not acceptable. Create 'an action plan' to communicate this and report back in three months to see if it has improved.

- tell people how important it is to share customer knowledge. Create 'action points' to achieve this.

- investigate the causes (perhaps via interviews and questionnaires) of why the CRM system is underperforming and communicate to all users the importance of using the system and the waste that the organisation is suffering.

In the above approach:

- each issue is treated in isolation and triggers its own action plan.
- communication of the problem and a rational appeal to people are emphasised.
- Implicitly, it is hoped that each of the issues can be improved as if they were independent.

This process is often reinforced further by the selection of 'sponsors', perhaps from the senior management team, who are bound to create teams, task forces or similar vehicles to tackle these problems independently.

The reason why the management team in this case decided not to go this way is because it was able to identify the underlying behaviours behind this list of issues. Collaboration, as a behaviour, simply wasn't there. If there was a mechanism to 'create' collaboration as a routine, established behaviour, that new behaviour would deal with ALL the issues at once.

Focusing on one, 'non-negotiable' behaviour had the potential for 'solving' most of the problems. This is the same way in which that team reached the conclusion for the other two non-negotiable behaviours which they, in their own terms, labelled 'Solutions Culture' and 'Final Decisions'. In other words, the management team chose as opposed to 'prioritised' in the traditional way.

3. AUDITING

We need to know how much of a gap there is between the desired behaviours for success and the current behavioural fabric in the organisation. If collaboration is needed big time but collaboration is not in the organisation's DNA (very typical, for example, for many sales forces created by the hiring of very individualistic people who then get rewarded for their individual success), we have a bigger challenge than if collaboration was somehow 'there' but hidden and perhaps not sufficiently reinforced. In traditional terms, if there is no 'culture of collaboration' and now collaboration is needed, well, 'cultural change' is required big time as well!

In the real case described, the management team was very aware of the lack of collaboration which they saw as a result of historical practices. They also had some 'employee survey' data that pointed in that direction, supporting their assessment. However, in some cases, particularly in large organisations, some sort of behavioural audit is needed in order to establish a 'baseline of behaviours'. The next step then is to be able to match the set of 'new desired behaviours needed' with that picture of the current reality.

There are many ways to do this. I use web-based screening questionnaires that can be assessed real time if needed. The following list contains forty behavioural drivers that research at The Chalfont Project Ltd has consistently found in different combinations as sources of enabling/blocking mechanisms in organisations. They are described at a high level, sometimes 'macromolecular', and therefore they will need to have further interpretations for a particular organisation. They are listed here as an example of behavioural patterns to consider.

1   'Admiring-the-problem': clear identification of issues not followed by behaviours conducive to solutions
2   Assessing, evaluating. Conscious efforts to conceptualise or qualify markets, customers, situations; entails awareness
3   Blaming, externalisation of accountabilities
4   Sharing of knowledge and information
5   Checking or auditing for consistency, as follow up
6   Collaboration, cooperation (or lack of), induced or spontaneous
7   Commitment (or lack thereof); generic behaviour to be further 'translated'
8   Communicating of goals, strategies, decisions

9   Competition (internal)

10   Compliance (or lack thereof) with requirements, rules,
        etc. Generic behaviour to be further 'translated'

11   Cynicism – attributional: attributed to others hidden
        intentions

12   Defeatism (acceptance or expectation of defeat);
        powerlessness. Related behaviours

13   Disconnect Behavioural-Reinforcement: not rewarding
        desired or rewarding undesired behaviours

14   Empowered behaviour: behaviour consistent with
        granted empowerment

15   Feedback: – provide feedback (or not) on information,
        data or knowledge gathered

16   Gathering or seeking information, such as background,
        goals, etc.

17   Individualism -personal

18   Initiatives - Reward of

19   Innovating: conscious efforts to create new ideas or new
        ways to explore alternatives

20   'Blind Input'. Provide – or request - input not knowing
        purpose or use

21   Input - Provide information (or not), input data or info
        into the system

22   Linking: conscious efforts to integrate people, ideas and
        teams

23   Non-Compliance not followed by consequence

24   Organising: conscious efforts to put things into place
        before action

25   Producing, delivering what is supposed to be delivered
        or actioned

26   Promoting or selling of ideas, results, achievements

27   Provide information feedback (or not)

28   Punishment; clearly identified as such or suspected as behaviour

29   Resistance; generic behaviour to be further 'translated'

30   Respect: behaviours consistent with presence of

31   Seeking commitment, endorsement or support

32   Short-term-ism: behaviours consistent with a short-sighted or short-term view of business, results, goals, etc.

33   Silo effect: behaviour consistent with silo life

34   Scepticism, behaviours consistent with scepticism as attitude

35   Standards related behaviours: conscious efforts to behave with pre-determined patterns of what's acceptable, desirable or expected

36   Talk-no-walk, behaviour inconsistent with verbalisation, behavioural disconnect, for example, with agreements

37   Trust-building; behaviour consistent with

38   Trust-eroding; behaviour consistent with

39   Trust-like: behaviours consistent with trust (or lack thereof)

40   'Walk-the-talk', behaviour consistent with verbalisations

As an example, in one case, the above 40 behaviours were grouped into seven even higher 'macromolecular' labels for the sake of further discussions with the team involved in a 'cultural change' programme. These 'seven drivers' became behaviours related to:

-     Assessing and evaluating
-     Action and execution
-     Defeatism and cynicism, detected via either verbalisations or behaviours
-     Communication and sharing

- Collaboration and participation
- Trust and respect
- Disconnects and reinforcements with focus on management inconsistencies in terms of rewards and recognitions

4. MAPPING

In the case study we are using, mapping was simple. It was the result of the 'visualising success and failure' exercise and the subsequent uncovered behaviours, plus a mixture of some new auditing and the data already available in house about employees' practices. Mapping represents the final set of behaviours on which to focus and, in this case study, these remained:

- 'Collaboration'
- 'Solutions culture'
- 'Final decisions'

Many others remained 'on hold' until the three described above were tackled. As mentioned in the previous chapter, an external distant observer may be forgiven for deeming this list to be pretty simplistic and no different from many other traditional 'action plans'. However, behind each of these high level labels were specific descriptions of what they meant and subdivisions into molecular and atomic behaviours, all of them susceptible of being 'visible' and 'reinforced'. And that's what makes the difference: the combination of relatively high level 'labels' and their operational descriptions, often at a very detailed, 'atomic' level.

5. REINFORCING EXISTING BEHAVIOURS AND 6. SEEDING NEW BEHAVIOURS

We have seen before how both 'new behaviours' and 'old behaviours are governed by the same rules of reinforcement. If a (desirable) behaviour is already present - e.g., the behavioural audit confirms that it is not 'alien to the organisation - it needs to be reinforced as well, or it will tend to fade.

So, potentially, the mapping of the desired behaviours needed may contain a mixture of 'new' and 'old behaviours'. For 'old behaviours', the next step is to apply reinforcement mechanisms as described before. These mechanisms, of course, play a pivotal role in what we will describe in the next chapter as 'behavioural diffusion', sometimes via imitation.

A different magnitude of challenge is the one posed by the need to establish (and subsequently reinforce) behaviours that are *not* part of the 'behavioural fabric' or 'behavioural DNA' of the organisation. To put it bluntly, that are not there! The conventional approach and wisdom would take you straight into 'preaching':

- *Explain* why collaboration is important; what we will gain by this, or what we will lose by not having it.
- The need to change the old individualistic *mindset.*
- Change people's *attitude.*

And so on.

An alternative is to talk less about the need for collaboration and 'seed it', so that it becomes a visible behaviour that can be reinforced, mirrored and 'infected' (see next chapter). Let me give you a real example. A typical case of the need to 'change culture' arose in a large pharmaceutical sales force that had been created with strong individualistic ethos. The company had historically hired people who were able to sell ice to Eskimos and had for years rewarded them with big bonuses for their individual sales performance.

They discovered that the Darwinian system that had worked in the past was perhaps not so suitable in the current environment where collaboration and sharing of information between people was key to their strategy. In their case, they had decided to combine two previously independent sales forces into one. In cultural terms, they had a great individualistic culture and wanted to change to a great collaborative culture, and still meet the targets. Previous 'cultural discussions' had taken them into painful territories. Taking the VIRAL CHANGE™ approach, they decided they would be better off 'forgetting the culture' and translating the change into behavioural change.

The new questions were now:

- what was it that the pharmaceutical sales representatives and their district managers now had to do differently?
- how were they going to reward the new behaviours?

But there was no habit of collaboration within the organisation. Literally, this had not happened before; not much between individuals, let alone between the two sales forces now combined. Waiting for a miracle wasn't on the cards!

> We wanted to show that - far from
> what an established 'mood of defeatism'
> was expressing ('not in a million years,
> we have no history of districts talking
> to each other, it will never happen
> here') - it was actually possible to
> 'see collaboration'. However, it had to
> be 'engineered'.

Through a simple process of mapping which small steps could be implemented soon, we helped management to implement a rather simple system of systematic sharing of small pieces of information between newly created 'user groups' These groups were created by asking each team to nominate one person who could act as a 'node' or recipient/distributor of the information. There were two user groups: one for 'competitor information' and one for information on 'use of marketing materials'.

Everybody was asked to send a simple weekly short email to their representative in each user group. One email containing a simple bit of competitive information ('company X is very active here and recruiting new people non-stop offering big salaries') and one for the other user group containing a piece of feedback on the use of promotional materials ('magazine article Y totally hopeless at convincing customers about message Z; anybody similar experience?') At that time, blogs didn't exist, nor did the company have a good intranet or, not surprisingly, electronic collaboration system, so email was the chosen vehicle. Today, company blogs and/or shared web-based spaces provide excellent vehicles for this.

The very initial reception of the initiative was frosty. The 'user groups' were instructed to reinforce any single visible behaviour consistent with their request, by sending short thank-you-emails to people sending the information, by consolidating that information (a mixture of tips, ideas, and complaints!) and by broadcasting to all both 'the news' and the amount and quality of the information shared. They were instructed to remain silent about the ones that for whatever reason didn't seem to bother to send the email.

In the first two weeks, the compliance with the request was poor. It picked up by the end of the first month, to remain stable at around 35% compliance. Towards the end of month two, it had suddenly reached 90% of people 'using the new system'. Qualitative records of people's comments read:

-   I was convinced that it would not be possible for districts to talk to each other like this.
-   It is incredible how this can happen. Are we all just sheep?
-   It is good news. It started with some teams saying that the information was really useful and then many others started to follow the same pattern
-   The most amazing thing is to see Mr X - who has never sent an email to anybody - now becoming addicted to the distribution of this information
-   I know of a district that suddenly became very active as if they thought, *"If everybody else is doing it, we should as well"*. Although I know that they never articulated it like that.

By the end of month three we had a problem. We had literally created it! There was 'too much information floating around'.

I suggested that 'it was a good problem to have', considering the company's history! From that point on, the user groups became more sophisticated in the way they filtered and disseminated information so 'the problem' was under control.

The nature of the information shared was in itself a positive asset for the organisation. But in socio-behavioural and viral terms, this was less relevant than the establishment of a new visible behaviour.

```
        Collaboration was not only
possible: it existed. And if it did
exist in this way (focused on those
engineered topics), then it could also
happen in a broader sense. It was not a
non-existing behaviour anymore. Sceptics
had been defeated! Collaborative
behaviour could now expand to other
topics and could be reinforced as
needed.
```

Morale soared. Many people expressed their joy of 'seeing things happening' in different ways. By the end of month four, people no longer identified themselves as belonging to sales force 1 or 2. People felt very positive about a move that just months before had been received with rejection and overall scepticism.

This example of *'behavioural seeding'* is vital to understand how this key piece of cultural change can be installed in a rather painless way. Again, following the same comments as before, had a distant observer commented on the original action plan, he could perhaps have exclaimed: "*Is that it? Sending weekly emails?*"

But that was the 'atomic' management' of a behaviour with a high 'molecular' destiny. The email traffic was the engineered excuse to break the defeatist vicious circle of 'it will never happen, we have never seen it done before'.

7. LIVING THE CONDITIONS AND 8. REINFORCING FOR SUSTAINABILITY

Now the behavioural plan is in operation, change is ready to follow the mechanisms that we will describe in the next chapter and that have already implicitly appeared in the case-vignette of the 'un-collaborative sales force'.

The message of this chapter is that a small set of behaviours is all that is needed to fuel the change. With my clients, I tend to use the term 'non-negotiable behaviours' to stress the importance of that small set. What happens with these behaviours is next...

'NON-NEGOTTABLE BEHAVIOURS' 10

1   VISUALISE SUCCESS AND FAILURE AND
    DESCRIBE THEM IN BEHAVIOURAL TERMS,
    NOT IN PROCESS TERMS.

2   UNCOVER PATTERNS AND
    COMMONALITIES.

3   CARRY OUT SOME SORT OF BEHAVIOURAL
    AUDIT TO UNDERSTAND THE TRUE
    BEHAVIOURAL DNA OF YOUR
    ORGANISATTON.

4   ASSESS THE GAP AND CHOOSE A SMALL
    SET OF BEHAVIOURS THAT HAVE THE
    POTENTIAL TO DEAL WITH THE KEY
    PROCESS OF CHANGE.

5   HAVE A PLAN TO REINFORCE EXISTING
    BEHAVIOURS WITHIN THE SMALL SET.

6   SEED THE BEHAVIOURS THAT YOU DON'T
     HAVE, BY DEVISING STRATEGIES THAT
     'SHOW' THEM AND 'PRACTICE' THEM,
     EVEN IF IT FEELS 'ARTIFICIAL'. YOU WANT
     TO MAKE THEM VISIBLE, AT ALMOST ANY
     COST. THEY WILL NOT APPEAR AS IF BY
     MIRACLE, NOR SHOULD YOU RELY ON THE
     HOPE THAT PEOPLE WILL EMBRACE THEM
     BY SIMPLE RATIONAL UNDERSTANDING OF
     THEIR NEEDS.

7   REINFORCE AND BROADCAST ANY
     PROGRESSIVE PRESENCE OF THOSE NEW
     BEHAVIOURS. EVEN IF ON A MINOR
     SCALE, THIS IS LIKE A 'PROOF OF
     CONCEPT' STAGE!

8   MAKE SURE THAT THE MANAGEMENT
     SYSTEM OF REWARDS AND RECOGNITION -
     WHETHER IT'S THE FORMAL
     PERFORMANCE MANAGEMENT AND
     APPRAISAL OR OTHER CORE INFORMAL
     PROCESSES - SUPPORTS THE NEW
     BEHAVIOURS.

9   OBSESSIVELY REFER TO THE SMALL CORE
     SET OF BEHAVIOURS AS 'NON-
     NEGOTIABLE'. MAKE SURE THAT PEOPLE
     UNDERSTAND THEM IN THEIR
     UNEQUIVOCAL MEANING.

10   ONLY GO BACK TO REVIEW THE SMALL
     NON-NEGOTIABLE SET WHEN THE NEW
     BEHAVIOURS ARE 'STABLE'.

LANGUAGE

NEW BEHAVIOURS

TIPPING POINTS

'CULTURES'

(10)

INFECTIONS, FASHIONS AND TIPPING POINTS: INFLUENCE IN ACTION

In the previous chapter, we have seen how the behaviours needed to create organisational or cultural change can be uncovered from a good understanding of what 'success' and 'failure' may look like. We have also seen that old and new behaviours need to be reinforced but that, in some cases, new behaviours need to be seeded first in order to make them visible and available. The next step is to understand how these new, 'visible-and-available' behaviours spread across the organisation and make the transit from 'what some individuals do and practice' to 'what the organisation does and practices'. The term 'socio-behavioural' that is behind VIRAL CHANGE™ contains two equally important words. 'Behaviours', as the

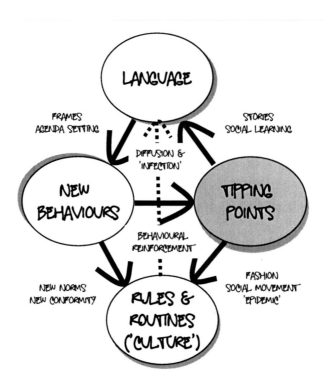

currency for the only real change, and 'social', for the mechanism needed to spread and sustain the change.

As we have seen, the conventional view of change (and the organisation itself) emphasises communication, a rational mechanism that travels down the 'plumbing system' of the organisation chart. The differences between this approach and the viral one have already previously been mapped.

Tsunami-change-management assumes that a big wave of communication and training sweeping across the firm is the main mechanism of change. It is the big-changes-big-process-of-change school of thought. We have also seen that when the organisation is seen as a living organism where non-linear mechanisms reign, butterfly effects (small, well-defined impulses or 'disruptions') have the potential of creating significant cultural change. So the next question is how individual behaviours become social routines! The word disruption is indeed appropriate because new behaviours disrupt the previous status quo.

>> HOW IDEAS AND BEHAVIOURS TRAVEL

The social sciences term for how new behaviours (individual, patterns, routines, 'practices') spread through the organisation is called 'diffusion'[33]. These new behaviours are either:

---

[33] Strang, David, Soule, Sarah, 1998, *Annual Review of Sociology*, Diffusion in organisations and social movements: From hybrid corn to poison pills, 24, pp. 265-290.

(1) *Directly observable*: 'I can see John now behaving in this way, or I can see team A focusing on completely different ways of doing things'

OR

(2) *Indirectly observable:* the consequences of those behaviours have been signalled ('these folks in the North district have done very well by practicing Z').

SOCIAL COPYING: DIFFUSION AT MACRO-SOCIAL LEVEL

At macro-social level, social diffusion has been studied in multiple areas of the socio-economic and political arena. To name a few: the spreading of strikes, collective activism, or how companies mimic reactions to mergers. This 'social copying' is a fascinating topic for people studying such diverse phenomena as fads and fashions or political activism.

Experts on 'diffusion' often split it between 'into a population' and 'within a population'. 'Into a population' includes innumerable studies looking, for example, at the role of the media. In the business arena, the role of academics, management consultants/gurus has also been looked at in the same context. Management fashions have been studied with some detail.[34]

We know, for example, that the coming and going of 'management fashions' is today understood to be a combination of multiple factors, including waves of

---

[34] Abrahamson, Eric, Fairchild, Gregory, 1999, Management Fashion: Life Cycle, Triggers and Collective Learning Processes, *Administrative Science Quarterly*, 44, pp. 708-740.

'rationality' followed by waves of 'normative thinking'. The former breeds fashions such as reengineering, or 'time-to-market' analysis, whilst the latter tends to breed more 'human relation' techniques and 'cultural engineering'. The role of the 'fashion-setting communities' (management gurus, management academics, consulting groups, etc.) has been described many times.

SOCIAL COPYING AT MICRO LEVEL: TEAMS AND NETWORKS

The micro-level ('inside the organisation', 'within a population') is the one we are interested in here.

In strong, cohesive groups ('strong ties') like teams, such diffusion may travel fast. The pressure for conformity is high. New ideas on ways of doing, or new behaviours declared as needed for the change, may sit very comfortable in a standard team once a few members of the team have adopted them. But the spread beyond the team is perhaps going to depend upon a 'weak tie'. Sometimes rumours and 'second hand information play a significant role in this type of 'weak tie' diffusion[35]. We previously discussed the role of 'weak ties' in innovation. The same mechanism applies to the diffusion of new ideas, new behaviours, internal fads and internal fashions.

To put it simply, VIRAL CHANGE™ in the organisation spreads via influence. And the 'influence chain of events' occurs by the collusion of three components: influence of individuals, influence at group level and the degree of receptiveness of people.

---

[35] Michelson, Grant, Mouly, Suchitra V., 2002, `You Didn't Hear It from Us but ...': Towards an Understanding of Rumour and Gossip in Organisations. *Australian Journal of Management*, 27.2

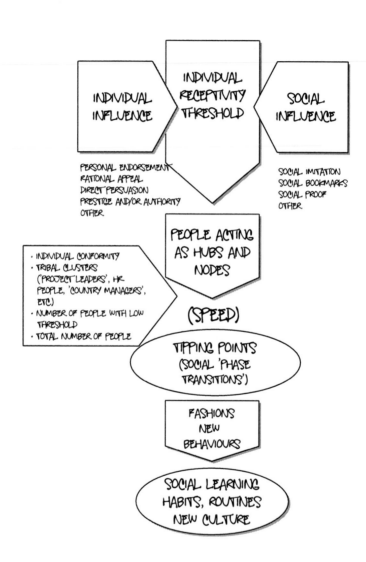

INDIVIDUAL
RECEPTIVITY
THRESHOLD

INDIVIDUAL
INFLUENCE

SOCIAL
INFLUENCE

PERSONAL ENDORSEMENT
RATIONAL APPEAL
DIRECT PERSUASION
PRESTIGE AND/OR AUTHORITY
OTHER

SOCIAL IMITATION
SOCIAL BOOKMARKS
SOCIAL PROOF
OTHER

PEOPLE ACTING
AS HUBS AND
NODES

· INDIVIDUAL CONFORMITY
· TRIBAL CLUSTERS
  ('PROJECT LEADERS', HR
  PEOPLE, 'COUNTRY MANAGERS',
  ETC.)
· NUMBER OF PEOPLE WITH LOW
  THRESHOLD
· TOTAL NUMBER OF PEOPLE

(SPEED)

TIPPING POINTS
(SOCIAL 'PHASE
TRANSITIONS')

FASHIONS
NEW
BEHAVIOURS

SOCIAL LEARNING
HABITS, ROUTINES
NEW CULTURE

>> TYPICAL FORMS OF INDIVIDUAL INFLUENCE

PERSONAL ENDORSEMENT

When a colleague in the organisation seems to adopt something new, a 'new behaviour' or a new way of doing things, this personalised endorsement is powerful in itself ("*I am certainly going to do it that way, it makes sense, about time we change gears, I am all for it*"). A simple mimic mechanism may prompt us to 'do the same' and endorse it as well.

PRESTIGE AND/OR AUTHORITY

This is endorsement at a higher level, coming from people who we believe, we trust; people who have gained some credible prestige or simply have a 'moral authority'. We are willing to follow or at least listen to them. They may simply be peers. They may be people higher up in the ranks, advisers, consultants, etc. The new, desired behaviours proposed as leading to organisational change may be legitimised by people of such (moral) authority or seen as a valuable 'role model'.

DIRECT PERSUASION

This is either 'rational appeal' at its best ("*this is a much better way, it will deliver X, we must go in that direction, are you coming with me?*") or other forms of persuasion, including pressure and coercion, whether overt or hidden.

THE UNEXPECTED ENDORSEMENT

This is the very powerful sceptic-to-convert transformation. There is something very potent about the endorsement of a new idea or new ways of doing things, or indeed broader organisational change, coming from a well-known sceptical or 'negative' individual. The 'conversion' sometimes convinces many people that the new directions are worth it, 'otherwise X would never support it'.

As you can easily imagine, very often there is a combination of these four mechanisms... and many others.

>> TYPICAL FORMS OF SOCIAL INFLUENCE

Social influence mechanisms are not completely self-contained either and do carry some degree of overlap. I'd like to focus on three of them:

SOCIAL IMITATION This is a generic phenomenon in connection with our conformity tendency that we will refer to later ('Team A is now doing X, they all seem to behave in a different way; maybe we should look at this').

SOCIAL PROOF This is the quintessential mechanism of social influence that works across both the macro and micro worlds ('everybody is doing A, it has to be good, this is *the* new way of doing things'). The new behaviour or pattern assumes legitimised status that way.

SOCIAL BOOKMARKS This term refers to some behavioural patterns seen somewhere in the organisation, but which are not necessarily widespread. People often refer to them as a 'good example of', even if the example hasn't become a norm across the organisation. Social bookmarks also function as **social clues**, pointing people and groups to phenomena to mirror or imitate. Many 'best practices' approaches work in that way, even if an organisation doesn't ever reach the same levels of performance defined as best practice. These act as mirrors and social role model.

These two complementary and constantly overlapping mechanisms of *individual* and *social* influence act upon each individual in the organisation. If individuals were all equals - like the very early network theory thought the nodes in a network were - then the combination of these mechanisms would trigger a rather universal effect. But we know that this is not the case! Some of us, for example, tend to adopt new things easier and faster than others. Also, some people seem to 'copy faster'.

>> THE INFECTION IN THE ORGANISATION'S PLAYGROUND

There are four further mechanisms that add complexity to the way diffusion - and therefore VIRAL CHANGE™ - happens:

(1) RECEPTIVENESS

We have our own 'individual receptivity threshold' for adopting trends, which either makes us one of those *'early adopters'* (ideas, gadgets, new technology…) or part of the *'late majority'*. This very individual component is key to understanding our differences. It may be related to individual differences in treating new information, or fears of what is not known or proven. Unfortunately these characteristics are often only visible by observing how individuals behave. We tend to ascribe some predictive value to this as well: if somebody has

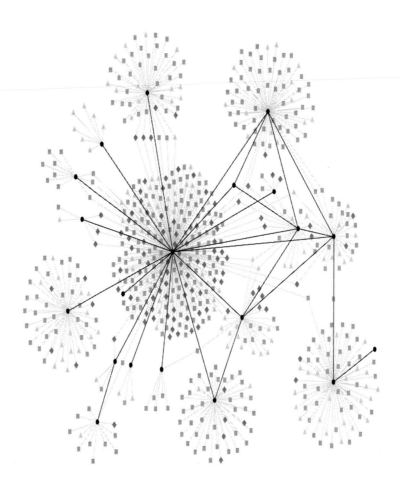

Dots:
New behaviours adopted and established
Diamonds:
Exposed, in the process of changing their mind

Squares:
Exposed, not changed
Triangles:
Unknown status

been an 'early adopter' before, we will infer he will do the same in new circumstances.

At any point in time of the diffusion of a new idea - or the spread of a new behaviour or pattern of behaviours, or new ways of doing things - there are people with different 'status' inside the organisation, as described in the graph on page 260. Some people (the black dots in the graph) will have 'adopted the new behaviour'. This cluster of people, small or big, may have appeared either spontaneously (emergent) or after some kind of orchestration, such as in the way we will describe in the next chapter. One way or another, this network will influence other people:

a. who are either 'receiving the influence', but who are still not changing, or convinced, or
b. who have received the influence but have not changed at all.

There will also be a part of the total organisation composed of people whose 'status' is unknown. Does it sound familiar? Probably yes. This could be a good Kodak picture of your organisation at any time of the implementation of a new change programme or an initiative, formal or informal. You don't know how the black dots in the graph got there. Direct influence by the top leadership? Maybe. You just know that those people are there. Just like you know that there are also others in different 'degrees of adoption'. It seems like a random Wednesday afternoon in the company. Right?

VIRAL CHANGE™

I am cheating. The graph is a reproduction of a picture from the Center for Disease Control in the USA. [36] It represents the spread of an airborne infection where the black dots are people with clinical disease, potentially infectious, the diamonds are exposed and incubating, the squares are exposed but not affected and for the triangles the status is unknown. It is the same as an internal infection inside the organisation where the agent is a new idea or a new behaviour leading to change.

(2) CONFORMITY In terms of receptivity and adoption, another mechanism, 'conformity' plays a role at individual level.

Conformity is the term used in social sciences to describe our tendency to adopt behaviours, from specific ways of doing things to the way we dress or talk. Groups have an enormous power to trigger conformity, which in turn makes us feel like we 'belong to' a particular entity, which in turn makes us feel protected from the exposure of being different or being rejected. Again, although it's a universal phenomenon, we all seem to be different in our degree of conformity or the ease and speed of adopting 'conforming behaviours'.

But the simple multiplication of what happens with one individual by the number of individuals in the organisation, doesn't explain the differences in speed of the spread of the changes or its stability. Diffusion seems to be more complex and intriguing.

---

[36] The original graph can be found at www.orgnet.com/contagion.html

(3) TRIBAL CLUSTERS A further multiplying effect appears by the apparent imitation among people who belong to a particular category, either in job description terms or shared standing in the organisation. I call this 'tribal clusters'. Example, what a project leader is doing (new behaviour, lexicon, change of style, new approach) may be 'copied' by other/all project leaders first as a mutually-reinforcing mechanism. It becomes 'a project leader thing'. Social sciences call these people *'structurally equivalent actors'* and this phenomenon has been applied to understand, for example, adoption of new drug treatments by doctors and the mutual influence of so-called 'opinion leaders'.

(4) CONNECTEDNESS A far *more powerful mechanism* of diffusion is the one carried out by the 'nodes' and 'hubs' of the organisation. These are the individuals described in previous chapters as those with a significantly high number of contacts or links.

As we have said before, these people are seldom represented in the visible, organisation chart or 'plumbing system'. They are often found, although not exclusively, in middle management and junior ranks. Their high degree of connectivity makes the spread of new behaviours to other nodes and other people fast. It is a cascade effect that is not linear. How they 'infect' other people is not often well-known and visible. Network sciences make us aware that this mechanism is similar to those involved in the spread of a disease in an epidemic or a computer virus.

The combination of these three 'forces':

- Individual influence
- Social influence
- Our individual thresholds for adoption, conformity, possible 'equivalence' (belonging to a defined group) and degree of connectedness (how much of a hub one is)

play a key role in enhancing the adopting a new behaviour or new pattern or, in general terms, 'change'.

Remember that previously we described three characteristics of the network:

(1) Power law (a few people/nodes have big number of connections, most people have only few).
(2) Matthew effects: the more you are linked and connected, the more you will be linked and connected.
(3) Tipping points: at some point in the diffusion, a 'phase transition' occurs.

These people at the peak of the power law (few of them, lots of links) are often the culprits of social infections, for better or for worse. They have the biggest number of connections and therefore they will get even more.

>> TIPPING POINTS

Which *routes* do new behaviours travel? From the nodes or hubs the spread takes place via the small worlds first, those clusters that we saw before. The infectious power of a new behaviour or pattern, somehow measured by its speed, eventually leading to major organisational change, depends on three variables:

(1) THE 'CONTACT' BETWEEN INFECTIVE PEOPLE AND RECEPTIVE PEOPLE

As in disease epidemics, susceptible people need to be in contact with infective people. Nodes, hubs or connector people are very good at infecting. In the next chapter we will see how VIRAL CHANGE™ often relies on an internal cluster of people, Change Champions, to induce that infection. In this model, an artificially created cluster (the Change Champions) is superimposed on the organisational network, *making sure* that spread will happen by:

a. declaring themselves as early adopters
b. using personal and social mechanisms of influence
c. reinforcing new behaviours
d. spotting 'fault lines' and repairing them if needed

(2) THE NUMBER OF PEOPLE INTERACTING

The number of people interacting will create a critical mass above a threshold that makes the behavioural pattern visible. Indeed, this threshold (or 'tipping point') may make initial behavioural and organisational changes invisible to the possible frustration of players. Then, suddenly, new things are present, change is visible. A cascade effect follows[37]. It appears as if, once a critical *number of people* have adopted something, an avalanche is inevitable.

---

[37] Duncan Watts and others have developed mathematical models to understand the numbers behind the concept of thresholds. This literature is very academic and only accessible if you have a good mathematical background. A mixture of academic papers, including historical ones, and more accessible summaries, can be found in a recent book:

At this tipping point, a true 'phase transition' appears, equivalent to the one described as a characteristic of the networks. Rational mechanisms seem to be overtaken by 'the new collective behaviour'. This initial infection (in enough numbers to tip), is followed by widespread acceptance. Welcome to the social life of fads and fashions.[38] Once triggered, the continuous propaganda effort could ease off without 'negative' (in terms of diffusion) effect.

(3) ENOUGH LOW THRESHOLD PEOPLE
In these small worlds, there must be a sufficient number of people with a low threshold for adoption, who will probably just copy or mirror a new behaviour from another colleague or small group. These 'low threshold' people correlate with 'early adopters'. Remember that there is not much rationality in the pathway from obscurity to celebrity. Just enough of us with a low-threshold but with high connections to infected people will do the trick.

>> VIRAL CHANGE™: INTERNAL EPIDEMIC OF SUCCESS (OR HOW TO MAKE SUCCESS FASHIONABLE)

A relatively small number of people have the capacity to infect a significant number of others in the organisation. Armed with a small number of infective agents (small set of non-negotiable behaviours) they will spread the ideas (from the rational communication to the emotional adoption) together with their own actions. They will do so through their small worlds first and also through their weaker ties.

Newman, Mark, Barabasi, Albert-Laszlo, Watts, Duncan, 2006, *The structure and dynamics of networks* ,Princeton University Press
[38] www.wikipedia.org has a list of fashions and trends organised by decade

Personal endorsement will be a key mechanism but other 'social copying' mechanisms will grow and/or take over. Conformity (with the new ideas, behaviours, norms or routines) will appear progressively but not necessarily in an even or visible manner.

At some point, a number of people will be on board and infected and a tipping point will appear where the new behaviours (and /or ideas and/or new ways of doing things) will look like norms of quite solidity.

A cross-sectional 'Kodak picture' of the organisation at any point will reveal different levels of infection. How other people get infected depends on their personal threshold (some people will be very receptive and others less), the level of conformity in the organisation, the existence of tribal clusters ('project leaders', 'country managers') within which the spread is faster and the total number of people with the potential to be infected.

How fast the infection of new behaviours will spread, will also depend on the quality and adequacy of behavioural reinforcement mechanisms. The small cluster of original carriers will play a key reinforcement role with their own endorsement, their own behaviour and the 'air time' dedicated to the issue.

Formal reinforcement mechanisms such as the ones behind reward and compensation schemes will be vital to support the new behaviours. But informal social reinforcement mechanisms, such as the nature of conversations or simply peer-to-peer mutual reinforcement, will be invaluable. New behaviours will be further reinforced by the spread of stories.

CHANGE = INFECTION =
INTERNAL EPIDEMIC OF
SUCCESS = FASHION =
FAD = MAKING (SUCCESS,
NEW IDEA, NEW WAY,
NEW DIRECTION?)
FASHIONABLE = CHANGE!

SMALL SET OF DISRUPTIVE NEW
BEHAVIOURS X (SMALL GROUP OF
ACTIVISTS + SOCIO-BEHAVIOURAL
REINFORCEMENT) X NETWORKS =
CHANGE

Embedded in the previous paragraphs is the idea that we have different possible players in this diffusion. And this is the next thing we need to address!

>> THE CREATION OF SOCIAL TIPPING POINTS: RETHINKING INFLUENCE

There are many ways of understanding the creation of social tipping points and there are some differences between the macro- and micro-social levels. It's a hot topic these days as each 'interpretation' has implications for many people involved in diverse areas such as marketing, health promotion, disease prevention, political marketing and social change of all sorts. My key point in this book and in my consulting approach to management of change in organisations is that, in the latter, the mechanisms of real change are not that different. But it is only when we start to understand the internal organisational management of change in the same way as internal infections or internal fashions that we are in a strong position to create lasting change.

Business and organisational management have incredibly thick skin, impermeable to the application of social sciences, despite the music you may hear from HR and OD departments. Inside the borders of the firm, life is usually mechanistic and predictable (top down and cascade down communication), whilst outside the borders, life is more organic, erratic and irregular. The firm usually understands its external markets and may segment customers well, but it's usually unskilled and very sloppy in understanding its internal market. Employee segmentation is rudimentary. I call rudimentary a system that categorises people into high performers, low performers and the rest (OK, you have more than three baskets, but that still doesn't change anything). Usually, a system like this is maintained to allocate money on an annual basis (a weak behavioural reinforcement mechanism) or to trigger command and control interventions ('managing the poor performers'). In many cases I know, the HR department dictates that it *must* be a Bell curve-normal distribution and that people *must* fit into it. That is, a small percentage *must* be either high performers or poor performers. And it is extraordinarily common to even decide those numbers a priori. Managers then have to fit their departmental populations into the pre-assigned Bell curve as opposed to assessing their population first and then figuring out what kind of Bell curve – if any – they have. The metrics police rules with an iron hand. In that process, true understanding of degrees and qualities of influence amongst employees gets lost. The power law of influence and connectedness (small number with high connectedness and potential influence, big number with low levels of those) doesn't fit into the Bell curve of the HR department.

We must bring the mathematics of networks back to the understanding of daily life in organisations. And along with the mathematics, we must bring an understanding and classification of employees in different terms, such as ability to influence, to be listened to or to model behaviours. That different segmentation is crucial to understanding how the behavioural tipping point creates internal social change ('new culture'). In my experience, there are four main mechanisms to create social tipping points:

1. **The Opinion Leader model.** Social infection starts with a small group of people who have a high level of

influence through what they say, how they say it, the rationale behind it and what they do. At macro-social level, these people can be found, for example, in scientific communities where, as I have described before, a Matthew Effect is obvious. Similar models can be found in community leadership, religion or political life. Within the organisation there are always 'opinion leaders', even if those opinions are exercised in the post room or the cafeteria. In some cases you can jot down the names easily; in others, 'opinion leaders' are more subtle and perhaps hidden. The Change Champions described in the next chapter fall under this criterium. In VIRAL CHANGE™, we use this model extensively, 'creating' a Change Champions' engine by finding its membership. In the Opinion Leader model, social tipping points occur when a critical mass is influenced and 'changed' by the Change Champions' activity (their endorsement of the changes needed, their articulation of the facts, their activist behaviour and their viral leadership – see later in the book). In a simplistic way, the change equation here is:

OPINION LEADERS X CRITICAL MASS = CHANGE

2. **The Critical Mass model**. It is easy to observe that many social changes, from fads to fashions to internal organisational routines (sub-cultures, ways of doing that have become 'part of the furniture'), seem to appear without being triggered by an Opinion Leader. When critical masses start to behave in 'phase transition mode', like a single node as described before, and several of those critical masses collide,

social change 'suddenly appears'. Let's take a simplistic example such as the use of the new Apple iPod. Mary bought one because she liked the feel of it and because she loved how different this thing is. Peter bought it because in his peer group at the advertising agency where he works most people have one. John is addicted to Apple any way so the iPod was a no-brainer. Pauline and Sharon are close friends and they just both did the same. Martin always buys anything new, sexy and slick - the iPod was a predictable choice. Uncle Peter bought two for his nephews after talking to a friend who did the same for his daughter's birthday. Picture all this, multiply it by a factor of 100 or 1000 and inject another million reasons and you have a critical mass of people walking/sitting around with two white umbilical cords in their ears. There was no obvious Opinion Leader trigger; they all acted as a mini-Opinion-Leader in their own merit by imitating, social copying or conforming to the norm (either a social norm or a norm in their minds). In a simple way, the social change equation here is:

CRITICAL MASS X CRITICAL MASS = CHANGE

3. **The Early Adopter model.** This one sits somewhere in between the two mentioned above. The Early Adopter model is a favourite in the technology arena as a way to indicate that some people are more prone than others to initiate usage of a new technology. But it doesn't have to be limited to technology adoption. Some of the examples in the iPod's case above could well be categorised under early adopters. The terminology is so well-known that it is impossible to

bury it in other models, but this model 3 borrows heavily from 1 and 2. The main subtle difference between the Opinion Leader and the Early Adopter is that the former is somehow more conscious and proactive, while the latter is more unconscious and reactive. The simple equation here would be:

EARLY ADOPTERS X CRITICAL MASS = CHANGE

4. **The initial Big Splash model.** Recently it has become fashionable to criticise the influencing models, particular the one represented by model 1. And all because of ... Duncan Watts, who's quoted in this book several times. He maintains that influencers are less influent that they think, because social media, social networks and any other forms of vehicle for an initial big splash (which he calls 'big seed') make the chain of influence work even if the conversion rate (influencer $\rightarrow$ enthused) is modest[39]. This apparent revelation made him appear in the Harvard Business Review (HBR) top 10 breakthrough ideas of 2007 (which tells us more about the HBR than anything else). My respect for Duncan Watts is not affected by the media hype created around the apparent war between him and Malcolm Gladwell, author of *The Tipping Point* and proponent of the power of many kinds of influencers. I take the airtime consumed by this in the media since the May 2007 HBR article with

---

[39] Watts, Duncan J., Peretti, Jonah, 2007, *Viral Marketing for the real world*, Harvard Business Review, Boston.
Watts, Duncan J., Sheridan Dodds, Peter, 2007, *Influentials, networks and public opinion formation*, Journal of Consumer Research

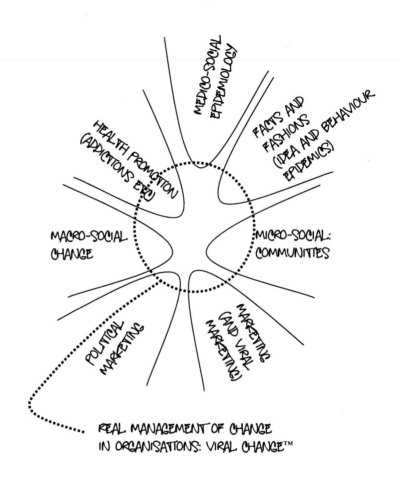

MEDICO-SOCIAL
EPIDEMIOLOGY

FACTS AND
FASHIONS
(IDEA AND BEHAVIOUR
EPIDEMICS)

HEALTH PROMOTION
(ADDICTIONS ETC)

MACRO-SOCIAL
CHANGE

MICRO-SOCIAL:
COMMUNITIES

POLITICAL
MARKETING

MARKETING
(AND VIRAL
MARKETING)

REAL MANAGEMENT OF CHANGE
IN ORGANISATIONS: VIRAL CHANGE™

a pinch of salt. The death of viral marketing and the death of the influencer - as many headlines read - have been grossly exaggerated. But I can understand the excitement: two big names, the pulpit of The New York Times and the blessing of HBR...it's simply too much to resist. Watt's equation could be described as:

INITIAL CRITICAL MASS (BIG SPLASH) X SMALLER CRITICAL MASS X BIGGER OR SMALLER CRITICAL MASS = CHANGE

Whilst models 1, 2 and 3 start small and go big, model 4 starts relatively big, then gets smaller (since the big splash is unlikely to produce a follower population of the same size) and then goes bigger in the same way as models 1, 2 and 3.

I believe that at any time, for any critical mass which is behaving as 'a single node' (3rd law of networks):

a) it is probably impossible to trace back the chain of influence.
b) all four mechanisms have probably acted at some point.
c) the people who wanted that critical mass to exist don't care much about the exact how and when or the combination of those mechanisms.

How can we translate all this to the inside of the organisation and VIRAL CHANGE™? The next chapter emphasises the use of Change Champions, which is model 1 of influence. Why? VIRAL CHANGE™ practitioners like myself can't afford to wait until 'stuff happens' (model 2), because we want to trigger the infection and spread it fast (model 1). So, VIRAL CHANGE™ asks the Change Champions (model 1 and described in the next chapter) to be early adopters of change by default (model 3). Their behaviours will create a critical mass (model 2) and the infection of change and success will spread. I am perfectly happy (and so are the Change Champions working with me) to accept the three points I have referred to above within the organisation:

a) When the new (sub)culture(s) is(are) active, visible, 'established'; when change has been introduced, I am not going to spend a lot of time tracing back to the particular influence of a particular Change Champion or a group of them.
b) Many mechanisms have probably played a role.
c) The Champions and I will be celebrating, even if the local weather, an invisible hand or providence has intervened.

INFECTIONS, FASHIONS AND TIPPING POINTS 10

1   ACKNOWLEDGE DIFFERENT STATUS OF YOUR PEOPLE IN THE ADOPTION OF CHANGE.

2   SPOT PERSONAL ENDORSEMENTS AND PROMOTE THEM IF YOU CAN.

3   LOW-THRESHOLD-FOR-CHANGE PEOPLE MAY BE A HETEROGENEOUS CATEGORY, BUT MAY INCLUDE THOSE WHO WILL SPREAD THE INFECTION FASTER AND IN A MORE POWERFUL WAY.

4   LOOK OUT FOR TIPPING POINTS.

5   REINFORCE THEIR EXISTENCE BY STORIES AND OTHER FORMS OF PUBLIC BROADCASTING.

6   EVALUATE YOUR INDIVIDUAL INFLUENCE. FIND EXAMPLES OF BEHAVIOURS YOU SEEM TO HAVE TRIGGERED IN OTHERS.

277

7   EVALUATE THE SOCIAL INFLUENCE MECHANISMS IN THE ORGANISATION. HOW MUCH IMITATION AND SOCIAL PROOF, FOR EXAMPLE, SEEM TO EXIST?

8   DO YOU HAVE 'TRIBAL CLUSTERS' AND DO THEY TEND TO BEHAVE 'IN SYNC'?

9   WHO/WHAT HAS THE GREATEST EXTERNAL POWER TO INFLUENCE YOUR ORGANISATION?

10   WHAT KIND OF SOCIAL REINFORCEMENT MECHANISMS OPERATE WITHIN THE ORGANISATION?

(11)

ACTIVISTS, DEVIANTS AND SCEPTICS: THE CHAMPIONS' VIRAL LEADERSHIP

In a previous chapter we have seen how personal influence is one of the mechanisms for the diffusion of new ideas. We have also seen how these 'new ideas' and their associated 'entourage' (language, emotions such as fear or excitement, expectations, rationality or irrationality of the appeal to change, new behaviours that need to be established for the change, etc.) travel well via the internal small worlds, and how those small worlds are connected with each other via those 'node-people' at the top of the power law graph. As you remember, we also saw how the organisation-network is far from a democratic-bell-shaped one. We said that in network terms there is no equality between people! These highly contagious people are causing daily infection without necessarily thinking about it. It is the very nature of their high connectivity that makes the infection spread.

The infection of new ideas, we saw, may look slow initially but, at some point, a phase transition/tipping point occurs and the epidemic is in the making.

>> CHANGE CHAMPIONS: INFECTION BY DESIGN

> Imagine now that we can create a network-within-the-network with people who are 'infectious-people-by-design'. We would not just rely on the passive infection pathways, but we would create new ones. This is the principal behind a 'Change Champions' group.

When I work with different organisations, they express a certain preference for specific labels and sometimes other words are incorporated (such as 'facilitators' or 'agents'), but the principle is the same.

Who are these people who have the necessary peer-to-peer influence? Well, here is a menu of characteristics to choose from. No 'Change Champions' group is composed of people with all the characteristics below. Indeed, it is that choice between the characteristics that makes Champions Groups differ from each other.

MOVERS, SHAKERS AND ACTIVISTS These people are well-known to you because of their ability to 'move things forward', to perhaps question the status quo, to stimulate and sometimes irritate. They are the anti-static engine in the organisation. In some cases their 'moving' and 'shaking' is purely of their own making. It comes naturally to them. In other cases, they seem more willing to do that 'shaking' by following more or less hierarchical objectives. One way or another, you know that they won't stay still! They make things happen, even though those things may not always necessarily be the things you wanted to happen!

MIRRORS These people possess some sort of prestige, and not necessarily because of their authority ranking in the organisational chart. People literally 'look at them' for endorsement, or for the opposite: signs of non-commitment. They may have been there for many years and command some sort of 'wise-man' quality. It is often the case that even in meetings or at the time of big announcements people will literally look at them to see their body reaction. They may or may not be conscious of their power. In some cases, they also have considerable role-model power.

SUPER-NODES These simply represent the network concept of high connectivity nodes. They have extensive links with everybody and seem to navigate the organisation with clear knowledge of its hidden map (which is obviously not the official map of the organisation chart). Often, but not always, these people have been around for a while.

SIMPLY HEALTHY RESTLESS PEOPLE These people seem to have a quality that makes them restless because of their innate - very often healthy - frustration. They have a more or less clear idea of the gap between where the organisation is today and where it should be. They may not be in a high position of authority and therefore feel a bit stuck. They will be happy to articulate the direction in which you should be moving! They portray themselves with a mixture of that frustration and at the same time commitment to make things better, to change.

There is some overlap between these categories on the menu. Well-connected people are often also 'mirrors' and project some authority of prestige. They may also be restless and frustrated with the 'need to change'.

>> FIND THE ACTIVISTS

How do you identify these people?

YOU KNOW THEM ALREADY In many cases you don't need to make much effort for identification: you already know them! If asked, senior or middle management, for example, could come up with a list very quickly. You may want to have a combination of the above criteria with more or less emphasis on certain angles, for example 'degree of connectivity' or 'anxious to change and make a difference'.

OPEN TO ALL You could open the 'role' to anybody in the organisation, or just invite a certain section! Then have an interview process to identify a subgroup, meeting a set of criteria. The advantage of this model is that you're open to all the possible help in an announced process of change, so you are announcing the (need for) change already! Everybody is invited! Since you will probably warn that this is something to be done 'on top of the day job', you may, by definition, hit a subpopulation of potentially committed people.

The disadvantage of this process is that it is very time consuming. You also need to be aware that you are bound to attract a sector of the population who 'always volunteer' or say 'yes'. Volunteer doesn't necessarily mean suitable. There are volunteer-prone people who would register themselves for just about any initiative! They may be very helpful, but some of them may turn out to be painfully unsuitable as well!

SNA?

You could, of course, use Social Network Analysis of some sort and map key connections, clusters and nodes within the organisation. Then, invite some of those nodes to be Champions, with or without further filtering.

SCREENING OR OTHER SELECTIONS

You could screen a population via other selection methods such as questionnaires. These may be useful in detecting the 'gap-conscious', the ones that exhibit more 'distance' between the level of current satisfaction and the vision of the desirable immediate future.

What I would <u>not</u> do is convert an existing group into Change Champions by decree. It doesn't work. You may be tempted to 'use' the managers or 'the direct reports of', or another pre-existing grouping. And you would probably be making a mistake. In my experience, every time that we have mapped some guidelines and asked a particular management group for some names, they have always been able to come up very quickly with those 'names'. Then you can refine or filter further but do not underestimate this simple method!

A combination of methods also works well. Once you have identified the Change Champions, you need to make a significant step: ask them for help! Because this group is your equivalent of 'patient zero' in epidemiological terms: this is where the infection starts.

>> MEET THE CHAMPIONS

You will need to explain the changes and directions that the organisation needs. Tell them that you are trying to find a cross-functional, cross-national (depending on your set-up) informal network that can help with the changes. Let them know that this may be a bit of an unconventional way to go about it, but that it will pay off! Let them know:

1. what you expect from them.
2. what 'the structure of things' is, how it is going to work.
3. what challenges they face.
4. how you are going to support them and what they should 'gain' in the process.

(1) EXPECTATIONS

You may want to use something similar to the graph on page 286 and take them through some core characteristics of this role:

- You need them to use the correct language and communication when discussing things with colleagues.

- You need them to express their endorsement to the process of change, whatever that means for your organisation. Of course, it has to make sense to them! But if it does, you expect them to be vocal about it and you expect them to be 'activists'.

- It is not just language and communication! They are not information-traffic-wardens! Their own actions have to be visible, so people can mirror them. They may or may not be comfortable with the concept of 'role model' so don't abuse it! Explain to them that 'emotional and rational copying' is a normal mechanism of diffusion (you'll find better words!) and that they need to play a big role in that.

- You'll ask them to observe what's going on and to detect any possible 'fault lines' that may occur. You or your behavioural change consultant are going to meet with them frequently, so there will be a continuous process of refinement on the messages and the reinforcement of the changes, incipient or not.

THE ROLE OF INTERNAL CHAMPIONS

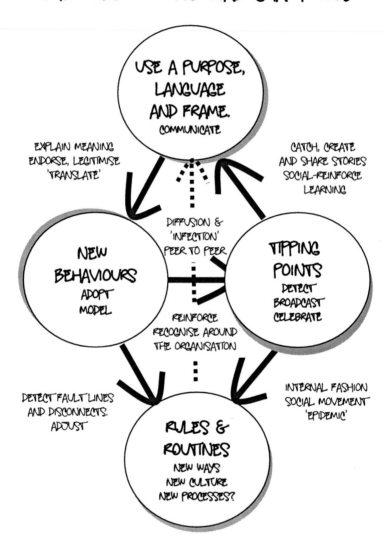

- Indeed, they will have to play a central role in peer-to-peer reinforcement of the desired behaviours for change!

- A frequent problem in many organisations is the disconnect between what people/management say and either what they do, or how they reinforce behaviours. The Champions network is in the best position to 'police the disconnects': i.e. to spot when people are being rewarded for A, while we are expecting them to do B.

(2) STRUCTURES

- You want to keep it as informal as possible. Initially, there will be a core set of 'rules of the game' which you will ask them to evaluate and propose to modify if needed!

- They will communicate with each other as much as they want and need to. OK, depending on the size of your organisation you may want to introduce some 'boundaries' but do not try to restrict their movement.

- Support this communication by facilitating the use of blogs, wikis or a protected space on your intranet. 'Protect' is the word. Resist calls for a democratic, open-to-all space where the entire organisation has access to their discussions.

- Promote un-structured ways for the Change Champions to work alongside more structured ones. Let them call some meetings. However, the power of the informal flow for discussions and sharing of ideas or progress must be respected. Remember, you want your Champions to work in a very, very, very long coffee break mode!

- They will have to work 'alongside management'. They are not 'substituting' the formal leadership but they are acting in parallel. This is an important item that will require a lot of care and clarification from both the formal 'management plumbing system' and the Champions themselves as a group and as individuals.

- The mandate for their role comes directly from you, the top leader, or from the top leadership team. It does not come from their immediate supervisor at divisional or section level.

- Their own managers are there to support them in their cross-territorial networking. The Champions group is an internal coalition, not a parallel management structure.

- Management should not abdicate their responsibilities as drivers, communicators and supporters of the change, but their support for the Champions is non-negotiable.

- There may be an expected discomfort and ambiguity problem! On many dark days, tiring days, bad days or even simple days... there may be an apparent conflict between 'formal management' and the internal coalition of champion-activists. Welcome it! Here is your chance to teach 'ambiguity management'!

(3) CHALLENGES

Let them figure things out! Don't pre-empt them! My own very short list is as follows:

- The above ambiguity: this is a role with 'core ideas' and 'aims', lots of support but not much structure. Working alongside a structured management system may not always be straightforward.

- Their own peer-to-peer interaction: many people may ask themselves why these people are doing this. They will find themselves in the spotlight of the peer network. This may not bother some of the Champions, but it may make others uncomfortable.

- All this is coming on top of everything else! They will have to carry on with their normal day jobs. Depending on the size of your organisation, the size of the Champions network and the type of job that they are doing, it may be prudent to establish some 'allowances', such as allocating half a day a week or something similar. Beware of getting this down into a formal structure, or else it will be converted into 'a second job'.

(4) HOW ARE YOU GOING TO SUPPORT THEM AND WHAT SHOULD THEY GAIN?

- Let the group know that there will be periodical meetings to update each other, and that they can come to you (or a designated team/consulting support) at any time.

- Make/protect time for the group to be able to express their feelings: you'll find a mixture of people who are very proud of what they are doing, honoured to be asked, enthusiastic, but also scared…

- This is a great opportunity for them to learn a bit more about management of change in real life, about tolerating ambiguity and about influence.

- They have a unique opportunity to experience and learn from real life networking. They should use this opportunity as part of their own professional and personal development, and you should be willing to discuss this with them at any time.

In my experience, many Change Champions end up in some position of promotion or job change after a period of hands-on 'activism'. This is good news and not so good news.

It is logical that after the extra visibility - and in particular if the implementation of some changes can be tracked to their intervention - that Champions are seen as 'successful' employees, and as such become candidates for promotion, for example. Not a bad deal for a Champion!

The structured part of the organisation as I have described before has a notorious ability to absorb or eat any 'good idea' or 'things that work'. Successful Champions may be seen as potential good managers, for example, as people who should be rewarded (which usually means promoted!). That may be good for some Champions, but not for all! But you'll have to pay the price of losing part of their hidden/invisible networking. The challenge for you as leader, however, is simple: find new ones!

>> SMART MOBS INSIDE: LEADERSHIP DISTRIBUTED

This internal group of Champions represents a true engine for organisational change. As such, the Change Champions are one of your most precious assets. Armed with their commitment and some sort of access to shared communication technology, they are on their way to creating change big time. Effectively, they will create a form of distributed leadership: that is, leadership that is not top-down or even bottom-up. As in the macro-social smart mobs, there is no central command and control for this group. The real-time communication, the sharing of stories, plus the adjustments that the group can make when they formally meet from time to time, de facto serves as a vehicle for a decentralised form of leadership that is self-reinforcing and socially-reinforced (look what we are doing here, what are you doing there?)

Incidentally, distributed leadership (and distributed intelligence) is at the core of many macro-social networks, including terrorist organisations! This comparison is something that you are going to hit! It is almost inevitable! You'll have to deal with it!

>> DEVIANTS

The following is a true story. A few years ago, community workers for the Save the Children organisation - an internationally recognised non-governmental organisation

(NGO) - made a clever observation. Working with communities where malnutrition in children was the norm, they discovered that a small group of very poor families were able to nourish their children against all expectations. All families shared the same resources and the same socio-economic status. Their limitations were the same. The community workers were fascinated by the apparent anomaly of that very small group that made them more resistant to famine.

What did these mothers do differently? They found out that in every case of successful anomaly, the mother of the child would go out to the paddy fields and collect tiny shrimps and crabs the size of one joint of one finger and add these to the child's diet, along with the greens from sweet potato tops. Although readily available and free for the taking, the conventional wisdom held these foods to be inappropriate, or even dangerous, for young children.

Along with the addition of the shrimps/crabs and greens, there were certain other positive deviant practices, such as the frequency of feeding and the quality of care for the child. It was apparent that the use of these foods and practices constituted enough of a difference to produce a well-nourished child.

The above account from the field practitioners is just one from a wealth of similar observations made in those kinds of mainly NGO programmes. They all fall into the same category of 'positive deviance'. Although the term has its roots in sociology and social psychology, it's the NGO community that has spread the concept around the world. Today, there are hundreds of communities and third world initiatives using positive deviance, many of them focussing on the big problem of children's malnutrition, others on prevention of HIV, family planning, prevention of human trafficking, etc.

The commonality of this approach in all these projects is always the same and can be described as follows: (1) most of the solutions are found within the community or the group already; (2) focus on finding out what 'the successful deviants' do that make them succeed and (3) transfer that knowledge to others. A standard methodology based upon these simple principles has been used by many in these now diverse projects.

'Deviance' and its opposite 'conformity' are terms used in social psychology to define levels of adjustment, adaptation or response to norms, whether in a community, a group or a particular environment. The word 'positive' associated with 'deviance' brings up some apparent contradictions. How can deviance be positive in the context of norms, following rules or playing by the book? The findings of the Save the Children people suggest that, in any case, ignoring these deviances is foolish.

I believe that the scope for the application of this concept to management - and in particular to management of change – is enormous. Our organisations are usually designed to follow rules and norms, with plenty of processes and systems that one has to adhere to. After all, these processes and systems ensure consistency of quality and homogeneity in the way of doing things. They are there for a reason. They have been proven effective in reaching some goals, achieving particular outcomes or providing management with some sort of control.

Conventional wisdom says that you would not run a company without rules, processes, systems and people sticking to them. Although this is obviously something that breeds success in many places, the reality is that in any organisation you will find people who do not follow the rules or the internal conventions. Some of these deviants may succeed, others may fail. Some of them may be difficult to manage; others may just be a bit of a pain.

Management attention is on the ones who follow, on the normative side of the organisation, on the creation of an even more robust system with processes that can be followed by anybody and that can be repeated again and again. Indeed, we have a term in English to call people who do not conform fully or come up with unexpected different ways of doing things. It's one of these prostitutions of the English language that we have accepted. We call them 'creative'. So when we say that Paul and Mary are good team players and are very committed, we usually mean they conform to the norm. When we say that Peter is 'somewhat creative', we sometimes do not mean creative, but non-conformist, surprising, often cutting corners and eventually getting away with murder. I am, of course, exaggerating here by using caricature as a way of proving my point.

>> BENCHMARKING DEVIANCE

What do we benchmark? We benchmark good practices, achievements, cost-effective processes and efficient ways of getting from A to B. We rarely, if ever, benchmark anomalies, deviations or non-conformity. We benchmark the perfection of current reality to make it far-better, but more-of-the-same. We discard deviations from the norm and we have labels for them: defects, difficult people, anomalies, lack of quality, unconformity, non-compliance, etc.

Yes, of course, organisations need quality systems, rules of management, processes and procedures to follow, etc. In some cases (such as pharmaceutical companies), regulators will provide an entire framework. Any deviance from this framework is punishable. It would be foolish to run a manufacturing department with no quality handbook or a regulatory division that doesn't pay attention to the regulatory requirements.

But the language of conformity, compliance, standard processes and systems, etc. is pervasive. It has the ability to create two things: a sometimes false sense of homogeneity and control, which is by default associated with good management practice, and blindness and rejection of anything else that doesn't conform or fit in.

> We should pay more attention to the deviants, the ones who have created success where others in similar circumstances have failed; the ones who didn't quite follow the rules but perhaps cut across bureaucracy and made

it; the ones who are 'different', but who are still achieving or are even achieving more. What do they have that's special? Can we learn from them? Can we transfer that learning?

I know that this may create loads of antibodies in conventional management but I suggest that positive deviance benchmarking - if we can call it like that - has enormous potential implications for learning. Any change management programme that does not integrate the ability to study internal positive deviances, and deviant people, would miss great power.

>> REVERSE-ENGINEERING OF POSITIVE DEVIANCE

In some cases, the ingredients for change may not only already be inside the organisation, but they may already have been 'experimented' with by those who - whether frustrated with the system or not - have tried different ways to solve problems, improve productivity, create innovation or speed up product development. And they may have been doing this not by complying with norms but by bypassing them. If this is true, you can't afford to fire these people because they don't comply. You should give them the job of showing you, as leader, what can be changed by not complying!

In summary, reverse-engineering of deviance allows you the following:

- To find people who have experimented with potential changes by bypassing norms that may represent sources of blocking precisely the kind of changes that you would like to see.

- Potentially, incorporate some of these people into the pool of Change Champions
- Learn about how internal networks of influence have played a role in the spread of the 'achievements' of those deviants.
- Understand how 'they got away with murder', because that will tell you a lot about reward, recognition and reinforcement systems within your organisation

My rule of thumb is that the more rules and regulations, the greater the opportunity for positive deviance. Here is my spectrum. On one end, in a theoretical organisational world with no rules, there is no deviance or deviant people because there are no clear norms. On the other end, a super-structured, highly normative environment ruled by rules and heavily mapped with processes and systems, is fertile ground for deviance which is easily highlighted in such an environment. The more rules there are, the greater the opportunity to break them.

Far from ignoring, dismissing, let alone punishing the rule-breakers, we should observe them with the same detached diligence with which the Save the Children volunteers looked at the few surprisingly well-nourished Vietnamese children. Maybe there is something there that holds the clue for innovation, for moving forward fast, or for simply being more effective.

>> SCEPTICS (AND 'FULLY ON BOARD PEOPLE'): SUSPEND JUDGEMENT

There is a third group of corporate citizens in this plot: the sceptics. Some of them may merit being called professionally sceptical, or chronically sceptical, or terminally sceptical. And many of them are simply a pain! They may have great social power, which can either be of positive or negative influence. On the negative side, they are often the ones who seed defeatism ('not in a million years will we change, it will never happen in this culture').

However, if you can get a notorious sceptic on board, you will have gained precious territory. In my consulting experience, when introducing VIRAL CHANGE™ in organisations, some sceptics - or at least some people perceived like that - become converted very fast once they see the commitment of others. This is especially true when some of them are invited to be part of the Change Champions network! Which is something to seriously consider!

My advice to clients is 'suspend judgement'. Some of your sceptics may become ambassadors for the change. And if this is the case, the advantages are enormous. However, you should be aware that it's also possible that some of those 'taken-for-granted' people, the 'always-fully-on-board' people, may not like it at all. And they could skilfully torpedo the change!

>> VIRAL LEADERSHIP: BEYOND COMMUNICATION

One of the big temptations in a diluted version of VIRAL CHANGE™ is to stop at the communication end of the process and simply use the Champions as information traffic wardens. This would be far from viral and would create something not even close to change. The viral leadership process (see the graph on the Viral Leadership cycle on page 300) follows a mixture of recurrent 'advocacy' and 'activism' mechanisms. It starts with the Champion-activist articulating the changes and the rationale behind them. Remember previous comments about language in chapter 6! Once this rationale has been expressed and communicated, the focus must be on the translation into behaviours and on the discussion and/or planning of how these can be reinforced. So far this is great advocacy work where many people would feel comfortable to stop. However, the real viral engine has only been just warmed up. At this point, the game starts with the Champion-activist getting engaged with other people and beginning some modelling:

- I am going to do X, what are you going to do?
- I am going to do X, will you join me?
- I am going to do X, if you do Y, can we meet again in two weeks time and see how far we got?

Now, this is activism and no longer just advocacy. The cycle re-starts when the person now engaged is able to act as a Champion himself. The ultimate goal of the Champion-activist is to pass the baton, not just to endorse the changes and communicate them to others.

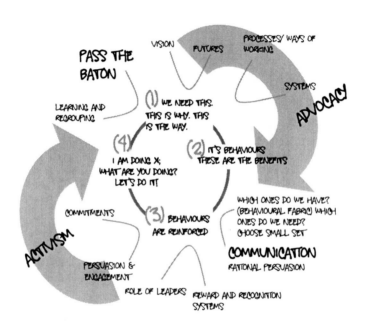

THE VIRAL LEADERSHIP CONVERSATION CYCLE:

Communication and mapping of actions tend to dominate the 'advocacy' part of the cycle. Activism goes beyond this to create engagement with other people and to ensure the baton gets passed. Many so-called change management programmes are heavy on communication ('advocacy') but weak on change of own behaviours and other people's behaviours ('activism')

ACTIVISTS, DEVIANTS AND SCEPTICS 10

1   CONSIDER CREATING AN INTERNAL GROUP
    OF ACTIVISTS OR CHANGE CHAMPIONS.

2   EXPLORE WAYS TO FIND THEM AND
    CONSIDER THE POSSIBILITY THAT YOU OR
    YOUR MANAGEMENT COULD IDENTIFY
    THEM EASILY!

3   CHAMPIONS NEED TO 'UNDERSTAND' AND
    MASTER THE RIGHT LANGUAGE FOR THE
    CHANGES.

4   CHAMPIONS NEED TO EMBRACE 'NEW
    BEHAVIOURS', ENDORSE THEM AND
    FACILITATE THE SPREAD THROUGH THEIR
    CONTACTS IN THEIR SMALL WORLDS.

5   MAKE SURE THAT THEY LIAISE, CONNECT
    AND WORK IN A SEMI-INFORMAL WAY.
    TOO MUCH OF A STRUCTURE WILL MAKE
    THEM INTO SOMETHING CLOSE TO 'A
    PROPER TEAM', WHICH WILL DEFEAT THE
    PURPOSE OF THEIR VERY NATURE AS A
    LOOSE NETWORK.

6   ACTIVISTS' REACTIONS ARE IMPORTANT:
      SENSE OF WORTH, COPING WITH
      DIFFICULTIES, SOME DEGREE OF
      AMBIGUITY WITH THEIR MANAGERS, ETC.
      DON'T SWEEP THEM UNDER THE CARPET.

7   CHAMPIONS SHOULD USE TECHNOLOGY TO
      COMMUNICATE AND SHARE IN REAL TIME
      IF POSSIBLE.

8   THE CHAMPIONS GROUP MAY CONTAIN
      SCEPTICS AND 'DEVIANTS' AS WELL.

9   LEARN FROM THE DEVIANTS. FIND THOSE
      WHO DO THINGS DIFFERENTLY AND BY-
      PASS RULES. THINK TWICE BEFORE
      DISMISSING THEM.

10   SUSPEND JUDGEMENT ABOUT PEOPLE
      WHO WILL NEVER CHANGE OR WHO WILL
      ALWAYS BE ON BOARD. SCEPTICAL PEOPLE
      MAY BECOME YOUR BEST AMBASSADORS
      AND THE ETERNALLY LOYAL MAY SWAP
      SIDES.

(12)

THE PLUMBERS (MANAGEMENT)

What's the role of the formal management structures in the creation and maintenance of VIRAL CHANGE™? It is, of course, crucial, but in socio-behavioural terms it contains some different angles when compared to the traditional view of change.

Let's summarise things that we have articulated in previous chapters. We need to recap them now to address the role of management. The traditional assumptions tell us that:

- Change must come from the top.
- Only if it happens at the top, it will happen elsewhere.
- The top creates a vision, strategies and objectives for the change.

- These will be cascaded down. Management layers below the top adopt and percolate them down the pipes of the organisation chart.
- All this will be done with heavy use of communication tools including activities such as workshops, etc. as a way to receive the information, interpret it, absorb it and integrate it into the day-to-day life of teams and divisions.
- Consistency is paramount so that at each step every component becomes a true representation of the well-defined strategy for change.

These assumptions have that distinctive mechano-hydraulic flavour of the push-from-the-top-down-the-pipes-change that produces outputs at the other end. This 'logical' approach is, however, responsible for the majority of fiascos seen in daily organisational life. The initial push usually produces some results. Yes, something comes out at the bottom of the pipes but, as in any plumbing system, as soon as the input stops, the output stops as well!

>> BLUEPRINT FOR THE PLUMBERS: THE FORMAL MANAGEMENT STRUCTURES

In VIRAL CHANGE™ terms, the role of management structures contains some elements of the above, but with different directions (see graph p. 306). It emphasises the launching of vision and objectives for the changes rather than the total command and control the process, or even a 'perfect interpretation' of those visions and objectives across the organisation. In fact, it acknowledges that a fair amount of re-interpretation (a) is going to happen and (b) is to be welcomed. In VIRAL CHANGE™ terms, a 'perfect outcome' for the change is not the deployment down the line of characters, plots and social routines in pristine consistency with what had been imagined at the top, but an enhanced version of the vision. Unpredictability is welcome at the table because it may bring extra added value! Please feel free to declare how much of it you are willing to take!

> Management structures facilitate the spread of change, mainly by obsessively supporting the *diffusion*, *infection* and *tipping points* created by the network of people linked by strong and 'weak ties'.

If a 'Change Champions' group is created - which is crucial in any medium or large-sized organisation - more time is spent supporting them than is spent on hierarchical meetings and workshops 'about the change' with the plumbing system characters. Example: let the Champions organise and run 'those workshops' as opposed to management. 'Let' meaning: suggest, foster, facilitate, visibly reinforce, devolve authority, 'let them loose'…

(1) LAUNCHING THE VISION

Management is responsible for the launch of the vision for change and is also ultimately accountable. The leadership is doing all this via the language and framing, visioning and feed-forward as described previously. Accountability is what leadership is paid for, so it sounds reasonable to assume that 'the buck will stop there'. Please note that it is also reasonable to expect this kind of push back: "*Total accountability requires total control, and we don't*

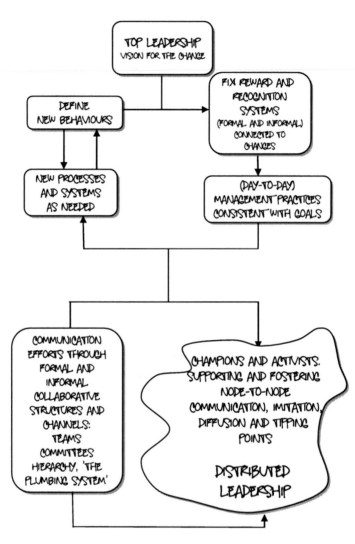

THE ROLE OF 'FORMAL MANAGEMENT' IN THE MANAGEMENT OF
VIRAL CHANGE™

have that if we have 'that bunch of people in the network'". In other words, if leadership is distributed through the Champions' network, how can the top leadership be totally accountable? Answer: because that's what they are paid for.

People are inevitably accountable for things, even if they don't have total control over them. But this connection between 'accountability' and 'total control' is somehow embedded in our management thinking. It is normal to seek control, to seek certainty, and we do that unconsciously. If I am going to be accountable, well, I'll tell you what to do. But, if we have acknowledged that VIRAL CHANGE™ creates a fair amount of re-interpretation during the infection process, and that there is some degree of unpredictability with continuous adjustments, management needs to figure out what 'accountability' in this different regime may mean.

> If it is more about supporting, resourcing and facilitating than about dictating, then accountability may mean ultimate responsibility for the protection of the network. That is, making sure that the Champions have the degree of freedom necessary to operate, group, re-group, spread the infection, produce imitations, create tipping points, detect fault lines, re-group again and re-infect.

Only deviations from the vision should make management shout 'time-out'. Otherwise, leadership of VIRAL CHANGE™ - including cultural change - is protection of fellow-travel-ship and a credit card for the Champions.

Frequently, my clients ask: "*How can we make sure that the infection is going in the right direction?*" Usually, this question comes after people have realised the great power of the infection! It is only natural to fear that they may lose control. But 'control' may mean different things to different people. The kind of management that needs to literally control everything and that has to do so via a strict process of objective setting, reviews and great formality of the 'performance management' is going to feel uncomfortable about VIRAL CHANGE™ and the ability (and power) of a small number of people to lead change across the organisation. In VIRAL CHANGE™, management does not relinquish its responsibilities. However, management acknowledges that the way change should happen (via network infection) requires a different attitude.

(2) PRACTICING ITS BEHAVIOURS

Management is responsible for the identification of the new behaviours needed to sustain the implementation of whatever new processes and systems may be needed. As we saw, a small set of these new behaviours may/will reach the category of 'non-negotiable behaviours'. As described before, some 'seeding' may be necessary if the behaviours needed are not part of your current behavioural fabric. Here, management has a social-engineering role, devising, if needed, initiatives (practices) that allow 'a new behaviour' simply to exist and to be visible.

You may remember the example of the un-collaborative sales force. We needed to start in a very un-sexy fashion by asking people to send an email to others with a piece of competitor and market intelligence, to be able to:

- create the behaviour of collaborating which didn't exist,
- make it visible to all,
- positively reinforce any single, 'small' piece of collaboration
- wait for some imitation,
- have enough people doing it and generating enough good stories
- create a tipping point.

At that point, collaboration would suddenly become de facto a widespread behaviour, triggering, amongst other things, a positive social reinforcement on a greater scale: we've done it! It's possible! We are collaborative people!

This was unashamedly engineered, de facto by-passing months of possible rational appeals for collaboration as 'a good thing needed' and a lot of praying for it to happen.

(3) REWARD AND RECOGNITION PRACTICES

Management is responsible for the design or modification of the 'reward and recognition system' so that it is directly connected with the change management process, perhaps leading to the desired 'new culture'. I am using 'reward and recognition system' in a broad sense, including:

- Formal processes such as annual or periodical performance appraisals
- Other formal or semi-formal management practices and processes such as coaching
- Informal 'management conversations'

As we saw previously, there must be a connection between the desired behaviours and their reinforcements. What you get is what you reinforce. To put it simply, if you are dealing with a cultural change process that requires new behaviours A, B, and C, and there is nothing in your performance management system that refers to or includes A, B and C, you'll fail.

Let me review again and expand on the example that we see very frequently in 'sales management' and that was pre-viewed in chapter 9, where we were talking about non-negotiable behaviours. Let me insist on the same scenario and repeat many things because it is very illustrative of the issue.

The ultimate goal of the sales process is to sell! To be frank, it includes other outputs such as continuous learning about the customer or gaining competitor information. But you could say that these things are also 'done' in order to sell.

Sales management also includes the use of tools and processes such as perhaps a CRM (customer relationship management) system or the use of market segmentation data. These are inputs. Your reps also spend a particular amount of time in the field and they have a particular customer visit frequency. These are inputs as well. The traditional management view 'logically' establishes a connection between inputs and outputs! Of course you need the outputs, people in that thinking mode would say. In order to get the outputs, the argument would go, we need sales people to comply with specific (input) requirements, such as number of hours in the field or the daily inputting of data into the CRM system. Consistent with the thinking model behind all this, traditional management will spend a considerable amount of time and attention (reward, reinforcement) on the input side, the 'power drill' side as we said before.

The mechano-hydraulic model of our 'engineer inside' tells us that by pushing input we'll get output. In this model, people will spend an ever increasing number of hours of management conversation and air time discussing the input: how many hours in the field, how much training, how many customers per week, etc. And this is what will be reinforced.

But the linkage input-output is more theoretical than you may think. Any good sales manager will tell you that there is a widespread difference between sales people, and that many successful reps achieve their targets with apparent independence from the 'average amount of effort'. In fact the picture looks more like Pareto's principle of 80/20: 80% of sales achieved by 20% of the people. Or, here we go again, the famous 'power law' that we saw in previous chapters!

We saw before that, in behavioural terms, if you reward input, you don't get output: you get more input. If you want output, this is what should be directly reinforced, regardless of the input that (you think) will get you there. But there may be good reasons why management may want to reinforce/reward input as well: set an example, homogenise practices, etc. But management should be extremely aware of:

1) what should come first
2) where the management efforts (air time, gratification, reward…) should be
3) what the risks are of rewarding something in the hope of getting something different.

In my experience, the reasons why sales management spends a ridiculous amount of time rewarding inputs are:

a) The above-mentioned mechano-hydraulic assumption that if they push inputs they'll get outputs. This is reinforced by two facts:
   - Our own traditional thinking
   - The pressure from vendors of input-tools. These days you can get very sophisticated market segmentation, market indicators, benchmarking data and so on. The assumption is that if you have ever increasing, sophisticated (and logarithmically more expensive) input data, output will happen.

b) Lack of trust in their own people: "*If we let everybody do whatever they feel like, people won't make the necessary efforts.*"

(4) NEW PROCESSES Management is responsible for the establishment of new processes *to be sustained by* these new behaviours, not the other way around, as previously explained. In this implementation, the issue of 'skills' or 'capability' usually comes up. You would be right in saying that so far we have mentioned very little about these 'skills' or 'abilities of people'. We have been emphasising 'behaviours' all the time and perhaps you would say we have simplified by tacitly assuming that the skill-thing is a level playing field. In other words, you may say or think that in any process of change - and leaving aside the issue of whether or not people are more or less resistant (we have dealt with this before) - some people may simply not be 'up to the job'.

You are probably right, particularly in the extreme cases. If your new processes require that the work done so far by Peter as a laboratory technician should now be done by a PhD in Chemistry, and if Peter does not have a PhD, then Peter is in trouble. Yes, in that case, you are right that you need to drastically re-skill your workforce! But a great deal of the change management and cultural change programmes that you have around may not entail such scenarios. In other words, I am not trying to dismiss 'the skill thing', but in many cases, we are not talking about that. It is the 'new-ways-of-doing-things' (the cultural change that you require, the famous 'change of mindset' and change of 'attitude'), not sending people back to University.

(5) COMMUNICATION DOWN THE PIPES

Management is responsible for the communication mechanisms 'down the pipes'. As we have discussed several times, the question is whether the plumbing system should take over as conduit for change; or in other words, is it better than the network? And the answer is: it's not.

For those of you with some mathematical background, think of the plumbing system (described by the organisation chart) as the *algorithm* pathways (or highways!). New ideas travelling down those pipes will go down established pathways and will have to use all the pathways in some sort of coordinated way.

Think of the network-based-spread-of-infection as a *heuristic* system where ideas bypass some pathways to go through channels that have a better probability for the successful travel (nodes with high level of connections). This is as simplistic as my own non-mathematical background can explain.

Interestingly, our brain is heuristic. Confronted with a 'decision', we do not explore all possible avenues and travel all possible algorithmic pathways as (our traditional view of) a computer would do. We jump straight into some ways or pathways and come to some conclusions (we jump between memory and learning nodes, we could say). We gain speed, we lose certainty. VIRAL CHANGE™ has that distinctive heuristic flavour!

(6) BACKSTAGE, SUPPORT AND UN-MANAGE CHANGE CHAMPIONS

Remain backstage and support the Change Champions. This is the crucial role of management in VIRAL CHANGE™ and one that very often triggers some conflict. The 10 commandments read as follows:

❶ Find the activists! Share your vision ask them for help.
❷ Create a common sense of purpose with them, give them a mandate and your confidence.
❸ Take them through the principles of VIRAL CHANGE™, one way or another. This is important because of the differences with standard processes. You should:
  • tell them about their role.
  • tell them about the role of management.
  • make sure that they don't see themselves as mere information traffic wardens or manipulated and passive actors.
❹ Launch the 'new behaviours' and your ideas on reinforcing them, plus what the organisation needs to achieve. Then work with them on the 'how' but don't impose a particular process.

❺ Let them loose and, backstage, you:
- protect their space and time.
- give them resources if needed (or rights to use them).
- endorse their work personally and in public.
- reward them.
- listen to their feedback and work with them again on any adjustments.

❻ Make sure that your own (management) behaviours are consistent with the desired changes: from the philosophy behind them to the day-to-day visible actions.

❼ Accept the inevitable degree of ambiguity that VIRAL CHANGE™ may bring when compared to the traditional change management process.

❽ Un-manage the Change Champions network but manage the assets that are being generated: the new ideas established, the new changes appearing through tipping points, the new routines being established...

❾ Do lots, talk less. One minute spent supporting a Change Champion -, who will induce the diffusion of the new behaviours and their infection - is worth one hour meeting with 'the teams' going over the 10 characteristics of the successful change and the 20 objectives we need to have in place.

❿ Celebrate, calibrate, celebrate.

>> MEASURING

We can't finish a chapter on management without referring to measurement! The first thing we have been taught, formally or informally, is that 'what we can't measure, we can't manage'. For many years, I have been in a minority challenging the solidity of this assumption. Then, at some point, I realised that the keyword that messed up everything was 'measure'. Our numbers-driven business world is often not happy unless we have lists of numbers in a spreadsheet. The scorecard movement has only partially softened this stance.

The reality is that we are still monitored and observed by the ROI Police and that many people in managerial positions refrain themselves from putting forward ideas or plans if they can not safely come up with the magic of an ROI worth the label. There is an old saying 'lies, damned lies, and statistics' that could easily be converted into 'lies, damned lies and ROIs'. But this is a conversation for another time. The reality is that many people use incredibly stupid reductionisms, such as measurement = ROI. Many of those want to look managerially correct. Many of them are precisely the 'how-are-we-going-to-measure-it?' ones, who will invariably ask the question no matter what the topic or situation.

People sometimes need to be reminded that there are… just a few things in the world that we can manage without asking ourselves what the ROI is. To name a few, I haven't met anybody who calculates the ROI when deciding to send their kids to school. And I am not trying to be funny. The same applies to calculating the ROI for repairing the photocopy machines in the office or even hiring a new director of Sales. The three things above have one thing in common: we make a judgement and then do it because we believe in it (educating the kids), we need to fix it (photocopiers) or we need somebody to lead a department (director of sales).

Measurement doesn't equal numbers and numbers don't equal ROI. In VIRAL CHANGE™, management needs to decide what they need to 'see', 'hear', 'feel', 'smell' and also 'count'. And there are hundreds of ways of doing so. Stories are a good vehicle. You can count them as well (!) if you are the kind of person that suffers from numbers-deprivation-syndrome.

Depending on the change aims, the leadership of the organisation will have a good idea of what to look for. The Change Champions are also a natural vehicle to help construct some 'metrics'. Measurement is not a problem in VIRAL CHANGE™. Numbers, for the sake of them, are useless without a judgement. VIRAL CHANGE™ counts on ongoing efforts to use judgement to re-shape the organisation with the help of some pre-agreed 'metrics'. I always remind people of the absurdity of some 'statistics-at-any-cost', by providing them with the statistic that 'the average human has one testicle and one breast'.

MANAGEMENT 10

1   LEADERSHIP TAKES CARE OF DIRECTIONS.

2   LEADERSHIP DEFINES THE NON-
     NEGOTIABLE BEHAVIOURS...

3   LOOK CAREFULLY AT THE REWARD AND
     RECOGNITION SYSTEMS: IF YOU REWARD
     A (CONSISTENT WITH THE CHANGES),
     SHOULD YOU STOP REWARDING B?

4   ALIGN 'THE PLUMBING SYSTEM': ANY
     MANAGER NEEDS TO KNOW ABOUT THE
     CHANGE CHAMPIONS. FOR EXAMPLE,
     THEY NEED TO UNDERSTAND THAT THEY
     DON'T MANAGE THAT NETWORK, BUT
     THAT THEY NEED TO BE FULLY ON
     BOARD WITH VIRAL CHANGE™.

5   DEVELOP PROCESSES AND SYSTEMS
     THAT ARE CONSISTENT WITH THE
     CHANGE SUPPORTING IT.

6 SUPPORT OF THE CHAMPIONS NETWORK
IS DONE BACKSTAGE, PROTECTING THEIR
SPACE AND TIME, FACILITATING AND
ENABLING THEIR POSSIBILITIES FOR
INFECTION.

7 CREATE METRICS (INVOLVE CHAMPIONS)
THAT ARE ABLE TO CAPTURE PROGRESS
WITHOUT BEING OBSESSED WITH A
NUMERICAL FORMULA. YOU MAY OR MAY
NOT BE ABLE TO CREATE ONE OF
THESE, BUT YOU NEED TO DISCOVER
WAYS IN WHICH YOU CAN 'SEE' PEOPLE
MOVING IN CERTAIN DIRECTIONS.

8 MANAGE THE AMBIGUITY, DISCOMFORT
AND POSSIBLE CONFLICT ARISING FROM
A DISTRIBUTED LEADERSHIP MODEL. THE
ROLE OF MANAGEMENT IN VIRAL
CHANGE™ IS DIFFERENT FROM THE ONE
IN TSUNAMI CHANGE.

9 BE EXQUISITE AT PRACTICING THE
DESIRED BEHAVIOURS THAT ARE AT THE
CORE OF THE CHANGES.

10   LOOK FOR DISCONNECTS AND ACT ON THEM. FOR EXAMPLE, WHEN YOU'RE DECLARING GOING IN DIRECTION A, BUT REWARDING GOING IN DIRECTION B.

LANGUAGE

NEW BEHAVIOURS

TIPPING POINTS

'CULTURES'

(13)

NEW CULTURES: IF NOT NOW, WHEN?

So new behaviours have now been established, new 'ways of doing' are present. You've seen the tipping points. You can see that transformation is in the air. You have some metrics. Or lots of stories. And now you are told (by your people, by your teams, by your consultants) that you need 'a period of stability'. This is a very sensible request. Unfortunately, it is your 'engineer within' talking. The one who thinks that all the pushing-down (or pushing-west, or pushing-east) has now produced its fruits, so we can rest.

Stability is the last thing you want. I know, people think that the opposite is simply chaos. This is not the case. You want some healthy instability or you might go back to a state of no change. The biological equivalent of that is called death.

I have shared with you how new cultures can be created 'now'. It is a question of weeks, not months, before you can start to see the first tipping points in the organisation. Those tipping points link with each other very quickly as well. There is no magic cut-off when your metrics suddenly say, "*We have a new culture.*" You'll see it. Your people will see it. Your Champions will tell you. Your stories will be abundant. If you created some form of metrics system, the indicators will start to show.

If anybody tells you that establishing sustainable changes in routines, 'new cultures', requires a long period of assessment followed by a long period of implementation, and that this business of 'culture change' is something to start 'seeing' in, say two, three years from now, he or she is one of the following:

- An internal or external ambassador of traditional, tsunami approach change.
- A genuine person using old mental models and repeating what he has been taught.
- A consultant (chances are, one with a big consulting group) ready for the tsunami, with an agenda for a very, very, very expensive exercise.

Or combinations of these 3! My rule of thumb is that initial tipping points can be seen in three months or less and that new cultures can be seen in six months. From that arbitrary, but relatively consistent, cut-off point of six months, further stability depends exclusively on the ability of the organisation to continue reinforcing desirable behaviours and to stop reinforcing incompatible non-negotiable behaviours. If it takes any longer than this, I must assume that we are doing something wrong.

>> YOU'VE GOT NEW ESTABLISHED BEHAVIOURS: YOU'VE GOT A CULTURE.

I'd like to refer again to the very original premise at the beginning of this book. Behaviours shape culture, not the other way around, as expressed in graph on page 314. OK, you are going to ask me to accept that you know 'a particular culture' that generates 'particular behaviours'. And my challenge to you would be to ask you why you say that. Let me tell you. Perhaps you say this, very rightly, because you see those behaviours on the ground. But there is no entity called culture, as we said at the beginning of the book. What you have is ways of doing, people referring to values and beliefs that inform those ways of doing (but still, you only have ways of doing), norms (that is, rules on which behaviours are and aren't acceptable), and also a set of attitudes and a collective mindset. And this mindset can only be articulated in terms of behaviours in a meaningful and unequivocal way. So, sorry, you don't have a culture, you have behaviours. That's why you only see behaviours.

And you may be very proud of them. But if you prefer to speak the language of attitudes, mindset, values and beliefs, that's fine with me! Because we can still have meaningful conversations as long as we agree on what we mean.

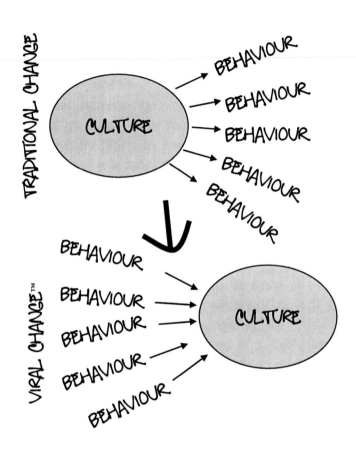

Example:
Traditional management of change: A culture of accountability produces behaviours that can be called 'accountable'

VIRAL CHANGE™: people - behaving in a manner that can be called accountable - create a culture of 'accountability'

>> FIVE EXAMPLES OF 'CULTURES' YOU MAY WANT...

We have treated culture here as a point of destination. After all, we have followed a process that looks like this:

ARTICULATION OF DESIRED CHANGE → LANGUAGE → NEW
BEHAVIOURS → DIFFUSION → TIPPING POINTS → CULTURE

But as the graph on page 328 illustrates, the conversation could easily have started with the description of a culture that you want to reach, a description which has 'informed' language, and followed by new behaviours, diffusion, and tipping points... The following is a very schematic and high level view of how to address the development of particular cultures, focusing on a small set of behaviours that can be spread via VIRAL CHANGE™. It is intended to provoke your own reflection, not to synthesise to the point of trivialising. But if you have followed me so far in this book, you'll understand what I mean.

The descriptions below are deliberately simplistic, just a caricature to stress that 'a culture of X' is created via installing behaviours A, B, C, reinforcing them, perhaps spreading them via an internal Champions network and provoking tipping points in which new routines appear and become established. These are real life cases of VIRAL CHANGE™ that I have lead. They do not correspond to a single client situation. The real cases have a mixture of all of them in different doses. Also, in all of them, new routines and 'cultures' appeared rather widespread between month 3 and month 5. In all of them, changes persisted beyond 12 months with different degrees of formal interventions.

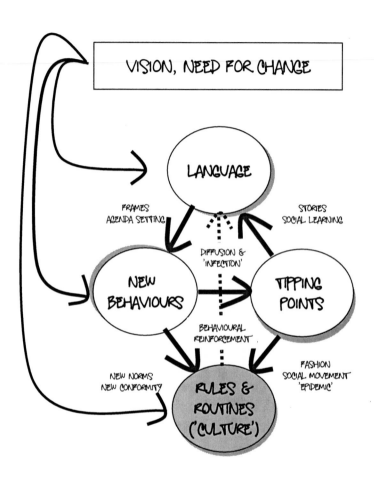

VISION, NEED FOR CHANGE

LANGUAGE

FRAMES
AGENDA SETTING

STORIES
SOCIAL LEARNING

DIFFUSION &
'INFECTION'

NEW
BEHAVIOURS

TIPPING
POINTS

BEHAVIOURAL
REINFORCEMENT

NEW NORMS
NEW CONFORMITY

RULES &
ROUTINES
('CULTURE')

FASHION
SOCIAL MOVEMENT
'EPIDEMIC'

EXAMPLE 1:

CURRENT CULTURE

Culture of complaints and problems. These are well-established themes of conversations and practices that are taking over organisational life

DESIRED CHANGE

To a 'culture of solutions', where problems are identified, but solutions (or articulations of efforts on the path to finding solutions) are 'attached'

WRONG PATHWAYS

Explain to people how negative and damaging this is and make sure everybody has been told that we need to change our mindset to a 'solution attitude'

VIRAL CHANGE™

Communications that highlight problems without a 'solution attachment' are ignored. That includes not replying to emails of that type. Install 'solution behaviours' by devising an (artificial) system where everybody brings up a (small) solution a month, no matter how small. At some point, the organisation will have enough solution language and solution-action to create tipping points. The shift will occur more or less suddenly and then needs to be capitalised on by reinforcing the new behaviours every time they are visible.

EXAMPLE 2

CURRENT CULTURE

'Broken windows' culture. Progressive but subtle decline. Unfinished business (mainly decisions) becomes the norm. The virus has spread by imitation and diffusion, in this case with negative consequences (see vignette 2 on page 332)

DESIRED CHANGE

To a culture of 'closure' where norms are respected and people have a sense of order and drive towards objectives, as opposed to a sense of drifting.

WRONG PATHWAYS

Explain to people that we have a problem and appeal to them to have more discipline with processes

VIRAL CHANGE™

Any norm, even if it's small, is to be respected. Highlight loose ends. Broadcast unfinished business (decisions). Show and publicly reinforce examples where the opposite is appearing (gratify closures and solutions). Role-model obsessively with exquisite follow-ups, 'closure of topics' or by fixing any other 'broken window'. It may look like a journey towards some rigidity but you need to reverse the 'broken windows' trend and this is the price to pay. And you need to do it by creating reverse-imitations, perhaps via Change Champions

EXAMPLE 3:

CURRENT CULTURE

Loose responsibilities. Confusion about who is accountable for, who is doing what. Sense that things are diluted in favour of groupings such as 'the team', and/or articulations such as 'we are all responsible'.

DESIRED CHANGE

To a culture of accountability where everybody knows where the buck stops and where there is clarity on who is driving what.

WRONG PATHWAYS

Explain to people the importance of accountability, the risks associated with lack of it and the need to change mindsets.

VIRAL CHANGE™

Install behaviours such as 'keep promises' and reward/recognise them. Reinforce every time clarity of accountability comes up. Lack of accountability in terms of behaviours should be associated with no air time whatsoever. Even if a project has finished successfully, if it has done so with total blurred accountability, it should not get recognition (If accountability is what you want to install!). Change Champions network may spread concepts and model behaviours very successfully.

EXAMPLE 4:

CURRENT CULTURE

Individualistic culture: lack of teamwork or cross-collaboration between teams, divisions or even individuals.

DESIRED CHANGE

To a collaborative culture where cross-communication and joining forces is preferred.

WRONG PATHWAYS

Explain to people the importance of collaborating, sharing information and knowledge, understanding other people's resources. Suggest/promote to share them

VIRAL CHANGE™

Devise collaborative mini-tasks if needed (as explained before). Reward any single collaborative behaviour even if small. Broadcast stories. At some point there will be a number of 'collaborative examples'. A tipping point will appear when people 'realise' that 'other people are collaborating', 'collaboration is possible here', etc. If a Champions group is in place they will model collaboration themselves, even if starting with small, almost artificial situations. Make collaboration appear and reinforce. Stop reinforcing individual contributions even if great. You'll be tempted to do both. You'll be wrong in viral terms.

EXAMPLE 5:

CURRENT CULTURE

'We-have-a-communication-problem' culture (widespread). The language of 'communication problem' has been installed very successfully probably by diffusion and imitation. The 'frame' is simply assumed all the time. (You have a communication problem because you have created one by assuming that you will always have a communication problem).

DESIRED CHANGE

We do NOT have a communication problem! We may want to improve and generate a culture of exquisite communication but we do NOT have a problem.

WRONG PATHWAYS

Explain to people the importance of communicating well, of involving everybody, of being sensitive to the needs of others, of being more inclusive, etc.

VIRAL CHANGE™

If needed (if very pervasive issue) do as in the 'collaboration' case. Artificially create small examples of good communication and publicise them. Do so through Champions plus their small worlds and/or ask everybody to show a small piece of good communication. Broadcast. Wait for the tipping point, when there are so many stories of communication that the assumption is reversed.

Try to reflect for a moment. Imagine your situation: real or possible, or simply worrying. Imagine that you have framed the need for change. This is not an in-depth exercise, but a simple prompt to take you to VIRAL CHANGE™ territory and imagine your possible pathways.

❶ DESCRIBE IN A FEW WORDS THE CHARACTERISTICS OF YOUR CURRENT CULTURE

❷ DESCRIBE THE CHANGES THAT YOU WOULD LIKE TO SEE BEING ESTABLISHED

NEW CULTURES: IF NOT NOW, WHEN?

❸ TRY TO IDENTIFY 3 BEHAVIOURS THAT, IF PRESENT IN THE ORGANISATION, REPRESENT EXACTLY 'THE CULTURE YOU WANT'. FOLLOW THE VIRAL CHANGE™ RATIONALE AND DEVISE A PLAN.

❹ LIST THE SPECIFIC ACTIONS THAT YOU MAY WANT TO TAKE AS A RESULT OF THE ABOVE IDENTIFICATION OF THE 3 BEHAVIOURS. DOUBLE-CHECK THAT YOUR ACTION PLAN IS CONSISTENT WITH THOSE BEHAVIOURS. IF YOU HAVE WRITTEN DOWN AN ACTION THAT SEEMS LOGICAL, BUT THAT YOU CAN'T LINK BACK TO THOSE BEHAVIOURS, ASK YOURSELF WHY IT IS THERE AND REVIEW YOUR CHOICES (OR START AGAIN!).

>> TWO CULTURAL VIGNETTES

There are innumerable situations of more or less dysfunctional cultures that are at the origin of the desire for change. It would be pointless to pretend a scientific classification or to describe them all in theory. I have chosen two cases for their pervasive presence in many situations in which I have been called upon to help with VIRAL CHANGE™. I wrote these two examples as two light articles a while ago and have preserved their original format. I am inserting them here on purpose to prompt extra reflection in this section about culture(s). These two cultures are particularly toxic.

I. MACDONALDISATION CULTURE

She is tall, immaculately dressed, wearing a name tag, extremely polite, and, fundamentally, very unlucky to have me standing in front of her. I am an angry customer, checking out after a three-day stay where everything that could go wrong, went wrong. The shower went from volcanic to polar temperatures with no warning, room service took an average of 70 minutes each time, the housekeeper thought the room was empty and stormed in during my post-jet-lag early bedtime, the TV screen told me that I would be charged for movies that I didn't watch, one of the telephones in the room did not work, and my next door neighbours had a 24-hour party which the thin walls broadcast to the world. And the price of the room was astronomical.

I look at her and describe the litany of problems, frustrations and near suicidal feelings. I am furious. I look and sound furious. She takes some notes on a little yellow pad whilst nodding at my list of problems. She even looks sympathetic for a fraction of second.

"Obviously, sir, I will let the manager know".
OK, great! Then she hands me the bill.
"Did you have a good stay, sir?"

I couldn't believe it at first, but it was something in her automatic pilot look that gave me the clue. The handing out of the bill must come, I thought, from their automatic pilot Customer-Happiness-Care-and-Services-Training, together with *"Did you have a good stay, sir?"* The fact that the customer has just given an apocalyptic account of the hotel does not figure in the manual.

"No, I didn't have a good stay. As a matter of fact, I have just explained to you for the last ten minutes that I've been on the verge of a nervous breakdown and those sorts of states are usually mutually exclusive with a 'good stay'."
"I am sorry to hear that, sir. Next time we will make sure that things are better".
"There isn't going to be a next time, my friend!"
"Excuse me?"
"Oh, forget it."

Then she looks puzzled. I have the bill in my hands and haven't put it away and I definitely haven't gone away yet. I am apparently in the process of exhibiting the strangest behaviour, that is, reading the bill.

"OK, all set", she sort of insists.
"No, it's not 'all set'", I said, stressing the 'all', –*"may I read it and see if I agree?"*
"Yes, sure, but it's all on your American Express card already."
"Tell me; is it common practice here to ignore the content of the bills?"
"No sir, of course sir, you are welcome (sic) to check it… but usually people here come on business."

338

I will spare you my comments on the incredible inference that 'people on business' are not expected to care about bills; they are all expenses after all and usually paid for with somebody else's money.

That lady at the front desk had a very precise mental (and physical) algorithm for what to do and what to say. It was all in the training manual, I suppose, and in some sort of Standard Operating Procedure where deviations are not allowed and judgement is not needed. A robot from Silicon Valley could have done a similar or even better job.

Management can be very similar to that front desk. In some organisational cultures things must happen in a standard way and deviations are a sin. Many managers are trapped in semi-religious attitudes to what is usually called 'the process'. Give me a good process and things can be repeated successfully, they seem to say. Even a CEO once told me there was no secret in business success: it was all a matter of having a good process and repeating it.

'A process' is always a pathway that usually takes you places. The more people follow that particular path, the higher the probability of reaching that particular destination. So, if anybody wants to arrive there through different ways, they must either have 'permission' or they will be considered loose cannons. When 'the process' is king, no spontaneous efforts are needed to reach the destination - this is why 'we have a process here', we say. But 'the process' runs the risk of creating an automatic pilot culture where people don't question things anymore and where work has been 'MacDonaldised'.
'MacDonaldisation' of work has been described as a way to ensure consistency and continuity well outside the fast food industry. How many times do we use the word 'consistency' in our daily management? Probably as many as we use the word 'objective'.

When was the last time you wanted to hire a manager who was inconsistent and subjective (yes, like your teenager daughter)?

Many management practices in organisations are there as a given, unquestioned, as part of a supposed 'body of good practice'.
The problem with any semi-obsessive process-driven organisation is that progressively it generates less and less need for judgement. Total Macdonaldisation equals end of judgement.

Judgement is in short supply. It requires exercise of the cortex in the brain. MacDonaldised management is mainly under paleo-encephalic, subcortical control. Management spends an enormous amount of time creating, designing, redesigning and changing processes. It's all a matter of having lots of well-defined pipes connected with each other to push things through.

Managers who believe that management is basically a plumbing system will make sure that the right things (ideas, money, time, products, molecules, memos, checklists or teleconferences) enter the system through the right input pipe. Then they'll go home and come back several times, until at some point things start to appear at the other end. Helas, here it comes: the project team minutes, the new hires, the amended SOP or the decision to proceed (to next set of pipes).

Henry Ford epitomised the Macdonaldised manager when he wondered: *"Why is it that each time I ask for a pair of hands, they come attached to a brain?"* He also produced the famous: *"you can have any colour of car you want, as long as it's black"*.

It would be easy to see the caricature in all this, the surface, the tip of the iceberg in these lines, and pretend that I am praising 'lack of processes'. Far from it. We need processes, and, dare I say, strong and solid ones. But they have to come with an equal dose of judgement, sometimes based on values and beliefs that may force you to bypass 'the process'. We are rich in pipes and poor in new ideas to flow through them. We can create enormous, fabulous, pristine and elegant plumbing systems that may push rubbish through. Add to that 'process' a 'time to market programme' and you will deliver rubbish faster. Not bad. And sad.

Management needs to be aware of the potential danger of the Macdonaldisation of work itself and management practices in general. There are no esoteric tricks here to fix it. Ask yourself, as many times as you can, the most important management question: "*what is the question that we are trying to answer?*" and its equivalents: "*why are we doing this?*" "*Is this the only way?*" "*What are the alternatives?*" Kids go through a period of personal development where they ask 'why?' every other second. Management could do with some regression to childhood.

Supermarket checkout at 4.30 pm. An enormous queue behind me. I have reached the check-out with the same pride as a climber planting the flag on the summit. I carry about 100 items in a basket designed to hold half a dozen of little packets. I look overwhelmed, exhausted and am praying for a magic trick that will automatically allocate my groceries to the right plastic bags. I have bought more things than I can carry.

"Would that be all, sir?"

And I thought of the girl at the front desk of the hotel. Somewhere in her subcortical system, the word 'bill' (or was it the noise of the printer) triggered the 'did-you-have-a-nice-stay' thing.
"No, it's not all. I just happened to be in the proximity of the checkout and I thought, hey, let's unload the stuff in bits and pieces. I am

going to leave all this here with you, I promise I'll be back, I am going for my second round. Just tell the other 20 people in the queue to wait."

I did not say that, of course. I behaved myself. I am getting increasingly intolerant of automatic behaviours. The supermarket assistant would invariably ask everybody the same question, regardless of the number of items, size of the basket, or any other variable. I have done the exercise several times, watching a few customers going through. Invariably, 100 out of a 100 customers would say, *"Yes, that's all"* (at least in my random sample of experimental conditions).

Next week, same time, same place, same assistant. Before he could say a word, I said *"That's all today"*. He stopped scanning. He looked at me. *"Funny you say that! I was just going to ask you"*.

My natural inquisitive nature, or my frustrated anthropologist within, leads me to ask the question:

- *"Why do you all say this all the time?"*
- *"You'd be surprised, sir, some customers ask for a pack of cigarettes once we have finished the transaction. That's why we ask if they are sure that it would be all, you see?"*
- *"But, you don't sell cigarettes here at this checkout!"*
- *"You have a point, sir, you have a point."*

2 'BROKEN WINDOWS CULTURE'

James Q. Wilson and George Kelling probably didn't expect to trigger a massive policy shift of colossal socio-political consequences when they wrote an article for *The Atlantic*

Monthly in 1982 entitled *Broken Windows: The Police and Neighbourhood Safety*. The authors had developed a theory based on their observations of a well-known sequence of events in some urban communities, summarising it like this:

"Evidence of decay (accumulated trash, broken windows, deteriorated building exteriors) remains in the neighbourhood for a reasonably long period of time.

People who live and work in the area feel more vulnerable and begin to withdraw. They become less willing to intervene to maintain public order (for example, to attempt to break up groups of rowdy teens loitering on street corners) or to address physical signs of deterioration. Sensing this, teens and other possible offenders become bolder and intensify their harassment and vandalism. Residents become yet more fearful and withdraw further from community involvement and upkeep. Some people leave if they can. This atmosphere then attracts offenders from outside the area, who sense that it has become a vulnerable and less risky site for crime."

Further to the publication, two things happened. First of all, a fuller theory emerged from what had been an observation of reality, one still too familiar in many of our cities today. Second, actions were taken in many places in the US, some of them counterintuitive, misinterpreted or controversial even now.

The glue that holds the 'Broken Windows' theory together, belongs to the behavioural and social sciences. I suggest that it is extremely useful - beyond the unpleasantness of some suburban life - to understand organisational decline in our safer and perhaps even cosier business organisations. As in suburban US, there are practical ways to deal with the organisational deterioration, or, alternatively, dare I say, get out before it's too late.

The 'Broken windows theory' suggests that relatively small - and in themselves often harmless - realities (broken windows, graffiti on walls, litter in the streets, etc.) have the power, if not addressed promptly, of creating big social changes by sending signals to the environment. These signals are interpreted as *"Nobody cares much around here, it is safe to break things, litter or vandalise, etc."*, and this makes the environment attractive to people who engage in this kind of behaviour. Prolonged harmless graffiti leads to more broken windows and wider vandalism because its message is: *"You can get away with destruction here"*, which opens the door to broader disorder. To put it bluntly, small deterioration can create irreversible decline. The theory was a pillar for what, years later, would be known as the 'zero tolerance' law enforcement policy in places such as New York, which has often been misunderstood, I suspect even by many who quote the policy.

The conventional wisdom of the action to be taken to fix these problems would read: don't let them get away with it, punish them. But in behavioural sciences terms, punishment has very moderate effects, at least if compared with what we call 'extinction', that is, making sure that if there are incentives for those engaged in the disorder, these incentives are removed. In behavioural sciences, we call behavioural reinforcement anything that, 'attached' to a given behaviour, has the ability to increase the probability of that behaviour. For the New York gangs engaged in massive graffiti on the underground trains, for example, the reinforcement could probably be understood in terms of a sense of power got from seeing the effects of their actions all over the place and the apparent immunity they enjoyed. Power, ego building, a sense of achievement, group spirit... Whatever it is or was, it is reinforcing those behaviours, that is, is motivating these people to do it again. While conventional wisdom and popular psychology would suggest that the police should find and punish those perpetrators, a truly behavioural sciences-based approach would favour the removal of the reward over the application of punishment. And this is precisely what authorities in places such as New York did. Instead of 'find them and punish them' they opted for 'find them and show them the futility of their actions'. How? By cleaning the graffiti as fast as they could, in same cases in front of the perpetrator's own noses. And, as a knock-on effect, overall crime declined. Big time.

'Broken windows' policy is far from a theoretical framework. It has clear consequences, as a commentator in the *Washington Post* described: *"The theory has spawned a revolution in law enforcement and neighbourhood activism. Broken windows? Get building owners to replace them. Graffiti on the walls? Scrub them clean, then get tough with graffiti artists. Abandoned cars? Haul them away. Drunks on the sidewalks? Get them off the streets, too"*. He also cites an official American neighbourhood website: *"These 'order strategies' such as those listed below help to deter and reduce crime: quick replacement of broken windows; prompt removal of abandoned vehicles: fast clean-up of illegally dumped items, litter and spilled garbage; quick paint out of graffiti; finding (or building) better places for teens to gather than street corner: fresh paint on buildings and clean sidewalks and street gutters"*. It couldn't be more prescriptive.

We have our own versions of graffiti and litter in our companies, and I am not talking about the cleanliness of the toilets. Organisational life is full of rules of the game, some of them explicit, others tacit, some necessary, some not, some enabling us to do our jobs, some plain silly and only created to satisfy big egos. In non-judgemental behavioural terms, rules create the borders of what is or is not acceptable, therefore serving as a map for people in the organisation. If the rule is stupid, people should be able to challenge it by trying to change it but never by simply ignoring it.

There is a trick here. Ignoring a stupid rule and being able to do so without being penalised, may have the intentional good consequence of making that rule less stable, which is good news. However, if an authority figure in the organisation ignores the rule, period, this is a graffiti signal to others saying: rules are not taken seriously here. This may be unintended, but it is potentially a powerful trigger for widespread lack of compliance. In the process of fixing A (by ignoring it), we have created problem B. However, many rules are not stupid. They simply guide efficacy or effectiveness or time management or information flow or quality maintenance. If you see a decrease in compliance, a progressive rise of loose ends, unfinished discussions, decisions only half-baked, delayed implementations, poor usage of an information management system or agreed actions not taking place, and, people are getting away with it, you may be looking at broken windows. As in the social theory described, these facts in isolation may not be big enough to make the firm collapse, but, whether you want it or not, they will have a multiplying effect with unintended consequences.

You may think that this is simply a lack of discipline, and you may be right, but this is unfortunately just a label that means very little in behavioural terms. The reality is that if there is no negative consequence (for the perpetrators) and the behaviours are reinforced by the fact that loose compliance, for example, is simply possible, before you know it, the place will attract other non-compliance realities of a bigger magnitude. Perhaps you could also call it poor management, period. You may be right, in which case management is more unlikely to see anything particularly wrong.

I am more interested in the utility of 'broken windows signals' in the organisation. These are symptoms that you may have spotted which, although not necessarily an expression of a true and full 'broken windows' environment, should be an early warning signal. They should ask you to make a judgement on whether there is something more serious behind those symptoms and signs. The greater the tendency for those loose ends, the more you should be alerted. Together with the examples given above, watch out for meeting minutes that suddenly disappear from the agenda and don't seem to be reviewed anymore; requests for issue input followed by progressive silence; deadlines that appear more 'flexible' than ever or are simply not met; circulated briefing documents that nobody really reads; sudden loss of clarity about who is accountable for what, perhaps associated with an increase in so-called shared responsibility; requested formats (for meetings, reports, input sought) that are ignored; repeated postponement of events due to the lack of quorum.

All those are 'broken windows' in the management system. They may not kill the firm by themselves but they are symptoms of underlying pathology. In the best of these cases,

347

there may not be death on the horizon but the firm's weak immune system will simply attract other infections. A worse case is one when all these things seem to be 'new' or not noted on the organisation's previous medical history. The firm has a temperature and the fever should alert you. And alert is a good word. While very poor organisational performance may rock the firm enough to shock the system and trigger immediate remedial measures, a more gentle increased tolerance for marginal performance is a sign of serious deterioration that can easily be overlooked. It is the equivalent of walking through the same street every day and not noticing the broken windows and the graffiti.

You may think that this is all very well, but that it's not happening or not possible in your organisation. After all, yours isn't one of those companies. For the eternal optimists, I would remind you of a social experiment in 1969 by Philip Zimbardo, now professor Emeritus of Psychology in Stanford. It is considered a precursor of 'broken windows' and you'll see why. Zimbardo left two identical 'vulnerable' cars on the street in two different places and waited for them to be vandalised. The one left in New York's Bronx was stripped bare in a day. The one left on the street in Palo Alto, California, remained untouched for a week. At the end of the week, Zimbardo himself put a hammer through one of the windows and, as a report put it: "*As though this act and its impunity were the starting gun they were waiting for, the Californians rallied round to destroy that car just as thoroughly*". All it takes is a broken window in your organisation. You decide what action to take, but here is a tip: don't bother with punishment.

'CULTURES' 10

1   REMEMBER: BEHAVIOURS SHAPE
    CULTURE, NOT THE OTHER WAY AROUND.

2   THINK OF CULTURE AS A POINT OF
    DESTINATION ('ONCE WE HAVE THESE
    BEHAVIOURS ESTABLISHED, WE WILL
    HAVE THAT CULTURE').

3   ONLY THINK OF CULTURE AS A POINT
    OF DEPARTURE WHEN YOU'RE
    VISUALISING A FUTURE ('IMAGINE THAT
    WE HAVE A CULTURE OF X WHERE
    PEOPLE BEHAVE LIKE A, B, C').

4   THINK SHORT-TERM: WHICH
    BEHAVIOURAL CHANGES CAN BE MADE
    NOW TO START TRIGGERING 'THE
    INFECTION'? BAN 'CULTURE CHANGE IS
    A LONG-TERM AFFAIR' FROM YOUR MIND
    (OR YOU'LL HAVE A LONG-TERM AFFAIR).

5   WHEN YOU DESCRIBE YOUR CULTURE (TO
    YOUR PEERS, STAFF, EXTERNAL WORLD)
    USE ANY LABELS YOU FEEL
    APPROPRIATE, BUT MAKE SURE TO
    ATTACH THE BEHAVIOURS BEHIND
    THOSE LABELS.

6   DETECT SYMPTOMS OF 'BROKEN
    WINDOWS CULTURE' AND ACT UPON
    THEM WITH DETERMINATION!

7   UNCOVER THE POSSIBLE
    MACDONALDISATION OF YOUR
    ORGANISATION. EVALUATE WHETHER YOU
    WORK UNDER 'THE TYRANNY OF THE
    PROCESS'.

8   PUT BEHAVIOURS BEFORE PROCESSES.
    TO ACHIEVE CHANGE, FOCUS YOUR
    ENERGY ON BEHAVIOURAL CHANGE, NOT
    PROCESS CHANGE. LET BEHAVIOURS,
    NOT PROCESSES, DRIVE THE 'NEW
    CULTURE'.

9   SPOT ANY 'NEW ROUTINES', DESIRABLE
    OR UNDESIRABLE, CREATED VIA TIPPING
    POINTS AND TRY TO UNDERSTAND THE
    VIRAL NETWORK BEHIND THEM.

10 FOR ANY 'CULTURAL CHANGE', MAP
    YOUR APPROACH BOTH VIA TRADITIONAL
    CHANGE MANAGEMENT AND THROUGH
    VIRAL CHANGE™. MAKE SURE YOU SEE
    THE DIFFERENCES IN FOCUS, PATHWAYS,
    LEVERS AND PLAYERS. THEN CHOOSE.

IN SUMMARY,
FOR ALL

(14)

VIRAL CHANGE™: PROCESS IN A BOX

Thanks for following so far! I sincerely hope that the principles shared in this book will be of benefit to you when introducing change in your organisation. Warning: if you have come to this chapter bypassing everything else, in search of the perfect summary, you are running a few risks, but welcome anyway!

The principles behind VIRAL CHANGE™ are clear. But you need to figure out how to use them. It's like cooking. So far, I have taken you through many pages, sharing ideas and 'methods' about the ingredients. There also some good recipes and this chapter is about sharing a final one with you. But only you can do the cooking. What matters most is that you are confident about the ingredients and about their logical combination…

In VIRAL CHANGE™ mode, many things are happening in parallel. So, to some extent, 'a process' in VIRAL CHANGE™ must have a different meaning from the standard one. And you know that the standard sounds, smells and feels fundamentally sequential. However, I am going to describe 'a process' that very much represents my experience and many of my engagements with clients. But your recipe may still look different from mine. You'll have to adapt things to the size of your organisation and to the nature of the changes that you want to implement. The principle ingredients will remain valid.

>> FOR YOU, THE LEADER…

- I am going to assume that you, or you and your leadership team, have already identified the need for change and have perhaps articulated some more or less specific objectives. You are de facto using 'language' (chapter 6). Be very aware of the frame you are choosing. We saw this before. It is not a trivial matter. If you chose 'a problem solving frame', everything you do will look solution-driven. You are then stuck with this. You'll end up surrounded by 'solution-delivering-consultants' and so on. All frames are legitimate. Just be aware that language matters and that frame… well, it will frame you.

- The articulation may have been spread to others, to direct reports or some teams. Many more people may be aware of the need to change things. 90 % of them, if not more, will have de facto a preconceived idea of what the process of change would look like: i.e. a tsunami! You may start suggesting alternatives. Discussing this book with a selected group - part of your leadership team, or the leadership team itself - may be the trigger for alternative thinking. It is a good way to start since in VIRAL CHANGE™ there are many unconventional things.

- If your organisation is medium or big sized, I strongly suggest that you choose the Change Champions route. It is a bit more difficult in very small organisations. In those cases, everything may look like a small world. You are going to have a mixture of different characters 'in the same room', so to speak. Everything that we have described in terms of non-negotiable behaviours and the need to reinforce them is valid no matter what size company you have/work for. But you need a certain number of people in your network to see tipping points appear, as mentioned before.

- Assuming the Change Champions route, your first port of call is to obtain buy-in from your colleagues in the leadership team or from your own subordinates at top level. Use chapters 1 to 5 (In theory, for the pragmatists) to take your people through the key concepts that need to be 'accepted'. Your goal as driver is to produce as many 'aha!'-moments as possible. The key concepts are:

    - The coexistence of designed and non-designed parts of the organisation, and the need for you to count on invisible parts like the internal networks.

- The richness of these invisible, non-designed forms of collaboration or internal networks.
- The existence of small worlds and everything that you can see once you open the curtains of the organisation chart.
- How networks work: the three principles of power law, Matthew effects and tipping points/phase transitions.

- Once this has been 'visualised', the corollary is easier: you are rich and have a network of people who have immense hidden power of influence, either because other people listen to them or because they have gained (moral, technical) authority or simply trust.

- The next step is crucial: we need to work alongside this network. We need to identify these people, ask them for help, work with them on the principles of our aims and devolve to them as much leadership as possible. And also: it is not conventional, it may look weird, it is not management versus them; management needs them if they want to spread change via the internal networks to create a fast new culture!

- You need to get your leadership team comfortable with the principles behind all this: what the organisation is about (In theory, for the pragmatists) and the four ingredients of VIRAL CHANGE™ and how they play their part (In practice for the theorists). I strongly suggest that you don't prolong the thinking process too much and that you establish a clear pace of change, or mechanisms to start the changes.

- This is a crossroads point, because you have two choices or pathways now. You are going to start uncovering behaviours and declaring your preliminary set of non-negotiable behaviours (chapter 9). Your choice is either to carry on doing this with your leadership team or to involve the Champions from now on. In most cases where I have been involved, the client prefers to involve the leadership only. If this is the case, you should, however, start the ball rolling in parallel to identify the Champions and plan for meeting them and welcoming them.

- You are now in a position to uncover those behaviours that you need to support changes (chapter 9). You are ready for that visualisation of success and /or failure that we have described before and the eventual choice of that small, powerful set. Remember a few things from this section:

    - Choice is a keyword. You will need to settle for a small set of perhaps five behaviours maximum. Remember that the introduction of these behaviours acts as 'disruption' of the system. Remember also that in VIRAL CHANGE™, this small set will have butterfly effects!

    - Another choice you have here is to rely solely on your (team) knowledge of the organisation and the (team) assumption about the current behavioural fabric. Alternatively, you can carry out some sort of audit to understand what the baseline looks like. You need to have a sense of the magnitude of the task. There are many things that can be extrapolated from employee surveys, for example, but many of them are not necessarily behavioural-based. The idea, however, is simple. You may recall the case of the creation of a collaborative culture in an organisational fabric where collaboration was not the norm. Obviously there was a big gap there. You will also recall that I gave you examples on how to 'social engineer' the behaviours so that it could be artificially visible.

- You now have a set of non-negotiable behaviours (and don't forget you need to have a set of appropriate reinforcement mechanisms) and are ready to start the infection. You will have identified the Champions in parallel by any of the mechanisms described in chapter 11.

- Meet the Champions. Be honest about your goals, in your request for help. Commit your support to them, explaining some measures that you will put in place to facilitate their work.

- Above all, allow plenty of time for the Champions to explore ways of doing things. Keep away from excessive formality. Yes, you will meet with them periodically to compare notes and adjust things…but resist the temptation of creating super-formal meetings with pristine agendas and lots of presentations.

- Needless to say, you will have decided how many Champions you need. There is no rule other than going back to the power law and the rest of the things we know about social networks. The geographical scope and structure of your company will inevitably play a key role in the decision. If you are organised by geographical territories with their own management, it will make sense to find some Champions for each of those territories. You'll end up with a group representing somewhere between 5% and 15% of the total workforce. I have developed a Change Champions network of 15 people for a 150 person division, a 20 people group for a 750 structure, or a 50 people group in a geographically distributed organisation of 1,000 people. They all work.

- The Change Champions need 'initiation' similar to the one your leadership needed, and that could happen the first time they meet as a group. Make sure that they feel the support from the start. Consider having some sceptical people in the network. Now, let them loose!

- Depending on the nature of the changes, and the set of non-negotiable behaviours, you may want to consider introducing these 'campaign style'. That is, phased over a few months so that every month or every two months, the Champions are 'given' and are 'embracing' a new behaviour. Although they will be very aware of the overall picture, you will ask them to concentrate on behaviour A for two months, for example, then meet again, review what is going on and introduce the next one, while continuing the infection and reinforcement of the previous one.

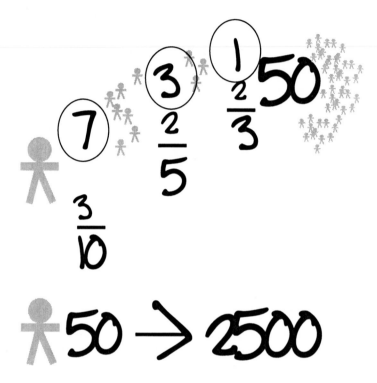

One successful Champion may influence 7 out of 10 connections. If each of those 7 manage to get 3 out of 5 on board and each of those 3 connects with 1 out of 3, the total impact is 50 well connected-and-infected people. 50 Champions would have the potential to 'touch' 2500 people. Even if we use more conservative figures, the power of influence is still enormous.

- Make sure the Champions have the means to communicate between them effectively and quickly. Blog is my preferred tool, although in the past I have used the protected, confidential space of the company intranet. The Champions network in itself can be infected! That means they need to reinforce each other with good stories of achievements or by sharing information about barriers and how they have dealt with them. These days this is a real-time event! Not something that happens at formal meetings every two months. You want to obsessively promote a flow of communication between the members of the network, so that the question 'has anybody encountered X?' is answered almost instantly by a remote Champion colleague with good ideas.

- As a leader, you are working on parallel tracks. On one hand, your focus is on the network of Champions, on the other hand you want your leadership team and other layers of management to support and un-manage (chapter 12). As we said, manage the assets, not the network. Remember that VIRAL CHANGE™ contains many counter-intuitive concepts and practices, Even people in the leadership team who have become convinced that this is the way to go, will be tempted to ask for components of the tsunami approach, almost unconsciously.

- For weeks, many things may be invisible, but tipping points, big or small, will start to appear. You need to broadcast them: it is happening. Hi-fi those changes. Let the world know. Systematically recognise any single small or big achievement by anybody. You must feel the infection. If you don't or if people don't: something is wrong somewhere.

- At some point, your metrics will tell you that changes and new routines are in place. That may mean four months, six months or perhaps one year from now to clear establishment. You and your leadership will have learnt a lot and may have had to make adjustments. The time may have come to 'stop the process'. But can you? Really? It is healthy to have a finish line, declare achievements and future challenges, say thanks and reflect. You could officially disband the Champions group as such, but you can't avoid them continuing as a network. At this point, the value of this group and process may have been highlighted and all sorts of people will come up with ideas to 'use those Champions'. Resist, unless it's the Champions idea. Which may happen. Otherwise, keep supporting their online meetings and listen to them about what they have learnt and what they could do next, if anything.

>> HOW DO I WORK?

VIRAL CHANGE™, conceptually and operationally, has originated within The Chalfont Project Ltd. This is how I personally do it from the outside. I help the leadership team in assessing the needs of the organisation and its desire for change. Then, I tend to design the components of a VIRAL CHANGE™ intervention with them, including the size and nature of an internal network of activists, if appropriate.

With the leadership team, I will map a process to visualise and gain a common, shared understanding of (1) the language to use and the frames to follow, (2) the uncovering of new non-negotiable behaviours that are needed to create the change (of processes, systems, culture, etc.), (3) the best mechanisms for diffusion, imitation, reinforcement of those behaviours and the conduit of the viral spread via an internal network, (4) the way to watch for and use 'tipping points' that create new routines or 'new cultures'.

I would facilitate those meetings with the leadership. I would therefore work with both a leadership team and an internal group of 'Change Champions', facilitating the balance between the two levers of VIRAL CHANGE™. In VIRAL CHANGE™, leadership is mainly distributed through the organisation (the Champions, for example).

The role of the external consultant is 'thought leadership': backstage, facilitation and coaching support all in one. This is what I tend to do. However, I play with the ingredients in the same way I suggest you do: thinking of different recipes for different types of cooking, as appropriate. Sometimes, things look a bit different from project to project. The idea of having a perfect map for the process of VIRAL CHANGE™ is in contradiction with the philosophy behind it. This doesn't mean, however, that there is no process, but it requires further cooking! There are lots of things you can do on your own, without external help. There may be other things where you may need the external support. But in any case, you are the cook. The graph on page 364 summarises this process.

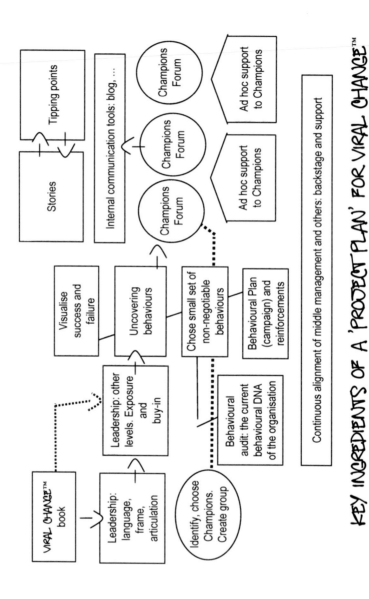

KEY INGREDIENTS OF A 'PRODUCT PLAN' FOR VIRAL CHANGE™

The diagram includes the following elements:

- VIRAL CHANGE™ book
- Leadership: language, frame, articulation
- Leadership: other levels. Exposure and buy-in
- Visualise success and failure
- Uncovering behaviours
- Identify, choose Champions. Create group
- Behavioural audit: the current behavioural DNA of the organisation
- Chose small set of non-negotiable behaviours
- Behavioural Plan (campaign) and reinforcements
- Champions Forum
- Champions Forum
- Champions Forum
- Ad hoc support to Champions
- Ad hoc support to Champions
- Stories
- Tipping points
- Internal communication tools: blog, …
- Continuous alignment of middle management and others: backstage and support

(15)

15 CHANGE MANAGEMENT ASSUMPTIONS REVISITED

In the introduction, I suggested you wrote down your position and experience regarding 15 statements on management of change. It is now time to review them. In real life, I would have loved to have this conversation in person and I hope it will happen some day. After all, we are only a few degrees apart. However, here is my review. As you will see, from a VIRAL CHANGE™ perspective, some of these assumptions may have been transformed, may look different or may perhaps be approaching the category of myths.

1. BIG CHANGE REQUIRES BIG ACTIONS

This is the commonly held belief that is behind the majority of so-called 'large interventions' or comprehensive, massive, expensive change management programmes. It is logically assumed that a significant change in the organisation (whether it's change of culture, ways of doing, etc. or a completely new direction) needs proportional efforts. And proportionate here means massive.

As we saw in earlier chapters, this model is consistent with 'linear thinking' or 'linear dynamics', something very much embedded in our way of managing organisations. The reality is that we are surrounded by a non-linear world, where there is no apparent proportionality in the cause-effect as we see it. For example, in organisational terms, trust is not a terribly linear thing! Small things can generate high trust and small breaches can destroy it completely. There is no proportionality there!

Interestingly we all have examples of day-to-day life where 'small things' create havoc. I often warn my clients of this 'tyranny of small things': some rules, some bureaucracy, a few people creating disruption. We are used to this dis-proportionality but seem to have difficulty accepting that management of change travels on disproportioned highways.

VIRAL CHANGE™ knows all of the above very well and banks on the power of a small set of levers, behaviours, that can generate great change in a non-linear way. And we know that the organisation highways for these behaviours contain things such as imitation, diffusion, infection and tipping points.

Change is most likely driven by a broad distributed leadership (Change Champions, for example).

2. ONLY CHANGE AT THE TOP CAN ENSURE CHANGE WITHIN THE ORGANISATION

Sure, you need change at the top. You wish to see that the top leadership takes things seriously and that they are on the path of change. It may be that they themselves have declared these intentions, conscious of the importance of their role modelling. If it goes that way, bingo! But sometimes it doesn't. There is a spectrum of leadership-at-the-top behaviours. On one end: total support, clear leadership and a pristine role model with high awareness of the importance of their behaviours. At the other end of the spectrum: total blockage, lack of support and unhelpful behaviours that jeopardise change efforts made in many other parts of the organisation. Success at that end of the spectrum happens despite leadership, not because of it. And there are, of course, situations in between! Conventional wisdom says that there is a good correlation between leadership and changes, but reality tells us that it is not often the case.

'Change at the top' is obviously desirable, but VIRAL CHANGE™ does not wait until this is happening. The power of the distributed leadership - mainly across the Champions network – often leads to advances on the ground not mirrored at the top. Of course, this may be a problem. I am used to Champions telling me about these 'disconnects' and their worries about taking risks with no consequent support. My general advice is usually one of 'suspend judgement'. Unless there is notorious toxicity in the system (leadership does NOT want the changes, no matter how much of a distributed leadership is pushing for them), many so-so leadership teams - which were supposed to lead but didn't jump on the wagon at the last meeting - will see tipping points and changes occurring when they open the windows. And then they will suddenly become fully supportive and they may, dare I say it, even try to take credit for it.

3. PEOPLE ARE RESISTANT TO CHANGE

There is nothing in our biology that makes us resistant to change! We are not resistant to change. We are change. But we can act in defence of things that can disturb our level of control over things. And this is a very different matter. We saw in an earlier chapter of the book that this is one of the assumptions that have become part of the furniture in the change management field.

However, we know that resisting behaviours, which come in lots of forms and shapes, always mean something. We need to look beyond the 'it is human nature' parapet and see why things are happening that way. To assume there is resistance by default is not healthy.

VIRAL CHANGE™ proves that behaviours that could be called resistant disappear when alternative behaviours are reinforced. In VIRAL CHANGE™, we make extra efforts to lead that assumption out the door and to suspend judgement. When people see the endorsement of peers, some behaviours-of-change in other parts of the organisation, the incipient tipping points... many resistances will unexpectedly disappear.

VIRAL CHANGE™ also asks you to suspend judgement until you see how the infection spreads. Some notoriously resistant people - possibly labelled like that from the start ('Mary will never change') - may become converted ambassadors, while some 'safe people' ("*John and Peter are OK, they will jump in.*") might become difficult and truly 'resistant'.

4. CULTURAL CHANGE IS A SLOW AND PAINFUL LONG-TERM AFFAIR

This is also a strongly held belief. It is just natural that people think that way. Our view of the culture is one of that one macro-frame that is 'the cause of everything', so any attempt to change 'that thing' surely has to come associated with parameters such as long-term, pain, difficulty, etc. And we all know one example or two of this. People with this kind of experience have difficulty seeing things differently. And how could they?

The trick is to change the paradigm, excuse my language. And instead of seeing culture as the cause of 'the behaviours', we should focus on behaviours and manage/change them to see cultural change. The introduction of this book is entitled *Change behaviours, get culture.* VIRAL CHANGE™ takes a pragmatic approach and sees that when a small set of non-negotiable behaviours is installed in the organisation and becomes stable and widespread, these behaviours will have the capacity to create new routines, rules and norms which will equal 'cultural change'. These changes are possible in short time frames such as three or six months. VIRAL CHANGE™ is very adamant that if we can't see those 'cultural changes' happening in those timeframes, something is wrong.

The power of the internal network to spread new behaviours is immense. Cultural change doesn't have to be a long-term, painful affair. It is not something that is so big that we will have to postpone it until we have some serious time. That is, not this year, next year, maybe…

5. EVERYBODY NEEDS TO BE INVOLVED IN THE CHANGE

This is an obvious desideratum. But very often it's unrealistic. Conventional management approaches tell us that we have to communicate to everybody so that everybody feels involved. There are different versions of this. In some cases what it means is 'we really need to involve everybody'. In other cases it means we need to 'reach everybody' so that (a) everybody has a chance to jump in or (b) nobody can say that he hasn't been 'involved'..

Since traditional management and conventional management of change use 'communication-to-all' as a default vehicle, it is not surprising that the tsunami approach is the prevailing one. However, we have seen how our understanding of networks in general and social networks in particular has changed things forever. A small percentage of the organisation is highly connected and potentially of high influence. Communication-to-all is the most ineffective way to convey the rationale for changes and for expecting that involvement will follow.

You are better off using networks as a vehicle. I am not suggesting that communication is not needed. It is, but we usually have 'massive communication' as the single mechanism of hope. VIRAL CHANGE™ uses the power of internal networks and their small worlds to effectively reach everybody, but not in the supposedly democratic way of the Town Hall meeting roll-outs. At any point in time, there will be different levels of 'receptiveness' in the population and the spread will happen in an erratic way. However, when this is happening, it is not just 'communication' as a currency that will follow through. It is endorsement, new behaviours, reinforcements and changes, all in one. VIRAL CHANGE™ likes to talk less and do more.

6. COMMUNICATION AND TRAINING ARE THE VITAL COMPONENTS OF CHANGE

It is very much related to the topic above. It was a trick statement. I said 'the' vital component, as opposed to 'a' vital component. But I did this for a reason. Many change management initiatives look like communication and training programmes. Even people who would agree with you that this is 'a part', may be leading change programmes in which communication (and training) seems to be 'the' key, at least in size! It is easy, or easier, to develop hundreds of PowerPoint slides explaining the ins and outs of the change, the need for change, the alternative to change and the cost of no-change, etc. But the key question is: would people do things differently, once the communication and perhaps training programme has ended? The answer to that question is: maybe they will and maybe they won't.

VIRAL CHANGE™ tells us that communication and training are components of the change, but that we really need to focus on behaviours. Behaviours can't be taught, at least not in the same way we teach people how to use a spreadsheet or how to do a business plan. You can only say you are teaching when the environmental circumstances are very concrete, rigid and 'controlled'. For example, sales persons are 'taught' how to handle a conversation with a customer, how to close the sale or how to respond to expected objections. In those circumstances, people 'learn' how to respond, what to say, when to say it, etc. It is usually crafted in an almost algorithmic way: if A is true, follow path B, if B is true, follow path C, etc. This is very different from 'teaching' accountability or collaboration or competitiveness. Although you can provide theoretical frameworks for those themes, the only way to 'teach' them is through reinforcing specific behaviours that would be consistent with them. Behaviours and the rationale of 'values', 'attitudes' and 'mindset behind them can indeed be explained, but behaviours occur through reinforcement mechanisms: by management, by peers (as in the peer-to-peer Champions interactions), etc. If you reinforce 'understanding' and 'rationality' of the message, you'll get more understood messages, but not behavioural change. VIRAL CHANGE™ tells us that only behavioural change is real change. Communication and training must be adapted so that they support behavioural change. But communication and training per se will not create change as if by magic.

7. NEW PROCESSES AND SYSTEMS WILL CREATE THE NEW NECESSARY BEHAVIOURS

The establishment of new processes and systems often assumes that behaviours will follow as a consequence of those changes. It is expected. However, as we know, it is often the case that people just continue to do things as before. That is why we have all those incredibly big fiascos of new processes and systems implementations, often lead by a new IT system, which end up with 'poor usage and acceptance'.

VIRAL CHANGE™ tells us that the assumption is wrong. In many cases, we see temporary peaks of adoption, but with poor guarantees of sustainability. The role of behaviours in the process is flawed. New processes and systems do not create new behaviours. We need to have new behaviours in place in order to support new processes and systems. Remember the case of the un-collaborative sales force? New processes and electronic systems do not create collaborating. On the contrary, you need to have collaboration in order to support these systems. Just a small change of paradigm!

Many organisations are stuck with this flawed process and it is not until behaviours are 're-placed' that we start seeing the light. As described in the book, the biggest fiasco area I know is CRM: an area where the software and IT industry has produced very sexy tools and where the implementers use that incredibly weak assumption: 'it is so good, people will adopt it'. There is no behavioural science expertise in most of those areas so it is not surprising that the wrong assumption prevails. Even in those cases where people are aware of the naivety of the assumption, little is done to remedy it. Blaming IT or the specification or the project teams is a useful alibi. Blaming lack of stakeholder involvement is another one, a funny one, particularly when the implementation has been done through a myriad of project teams, user teams and stakeholder Task Forces.

8. PEOPLE ARE RATIONAL AND WILL REACT TO LOGICAL AND RATIONAL REQUESTS FOR CHANGE

Yes, we want to believe that. Rational appeal (B is better than A, we should go with B) is a logical, pervasive mechanism. We use it all the time. And so we should. But in itself it doesn't ensure change. People are able to understand the rationality of things and do appreciate that they are told things that way. But rational understanding does not guarantee (a) emotional integration or (b) behavioural change. How many times have we used the expression: 'he or she doesn't get it', as if the intellectual and rational click has not been heard inside the brain.

We spend an enormous amount of time appealing to rationality, perhaps because we have a too high regard of ourselves as rational monkeys! We also spend time and energy on emotional massage: the country-house hotel with 'motivational speakers' is an example of this. What happens after the initial injection of rationality and emotions? Energy levels go down and reality takes over. Unless we have a daily motivational speaker and a daily meeting to appeal for rational change, we have a weak case for 'change will follow'.

VIRAL CHANGE™ tells us that what really matters is behavioural change and that this is only going to happen if particular behaviours are reinforced (reward, recognition, airtime, any good reinforcement). This reinforcement comes from (a) management and (b) peers. As you may know by now, VIRAL CHANGE™ attempts to get management reinforcement as a given (which is sometimes a lot to ask, I admit!), but it banks quite a lot on the power of peer-to-peer reinforcement, mainly through the internal (viral) network of the Change Champions.

Appeals for rationality? Great as a one-off. Then behavioural reinforcement is the only thing that will make the change happen.

9. THERE IS NO POINT IN CREATING CHANGE IN ONE DIVISION WITHOUT THE REST OF THE COMPANY PARTICIPATING

Even people in a part of the organisation who feel passionate about change and embrace the principles of VIRAL CHANGE™ often have this nagging feeling about what the extent of it all will be, if the rest of the divisions (or the corporation, or headquarters, or everybody else) don't do the same. In the worst case, this thinking leads to paralysis or a delay in the 'change process' until – or so they hope - others have understood and bought in. Which, incidentally, may never happen!

There is little doubt that changes in one group or division have the potential to create antibodies in the rest, or will simply be rejected or alienated. It may be tough. However, as leaders, one has to ask the question: what can I do that is under my control? Simply asking this question many times results in revelations such as: actually, a lot. Organisations have great capacity to host models in a symbiotic way. Change needs to start somewhere.

VIRAL CHANGE™ focuses on the spread of changes via internal viral networks. In many cases once the tipping points have occurred, their visibility goes beyond the borders of the organisation, and other divisions or groups may copy or start thinking about copying the changes. There is so much you can do via VIRAL CHANGE™ within the borders under your control.

People who accept the idea of 'try-and-see-what-happens' have invented the word 'pilot'. It seems as if 'piloting' is acceptable, but 'here-we-go-for-real-change' is not. VIRAL CHANGE™ could be done through pilots, but we would be prostituting terminology. There are no 'pilots', only real life spread of infections. My advice is: start now!

10. SCEPTICAL PEOPLE AND ENEMIES OF CHANGE NEED TO BE SIDELINED

We all have our share of 'difficult people'. Conventional management of change has taught us that there is always going to be a group of 'no-hope' people and another group of 'maybe-but-very-sceptical-people'. It smells like a bell curve! There is nothing wrong with the talk. We all know what we mean by it. My warning is against premature labelling and self-fulfilling prophecies.

A converted sceptic is worth 100 disciplined followers, because (a) an imitation of his 'conversion' may draw a small world of its own into the change and (b) the 'conversion' itself is social proof and legitimisation. ("*If Peter is involved, maybe this is for real at last*", I heard in a client meeting). Our 'internal segmentation' often reads like this:
- Good guys: going for it, get them all on board.
- Resistant guys: they will never change, be prepared to let them go.
- Sceptical guys: mainly a pain, either they will 'get it' and change, or else'.

VIRAL CHANGE™ has the following words of wisdom: suspend judgement, be willing to be surprised and, above all, don't write off the assets that quickly. Mary, the one who is systematically sceptical, may well be so for a reason. And she may see VIRAL CHANGE™ as a real opportunity for real change and see a role for herself in its model of distributed leadership. A sceptic may be one of your best Champions. Alice, a wonderfully loyal employee, always ready for change, may have been taken for granted. But Alice, recently promoted to section manager, may not fancy the idea of Change Champions going around apparently bypassing her hierarchy. She may become a wonderfully unhappy and unsupportive employee. Do not sideline anyone! Let's first see who the final characters are in the tipping points plots!

11. VISION FOR CHANGE NEEDS TO COME FROM THE TOP AND CASCADE DOWN

I don't know whether 'it needs to' or whether it just happens to be the observable norm. It really depends on the use you make of the word 'vision'. If your vision is something close to the ultimate managerial clairvoyance only hosted on the executive floor, then… well, it may cascade down. I think the main reason why an executive floor is at the top of the building is so the cascading down of the vision takes place with the full use of the forces of gravity! If vision is a clear point of destiny, then there is no point expecting this to come from the Post Room (and this is not a judgement about the ability of people in the post room to have a vision).

If your view of vision is more one of directions that can be refined, can grow, can benefit from the 'none of us is smarter than all of us' philosophy, then VIRAL CHANGE™ is something you'll be very comfortable with. VIRAL CHANGE™ creates waves of infections and emergent tipping points. Allowing for (real) distributed leadership means that there is no 'pre-defined final outcome' (a scary thought for those in the command and control arena), but unpredictable, non-linear and potentially incredibly better outcomes.

In VIRAL CHANGE™, initial vision may come from the top leadership itself but it doesn't follow the forces of gravity. Oh horror! How do I know that people are going in the right direction and aren't drifting? Well, get involved! You are defining the non-negotiable behaviours and therefore you are the master of those hot topics. If they are reinforced as planned, you'll have an incredibly hi-fi machine. At which point, 'the top' as a geographical signpost becomes irrelevant.

12 AFTER CHANGE YOU NEED A PERIOD OF STABILITY AND CONSOLIDATION

Or so the troops sometimes say. After the third reorganisation and the fourth quality programme and the second change management initiative, the cry is loud: give us a break! Yes, stability would be nice. But the last time we had stability was around 1756 (give or take a 100 years). The current world is instable. The business environment is a chaotic moving target. You have to be very careful about the word 'stability'.

Although the linguistics are logical, we must accept that real consolidation and real stability are not going to be a sort of 'steady-state'. Many people in managerial ranks spend their life in rehearsal mode: I'll do this when I have more people, when my headcount is full, when I'm given a new budget, etc. But in the meantime: things happen!

VIRAL CHANGE™ provides a mechanism for a continuum between changes (from tipping points) and establishment of new behaviours as a routine. It also gives us the power of internal (viral) networks and their perception of 'stability' or 'change'. It is legitimate to place borders and timelines on processes, but they are only useful as part of a code language. As we said in the previous assumption, it is only when 'destination' is absolutely fixed and unmovable that 'the end of the change process' makes sense. If you have reached X, well, that's it! But if vision is more of a journey with the possibility of new discoveries, then when exactly would you be able to say that you have reached terra firma?

VIRAL CHANGE™ forces you to see waves of change, more than a sequential journey from A → B → C. Your concept of stability or consolidation may never be the same!

13. SHORT-TERM WINS ARE TACTICAL BUT THEY DO NOT USUALLY REPRESENT REAL CHANGE

Obviously, some people don't like 'short wins'. These are usually the same people who do not consider change a valid label unless a big M&A has taken place. There is a semantic implication of 'not-really-serious-change'. The world is rather bipolar here: some people love these short-term wins, others hate them.

Short-term wins are very much welcomed by VIRAL CHANGE™. We have said all along that small changes can lead to a big impact. So it is only natural that short-terms wins, or 'win-wins', are part of the picture. The difference between the win-win/short-win in VIRAL CHANGE™ and the one in conventional management of change is that in the latter, it usually means let's fix what is small, visible and will make many people happy, a sure-sure bet, doable, sexy, it's going to be rewarding. In VIRAL CHANGE™ mode, small win-wins may be small, visible and will-make-many-people-happy, a sure-sure bet, doable, sexy, it's going to be rewarding, or it may not be. This is not the judgement to make. In VIRAL CHANGE™ it's not the easiness of the task that defines the 'small' quality. It is perhaps an atomic behaviour that by being reinforced creates a sense of possibility and that - when many of them are visible and 'available' - creates a tipping point of significance. There is small and then there is small: two types of small, two types of win-win. The statement above uses the word 'tactical' implying that there are strategic things and tactical things. VIRAL CHANGE™ does not host that distinction. Apparently tactical things (the wide spread of a simple behaviour) have implications well beyond day-to-day tactics.

14. THERE WILL ALWAYS BE CASUALTIES – PEOPLE NOT ACCEPTING CHANGE – AND YOU NEED TO IDENTIFY AND DEAL WITH THEM

This assumption, and its equivalent below, contains quite a lot of common sense. I have warned you several times before about preconceived ideas and I suggested a 'suspend judgement' policy. Yes, there will always be casualties, but you don't know which ones. This assumption cries for leaders with significant emotional and social intelligence skills (in short supply), leaders who are able to read beyond the obvious and ask the question 'why?' Why the casualty? Happiness and unhappiness are part of our human nature. You can't make people happy or unhappy. People make themselves happy or unhappy. I prefer happiness to unhappiness but can't run a client engagement assuming that everybody is going to be happy. Unhappiness sometimes comes on the back of difficulty. What people might be saying is: "*This is tough.*"

Again, I would think twice before labelling the casualties. The death of many unhappy employees is sometimes grossly exaggerated. The statement also includes the words 'accepting change', so it contains the hidden famous assumption that people are resistant to change, which we have dealt with several times before. VIRAL CHANGE™ asks us not to make early assumptions. The power of internal networks enables them to deal with 'receptive and non-receptive people' far better than the managerial plumbing system. Inclusions and exclusions become very obvious after the peer-to-peer influence. If some people do leave, make sure you take some time to look beyond the obvious 'exit interview'. In such an exit interview, people tend to pay excessive attention to 'what was wrong'. Incidentally, I prefer 'stay interviews', i.e., asking people why they are still here. From those who finally exclude themselves, we can learn not only what was 'wrong', but perhaps also what is going so well, that they can't integrate it!

15. PEOPLE USED TO NOT COMPLYING WITH NORMS WILL BE EVEN WORSE AT ACCEPTING CHANGE

The assumption has little ground. We have seen in chapter 11 how deviant people can teach us a lot. People who are traditionally bad at accepting norms from the managerial plumbing system may, however, be good adopters of infections when particular behaviours have been reinforced in the peer-to-peer internal network of Champions. My anecdotal experience is one of inverse correlation. Non-normative people often make good Champions! VIRAL CHANGE™ is using completely different highways to establish 'norms'. They come up as a consequence of behavioural routines that have been established after tipping points. So they come in with their reinforcement mechanisms attached.

I'm not suggesting that you should agree with my comments on these 15 assumptions! I'd like you to read them as my view of these assumptions, as seen through the glasses of VIRAL CHANGE™. Make your own judgements. What matters is that you accept that a lot of mythology exists around change and its management. The above 15 are examples of how there are many assumptions that contain truth and fallacy at the same time. Take a look at your original notes and reflect upon the potential changes or modifications that you may have made after reading this book. Look at the rationale behind your possible 'change of mind'.

I'm convinced that this is a good list, an exercise, to help you instruct others in your organisation or to allow you to start having a conversation about the myths behind management of change.

EPILOGUE: 'HI, THIS IS A CULTURAL CHANGE PROGRAMME, AND THIS IS THE LAST TIME WE MENTION CHANGE OR CULTURE'

The best thing that could happen to a 'culture change' or 'change management' programme is losing the labels! Maybe, by doing just this, we are already 10/20/30% further along, who knows? You will recall how I shared with you ideas about language and frames, and how I suggested that 'you'd better pick the right frame, before the frame picks you'.

Change management labels, including cultural ones, create a significant level of antibodies in the organisation. 'Here we go again' seems to be in the air. It would be naïve to think that we can avoid labels completely. After all, if it's not called 'culture change' it may end up being called 'an organisational transformation programme' or a 'company renewal', or something like that. So, does it matter? I'd like to suggest that it does, because enormous historical baggage is included with many of those terms. I have suggested in the early chapters that we need a terminology clean-up precisely because there is such a broad spectrum of 'initiatives' under those labels.

You may want to create VIRAL CHANGE™ and install new behaviours, and perhaps you may not need to call it anything. It may be, however, that you are 'forced' to do so in the context of - alas - many other parallel 'initiatives'. You may try to resist, but in the end you may need to reply to *that* question: "*How do we call this thing that we are doing? You know, the culture thing, the viral thing?*" And before settling for 'the culture thing' you may want to consider an alternative. I don't have a ready-made answer for you, but I stand by the philosophy behind my flippant proposition: "*This may be a cultural change programme, but this should be the last time we use 'change' or 'culture'!*"

One of the most distinctive features of VIRAL CHANGE™ going well is how much it progressively gets embedded in the life of the organisation without the need to refer to it as 'a programme'.

Believe me, this is a good measure of success! When people are using expressions such as 'if we have these behaviours, if we all did things that way, the new culture will follow', then you are on an excellent track for success.

When I'm working with clients on VIRAL CHANGE™ I do try to avoid labels such as 'cultural change' or 'change management programme', but, of course, we always end up using others.

That's OK, as long as we try to avoid getting too close to the formal, standard, mechanistic tsunami change. I have no problem with describing that we are focusing on increasing productivity; or that we're creating competitiveness; or that we're aligning two merged organisations; or that we're adapting to a new environment; or that we're establishing a new behavioural fabric; or that we're rethinking the way we do business. These are all labels I have used in the past. And they're great!

For the same reasons described in the chapter about language and frames, the branding of an initiative of change may be useful. It all depends on its sincerity and simplicity. People in organisations - particularly in large companies with multiple layers of 'programmes' and 'frameworks' - are very cynical. Finding the right articulation is key.

I am stretching the argument. You may need/want to find a balance and use the 'c' word (culture or change) because you feel it is precisely what people need to hear. It is your call! It is your organisation, and most likely you are paid to make those sorts of judgements. I am perhaps too cautious. If you have patiently followed me through this book, you'll understand my point. It is the elevation of efforts and commitments to the category of a 'programme', which has to share its air time with another five or ten programmes, that bothers me; not the use of the language of culture or change in itself.

>> FINAL WARNING

This book may infect you. If it does, your understanding of organisations and management of change will never be the same. If you become infected, you will want to spread the practices of this book by infecting others in your organisation. If you're seriously infected, you will drive and implement changes this way from now on.

However, this infection can be treated. Medicines come in many forms and shapes, such as pretending that this is just clever talk. To combat the infection, you can also try 'my line manager will never buy into this stuff', 'not in a million years!', 'the CEO won't like it' or 'too bad, we have just started a total, all-inclusive, multi-million-dollar engagement across all divisions'.

If you don't treat the infection, you will become a carrier. Unlike other contagious diseases that you may get, this one is not only clinically silent but it has a beneficial side. It will generate good levels of antibodies that will protect you for life against other really, really serious terminal illnesses, like, for example, the 'Massive Change Communication and Training Programme', a 'disease' has a three year roll-out, trillions of post-its and an incredibly expensive budget and will end in death by PowerPoint.

I really wish you success in creating VIRAL CHANGE™ in whatever organisation you work for (= spend most of your time). In creating that wonderful, distributed leadership across the organisation, in which networks of small worlds lead in all directions, all the time, without the reference to a command and control centre. In mastering the power of language, behaviours tipping points, creation of infections and new cultures. In creating a fashion for success, creating wealth and building an environment where people are looking forward to Monday morning. Good luck.

ABOUT THE AUTHOR

Leandro Herrero practiced as a psychiatrist for more than fifteen years before taking up senior management positions in several top league global companies, both in Europe and the US. He is co-founder and CEO of The Chalfont Project Ltd, an international consulting firm of organisational architects. Taking advantage of his behavioural sciences background – coupled with his hands-on business experience – he works with organisations of many kinds on structural and behavioural change, leadership and human collaboration. His books include *The Leader with Seven Faces, Viral Change, New Leaders Wanted: Now Hiring!* and *Disruptive Ideas.*

The Leader with Seven Faces:
Finding your own ways of practicing leadership in today's organisation
By Leandro Herrero

After all the books written about leadership, you'd think we know a thing or two about leadership. However, nothing seems to be further from the truth.

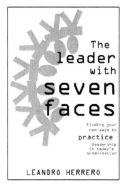

The Leader with Seven Faces provides a novel approach to leadership where the questions to ask (about what leaders say, where they go, what they build, care about, do, how they do it and 'what' they are) take priority over producing 'universal answers'.

For anybody interested in leadership of organisations… and in seeing things through a new pair of glasses.

You can read excerpts, reviews and much more information about the book at **www.meetingminds.com**.

The Leader with Seven Faces is available from Amazon, Barnes and Noble, Blackwell, WH Smith, Borders, Books Etc. and many other (online) bookshops, as well as from www.meetingminds.com.

New Leaders Wanted: Now Hiring!
12 kinds of people you must find, seduce, hire and create a job for
By Leandro Herrero

A small percentage of the workforce has the key to success. A selected group of managers make all the difference. But what are the skills these people have that enable them to create business success?

The job advertising pages don't often describe those new skills. There is a tendency to play safe and look for people with a conventional set of skills and a proven track record. However, to get spectacular success, you need an 'internal engine' of people who think and behave differently. Who are these people? Where could they be? Do I have them already or do I need to find them? You cannot ignore these questions and your number one priority should be to find these people.

New Leaders Wanted explores those new skills and new approaches to reality and will guide you in your search to find those people.

You can read excerpts, reviews and much more information about the book at **www.meetingminds.com**.

New Leaders Wanted: Now Hiring! is available from Amazon, Barnes and Noble, Blackwell, WH Smith, Borders, Books Etc. and many other (online) bookshops, as well as from www.meetingminds.com.

Disruptive Ideas
10+10+10=1000: the maths of Viral Change that transform organisations
By Leandro Herrero

In a time when organisations simultaneously run multiple corporate initiatives and large change programmes, *Disruptive Ideas* tells us that - contrary to the collective mindset that says that big problems need big solutions - all you need is a small set of powerful rules to create big impact.

In his previous book, *Viral Change,* Leandro Herrero described how a small set of behaviours, spread by a small number of people could create sustainable change. In this follow-up book, the author suggests a menu of 10 'structures', 10 'processes' and 10 'behaviours' that have the power to transform an organisation.

These 30 'ideas' can be implemented at any time and at almost no cost; and what's more...you don't even need them all. But their compound effect will be more powerful than vast corporate programmes with dozens of objectives and efficiency targets...

You can read excerpts, reviews and much more information about the book at **www.meetingminds.com**.

Disruptive Ideas is available from Amazon, Barnes and Noble, Blackwell, WH Smith, Borders, Books Etc. and many other (online) bookshops, as well as from www.meetingminds.com.

meetingminds
ideas worth printing

To order extra copies of VIRAL CHANGE™ or any of our other books, visit our website at www.meetingminds.com. It is also available from major online bookshops such as amazon.com, amazon.co.uk, amazon.ca or barnesandnoble.com. For bulk orders, please contact us directly for more information on discounts and shipping costs.

Customised editions: These are special editions created for a particular audience such as a specific **company or organisation**. The core materials of the book are maintained, but relevant company-specific resources - such as in-house case studies or tool-kits – are added. A **special foreword** or tailored introduction - written either by the author or by your company's leadership - may be added as well. The book cover could also be adapted. Using modern printing technology, we can supply all the above in any number of copies, from small runs to bulk production. If you are interested, please contact us.

Continue the conversation: There are many ways you can engage the author, from speaking opportunities to consulting services facilitating a change process and/or enabling your internal resources to drive VIRAL CHANGE™. Details can be obtained via **www.thechalfonproject.com**, through which you can also contact the author.

PO Box 1192, HP9 1YQ, United Kingdom
Tel. +44 (0)208 123 8910 - **www.meetingminds.com**
info@meetingminds.com

Index